Praise for *In Between the Magic*

"Those who are lucky enough to have been love-struck in their teenage hearts know that it's a pain they would never exchange for anything else. My days of romance and dance in the late sixties were populated by a handful of beautiful, freedom-loving creatures—one such ephemeral soul was Juliette Bora (that was her name then). I remember the Beatles' 'Hey Jude' playing while out clubbing together in Tramps and 'Everyday People' by Sly Stone down in the Cromwellian, but were we totally conscious? My journey of life with her ended in a slightly regrettable way. She would admit we were on different paths. I didn't even cotton that she was a Muslim—but then religion didn't actually matter in those days—but I knew she was Turkish, and she knew I had a Greek streak in me. How ignorant we were in those unhinged days. Songs still manage to preserve those feelings, don't they? We did link up again briefly in LA while I was on an earnest search for a wife in the late seventies. Her recollection may be slightly different from mine, but we both agree it was kismet, wasn't it? Love and peace."

—**Yusuf/Cat Stevens**

"Some people imagine lives but never live them. Juliette has lived a life that can only be described as incredible, unbelievable yet absolutely true. To be able to survive, then prosper and succeed doing so many things other people would only dream of, is one thing. To be able to chronicle it in this autobiographical narrative requires a deep understanding of yourself that most people do not arrive at in life. Her story, *In Between the Magic*, shows us the inspiration and indomitability of her spirit."

—Terrence Mann, Tony Award–nominated actor, singer, and theatre director (appearances include: *Cats, Les Misérables, The Scarlet Pimpernel, Beauty and the Beast,* and *Pippen*)

"As a husband, father, peak performance coach, and close associate of Tony Robbins, I proudly endorse the real, raw, and empowering lessons *In Between the Magic* unveils. The crafty combination of storytelling, drama, truths, humor, and psychological framework reminds us how to unlock one's inner power by aligning determination with the mind, body, and spirit. Juliette pulls no punches with sharing her wildly authentic story centered around courage, finding your inner strength and true self when the world does its best to condition and program us to be something we are not. *In Between the Magic* is the real-life playbook for transitioning from a survival mode mentality to a thriving existence and will help a lot of people who desperately need it. Enjoy the ride!"

—James Cunnings, senior platinum coaching executive for Tony Robbins @ Robbins Research International, Inc.

"This book, *In Between the Magic*, is beautiful, sad, poignant, hilariously funny, and a bit bat sh*t bonkers . . . but more than anything, it's totally Juliette."

—Barry Ryan, renowned photographer, musical artist, London, England

In Between
the Magic

My Life *from the* Playboy Club
to Beirut *and* Beyond

JULIETTE WATT

RIVER GROVE
BOOKS

This book is a memoir reflecting the author's present recollections of experiences over time. Its story and its words are the author's alone. Some details and characteristics may be changed, some events may be compressed, and some dialogue may be recreated.

Published by River Grove Books
Austin, TX
www.rivergrovebooks.com

Copyright © 2023 Juliette Watt

All rights reserved.

Thank you for purchasing an authorized edition of this book and for complying with copyright law. No part of this book may be reproduced, stored in a retrieval system, or transmitted by any means, electronic, mechanical, photocopying, recording, or otherwise, without written permission from the copyright holder.

Distributed by River Grove Books

Design and composition by Greenleaf Book Group and Mimi Bark
Cover design by Greenleaf Book Group and Mimi Bark
Cover image used under license from ©Shutterstock.com/N_jay;
©Shutterstock.com/slhy
Photograph of roulette players on page 48 used under license from © Getty Images
Photograph of Sammy Davis Jr. on page 63 © Evening Standard Ltd
Photograph of Paul and Barry Ryan on page 77 used under license from ©Shutterstock

Publisher's Cataloging-in-Publication data is available.

Print ISBN: 978-1-63299-673-2

eBook ISBN: 978-1-63299-674-9

First Edition

To those who've endured the slings
and arrows of life's hardships and heartbreak and
to the millions of women who are emotionally
shackled to a life they never chose . . .

I wrote this for you.

For those of you who've had a mother sucking
the very spirit from your soul, a spirit you didn't realize
you had until it was almost gone . . .

I wrote this for you.

For those who've had only themselves to depend on—
for survival—for life—for the very air to breathe . . .

I wrote this for you . . . to believe . . .

"You're not ordinary, you are extraordinary."

JULIETTE WATT

For Barry Ryan.
This is for you and our fifty years of crazy friendship.
I love you—always.
I will miss you—forever.

Contents

CHAPTER 1: The Beginning and the End 1
CHAPTER 2: A Horse Called Amber 19
CHAPTER 3: Lessons at the Ice Cream Van 27
CHAPTER 4: Bury My Heart in Rock and Roll 33
CHAPTER 5: Carnaby Street 39
CHAPTER 6: The Playboy Club 45
CHAPTER 7: The Bunny Costume, Mr. Bojangles,
            and the Chairman 53
CHAPTER 8: Helter Skelter 65
CHAPTER 9: Cat Stevens 69
CHAPTER 10: Eviction to Misery 79
CHAPTER 11: Why Can't I Fly for the USAF? 83
CHAPTER 12: Behind the Iron Curtain 89
CHAPTER 13: Istanbul 99
CHAPTER 14: 1969 Cabaret in Cairo 107
CHAPTER 15: Werewolf Eyes 115
CHAPTER 16: Bifocals and Very Big Guns 119
CHAPTER 17: The Driving License 127
CHAPTER 18: Gun Running and Spiders 137
CHAPTER 19: Paradise Lost 145
CHAPTER 20: London and a Broken Heart 157
CHAPTER 21: The Swiss Adventure 165
CHAPTER 22: The Ball and Chain of Mother 181

CHAPTER 23: Cabaret and the Bailey's Circuit 191
CHAPTER 24: Le Maquereau. 201
CHAPTER 25: Revenge 205
CHAPTER 26: La Vigilante. 217
CHAPTER 27: How Not to Become Famous 221
CHAPTER 28: Words of Wisdom in Scotland. 229
CHAPTER 29: *The Judy Garland Story*—Italian Style 235
CHAPTER 30: Las Vegas and Rachmaninoff 241
CHAPTER 31: The Scam. 249
CHAPTER 32: Los Angeles 257
CHAPTER 33: The Kindness of Strangers 265
CHAPTER 34: Yusuf Islam 273
CHAPTER 35: Goodbye to the Stars in My Soul. 279
CHAPTER 36: Hugh Hefner and the Playboy Mansion . . . 287
CHAPTER 37: By Invitation Only 295
CHAPTER 38: Meet the White Wizard 301
CHAPTER 39: Feeling the Burn 307
CHAPTER 40: The Audition 315
CHAPTER 41: Leaving Is the Hardest Word 327

ACKNOWLEDGMENTS 335
ABOUT THE AUTHOR 337

Chapter 1

The Beginning and the End

For want of a clever and witty way of beginning this story, I decided to go with ordinary and straightforward. Notwithstanding, while ordinary and straightforward did exist briefly in my life, that existence inevitably came to a swift and abrupt end.

I was born in London, England, on June 3, 1951. My mother, Helen, was an Anglophile French woman and my father, Sureyya, was Turkish. After a brief courtship sustained mainly by letters, they married in Istanbul, Turkey, and then moved to Ankara, where my father was working for the United States on a secret, classified CIA Air Force base called TUSEG. When my mother discovered she was pregnant, my father sent her back to London, determined that I would be born British. Shortly after my birth, we went back to Turkey, which meant making the 1,900-mile journey. To get from London to Istanbul, you flew the famous Douglas DC-3—a spectacular, gleaming machine of which Henry M. Holden, author of *The Legacy of the DC-3*, said, "The journey became the destination."

Of course, as a baby, I was far too young to appreciate this new and awe-inspiring form of travel, but when we later moved back to London and were taking our yearly vacation trips to Turkey, I used to count the days until we were once again climbing the airplane stairway to take to the skies. Mother

Father and Mother in front of the DC-3

wore her gloves, along with matching shoes and handbag, and we were escorted to our seats by either the captain or a stewardess. Along with the other passengers, we entered a cosseted world of supreme customer service, one that might be inconceivable to today's beleaguered air traveler. Gourmet food and wine was available in plenty, and at cruising altitude, the captain strolled the aisle and chatted with passengers, who were called "visitors" or "guests." On transcontinental sleeper flights, curtained berths were available with goose-down comforters and feather mattresses for the night leg of the flight. Breakfast choices usually consisted of pancakes with blueberry syrup and julienne-of-ham omelets. The plane held around twenty-three passengers, all seated in comfortable lounge chairs, creating a journey nothing short of delightful. From my first flight at three years old and for all the trips to Turkey thereafter, I was always given a "wings" pin, and from four years old and on, I spent most of the time on the spare seat in the cockpit, sitting with the pilots for at least two legs of the journey. I was in heaven, and I think it sparked my love of airplanes and sowed the seeds of being a pilot—which I became many years later. And, in retrospect, I think my mother was happy not having me with her for the better part of a two-day flight. After all, she had neither the time nor patience to care for a young child, so any opportunity for someone else to take care of that being was always welcomed with relief on her part.

In 1954, everything changed—just as Mother had finally settled into a comfortable life within the prominent, high-society social scene of Ankara. I was being cared for by a lovely Turkish nanny, and my only memories of my mother from that time are wafts of Femme perfume and the rustling of her silk dress as she kissed me good night. In the midst of that seemingly perfect state, my father made a sudden, firm, and final decision. We were leaving Turkey, and England was going to be our permanent home. The change was a horrible shock.

Mother was almost hysterical as she cried and pleaded with him. "Please, Sureyya!" she begged. "Not back there . . . please! Please can't we stay here? Please!"

"No," he told her, and that was that. There was absolutely *no* further discussion on the matter, or any explanation. In general, my father was the kindest man I have ever known. He was terribly handsome, spoke six languages fluently, dressed like Cary Grant—yes, he owned spats—and lived his life exactly the way he wanted, although we had no idea how that was, as his life was a huge secret. He was also very tough and precise in his instructions, or commands, and not to be questioned. Our lives were run his way, which wasn't necessarily awful, just quite unpredictable for us at times. After leaving the CIA—which, at least to our knowledge, he did—he traveled extensively as a ship buyer's agent. By the time we moved to England, his job involved numerous trips to Norway and other places, facilitating the exchange of tens of thousands of dollars in the buying and selling of oil tankers. Even though I was a child who knew basically nothing about money, my mother would carefully explain how large sums would come and go from our own family bank account, but she trusted my father, as we always seemed to have plenty ourselves, so there was never a need for any concern.

What really irked my mother was never knowing where my father was in the world at any given time—after all, this was the 1950s, and international communication was sparse and difficult. My mother had to rely on letters and the occasional overseas phone call—a monumental affair of waiting hours by the phone and yelling numbers at an operator who could barely hear her over the static. When she finally did get through and the number was ringing, if my father was unavailable, the call was over, and she would have to wait sometimes a week in the queue to place it again. I do remember, on many occasions, and upon my father's return from parts unknown, hearing raised voices from behind the kitchen door as my mother would grill him on his recent whereabouts. Her voice would get louder, demanding to know where he'd been and why. My father would stay silent, closed like a locked door, which was usually when Mother would finally slump in a chair, exhausted by her efforts. His response to her was always calm and reassuring, but also entirely vague.

"It's business. Nothing for you to worry about—just look after our precious child."

Everyone liked and deeply respected my father. He conducted all his business on a handshake, believing a man's word was truly his bond so contracts weren't necessary. For some inexplicable reason, no one ever challenged that statement—no one doubled-crossed him, backed out of deals, or doubted anything he said or did. When he walked into a room, you felt his presence. He was charming, diplomatic, and very smart. He handled my crazy maternal grandmother brilliantly, and my sweet grandfather worshipped him.

Mother, on the other hand, baffled him. I think my father eventually realized—and I merely surmise this—that her mind was not right, nor was it ever going to be. I believe that, not too long into their marriage, he realized he'd made an enormous mistake. I have a clear memory of us standing outside my mother's bedroom door. Father was holding a cup of tea, the cup rattling on the saucer almost in time to the violent and rhythmic banging on the wall from inside the bedroom. My mother's head made contact again and again with the rose-patterned wallpaper as she tried in vain to beat the demons out of her broken mind. I remember looking up at his stricken face, his fear and shock palpable. This was completely outside his realm of understanding. Turkish women did not behave this way; who had he married? I felt him reach down and put his hand on my head as if to remind himself there was a reason he was here, and that reason was a small five-year-old child.

My father had married a pretty English girl he'd met one afternoon on Brighton Beach in the South of England, during the summer of 1948. Mother was spending a week there with her aunt Margaret and ran into him on her daily stroll. He asked where he could get a cup of tea, and she walked him to a café on High Street. He invited her to join him, and they made conversation where, for about an hour, she lamented the loss of the love of her life—a Russian lieutenant who'd been killed by the Nazis during the war. My father listened and patted her hand as she openly sobbed into her teacup. He then asked if he could write to her. She said that would be fine, and off they went their separate ways.

They wrote to each other for two years until, finally, they saw one another once more for a second cup of tea, this time at The Ritz Hotel in London. Then, out of the blue, came the letter proposing marriage. She wrote her acceptance and, with lightning speed, packed her bags and left two quite stricken parents on the front doorstep, half waving as the cab pulled away. They were mortified. Who was this *foreigner*? Without a backward glance, Mother boarded her first DC-3 for Turkey, and two weeks later she married a total stranger at the Palace Hotel in Istanbul.

When I arrived two years later, things changed. My father absolutely adored me. He showed me affection; I was a completely loved person. I was cared for and I was safe. Both he and my maternal grandfather thought I was an absolute miracle of perfection, and I believe I was the main reason my father stayed with my mother. We had a bond from the day I was born, and that made my mother happy.

A few weeks before we were due to leave Turkey for the move to England, my father announced that my mother and I would be going first and he would follow later. When was later? Who knew? Once again, there was no discussion between them on the details. I was only three years old, but I remember my mother crying hysterically when the taxi arrived to

Father and Mother, Palace Hotel, Istanbul, 1950

pick us up. As he opened the car door, he patted her on the shoulder and kissed me on top of my head.

Leaving Turkey was my mother's greatest nightmare come true. London housed her parents—her mother, to be precise—and arriving back to London on a gray, chilly evening in September was just plain depressing. Of course, we had nowhere to live, so we moved in with them, thirty miles outside of London, in Hatch End, a dull, lifeless little town. It was the typical gloomy suburbia of the fifties, with row upon row of square, red-bricked houses spawning identical square-lawned, flower-bordered front gardens.

My father arrived about a month later. It was a brief visit, and then, again without discussion, he was gone again on another mysterious business trip.

My grandfather, Clarence, was a sweet Irish man who didn't drink and didn't argue; peace and serenity were his life at whatever cost and, of course, you could also throw in the occasional good game of chess and a good laugh. His entire family had been drunks, cementing his decision to live his life present and sober. A tailor by trade, he worked in London at Gieves & Hawkes, a prestigious store that made the uniforms for the queen's mounted guards. For thirty-six years, he kept the same routine, taking the train to London, having lunch at the Moulin Rouge Café on Tottenham Court Road—owned by the father of Steven Georgiou, who would one day become Cat Stevens—then home at the end of the day.

When my grandfather was a single man, vacationing had been his passion, and he loved going abroad. For five consecutive years, he'd spend the first two weeks of July in Juan-Les-Pins in the south of France, and each year another family from Paris, the Morrisseys, vacationed on the same beach. They were a large family with four daughters, and they always stayed in the same hotel as my grandfather. Eventually, after a couple years, he became friends with the family and accompanied them on their daily beach visits. He would play chess with Pierre, the father, and they would all go on a daily walk down the beach to get ice cream. Alice was the eldest daughter, and my grandfather often, by chance, found himself walking beside her. They made polite conversation, and she would sit beside him on the sand as they all ate their ice cream. After five years of enjoying his summers with them, he decided he wanted to go to Egypt to see the pyramids for a change and, being polite, he dutifully wrote the family, informing them that he would not be coming to France that summer.

"Perhaps I'll see you in a couple of years," he wrote.

Back came a short and terse response to *his* parents, saying, "We had thought this would be the year Clarence and Alice would set the date."

He was thunderstruck. The poor man had no idea he'd been engaging in a five-year courtship, and his parents were adamant that he do the proper and gentlemanly thing. The rest is a tragic, awful story. Grandpa married a mentally sick and deranged woman who would make their forty years together a living hell, her unpredictable fits of screaming rage shaking the house to its very foundation. The only refuge was to hide behind closed doors, hoping extreme violence wasn't going to be the curtain call of the tirade. Sometimes it was, or sometimes she would just stop and calmly go into the kitchen to make tea or bake a cake. To the outside world, she was the wonderful Mrs. Healey who was so good in the garden and gave so generously at church every Sunday, but to us she was as close to the devil as one could imagine. With a Bible tucked under her arm, she would spout "God's Word" daily, then fall into long silences that could last a week, broken only by the banging of doors sounding out her rage. Food wasn't bought and, therefore, meals weren't prepared; fires weren't made, making wintertime a cold and miserable existence. Days would pass until she would decide to reenter the world, acting as if nothing at all had happened.

My mother was born in year two of their marriage, arriving on July 27, 1920, after Granny spent twenty-two hours in the blood and guts of childbirth—which she managed to blame on my mother, often reminding her she had been an abnormally oversized baby, thus being the sole cause of her lengthy and agonizing labor. My grandfather once confided to my mother that there were times, even early on, that he'd disliked Alice, and that he'd often seen a touch of meanness during those French beach walks, which had concerned him. It should have. She was a wicked bitch who had no business having a child and should have been locked away in a secure place. She was mean and cruel beyond belief—she repeatedly threw her baby, my mother, across the room until she bounced off the wall, lying motionless until someone found her—usually Grandpa or some aunt that happened to be visiting. She strangled my mother's little cat in front of her on the back-porch steps because it peed on the dining room carpet.

As an adult, my mother lived constantly perched on the threshold of madness, banging her head on walls to make the unbearable pain of her life go away. She lived her childhood in terror, her adolescence in trying to escape that terror, and her adulthood in the torment of pain and sadness.

In 1939, the first year of WWII, Mother fell in love with Frank Borchard, a young German who had lived in London for many years. Happy for the first time in her life, she used to sneak out to meet him at his apartment, and for a year their illicit liaison remained undiscovered. Then my mother got pregnant and they planned to run away and get married, but England had other plans. In the spring of 1940, there was an outbreak of spy fever and agitation against "enemy aliens": eighty thousand Germans, Austrians, and Italians who had been living in England for decades were, by the order of Winston Churchill, interned in camps around the country for the "safety of Britain." On June 30, 1940, the liner *Arandora Star* sailed for Canada, carrying more than seven thousand internees—most to Canada, some to Australia. Early on the morning of July 2, about seventy-five miles west of Bloody Foreland, the ship was struck by a single torpedo from a U-47 submarine, commanded by Günther Prien. The *Arandora* sank with the loss of 714 lives, including Frank Borchard's.

On discovering my mother's pregnancy, my grandmother beat her senseless and sent her away to have the baby in shame, at the Birdhurst Lodge run by the evangelical Mission of Hope. Seven months later, the child, a boy, was born and immediately adopted by a Christian minister and his wife, who whisked the baby home two hundred miles away to Manchester in Northern England.

My mother was broken forever.

To preserve his own sanity, Grandpa became a preacher at the local church and was rarely seen. He couldn't handle the darkness of his home, and since divorce wasn't an option, he did what he had to do to live the life he never chose. Grandpa went to work in London all week and then to God on weekends, only to return home in the evenings for dinner and the newspaper.

For me, living in my grandparents' home as a child, this unsettling life was disturbing, so I created a make-believe world of my own. I was always worried when I was around my mother and grandmother because I never knew who was going to fall apart. I could quickly shuttle All Things Scary to the back of my small Unaware of the Adult World Brain. Toys and playing took high precedence, and being an only child, I was already becoming an expert at self-entertaining and spent many hours two doors down the street playing skittles, jacks, and hopscotch with my friend Clare. Hanging out with her and her oh-so-happy parents, sliding down the stair banisters, eating raw cake dough from her mum's cooking bowl, and staring in awe at the thousands of old newspapers—that we were forbidden to touch—that Clare's dad had stored in every room in the house was my idea of happiness.

We would go on car trips to see the countryside and visit the horses in the various fields of nearby farms. They would always walk over to the fence in the hope of getting something sweet from my pocket. I used to touch their necks and let them blow on my hand, and that smell to me—to this day—is the smell of peace and serenity. I fell in love with these grand and gracious creatures, and still, even now, they are my truth and my guidance.

Relief arrived when my father came home from a business trip and announced we could purchase a house. We'd been living in Hatch End for six miserable months, and it didn't take long for my mother to find us a lovely five-bedroom home on Beachwood Avenue in Finchley, North London, costing the hefty sum of £3,000, the equivalent of about five thousand dollars in those days, and—just as a reference—that house sold in 2015 for £4.6 million. Mother had it redecorated, which put her in a brilliantly good mood for the duration of the renovations. Nevertheless, this new family dynamic did not diminish my father's constant traveling—always on business. To where? Who knows? As well as brokering oil tankers, he had the mysterious profession of "import and export," for which he was gone weeks at a time.

I remember always being in the state of waiting for him to come home. When he did, the front door would fly open and he would stand there, exuding exotic cologne and mysterious travel smells, loaded with presents up to his chin. Mother usually chose this time to become manic and blast him in a fierce Behind the Kitchen Door Attack, lecturing him on his persistent absence.

The poor guy didn't even have his coat off or the presents out from under his chin, but in the epitome of calmness, he would stand tall and say pretty much the same thing every single time: "I'm doing it for you and our precious child." Meanwhile he would hand her a beautifully wrapped box. "From Paris."

"What if something happens to you? What would we do?" she'd demand, waving the box in the air. He was again calm as he placed the rest of the presents on the table.

"You have this house. I have put it in your name. You will have money."

"But—"

His hand would go up, swiftly silencing her. The conversation was over. Sometimes she tried to continue, to resist, but the result was always the same—there was honestly nothing for her to say in the face of what presented itself as utmost love and sincerity, spoken with such strength and conviction. Leaving the beautifully wrapped boxes, she would weakly mumble something about dinner and head to the sink to peel potatoes or attend to some other meal-related task. I suppose it was hard for her when he was gone, having only the companionship of the intermittent Turkish visitors, her parents, me, and oh—yes—those chattering goblins in her head, although she did try in her own odd way to be a good mother. Sometimes she was kind and funny, which was frequently confusing, as "kind and funny" could turn "cold and mean" in an instant. Other people's opinions were of great importance to her—she required me to be the perfect child and would dress me meticulously in pretty dresses with shoes to match and take me everywhere, pushing me at people.

"Say hello nicely."

I obeyed, my forced "hello"s angelic in tone.

I also remember feeling especially important—as if my job were to keep Mother in good spirits by being perfectly behaved and making sure everyone was smiling. I spent the next fifty years trying to keep Mother in a good mood, and it almost cost me my life.

When the Turkish relatives and friendly import-export business guests would turn up, mother was the perfect hostess, arranging dinners and evenings out at the Talk of the Town, a popular supper club in Leicester Square. Sometimes she'd bring me along, as I was usually a big hit with the guests, and my well-trained "hello"s and angelic smiles guaranteed everyone would tell her what a wonderful, pretty child I was and *so* well behaved. Thus, Mother's good mood would prevail—at least for the evening. You never knew who was top of the bill, and from our coveted, front-row table—my father knew everyone—we saw Frank Sinatra, Sammy Davis Jr., Shirley Bassey, Eartha Kitt, Lena Horne . . . anyone who was anyone. Mother was the shopping shepherd to the Turkish visitors and relatives, creating endless trips to Harrods, the highbrow department store in Knightsbridge. She said she hated it, but she didn't.

Years later, when it was all gone and everything was gray shadows, she would constantly reminisce about the happiest times in her life—dancing on the tables at the Polish Embassy during the war and then, years later, shopping with the Turkish visitors and relatives at Harrods. World War II was a vivid, almost daily topic of reminiscences; she would become teary and nostalgic as she talked about the daily bombings in London and making cups of tea down in the shelters with all her friends. She used to talk about "The Blitz of London" as if it were a romantic movie she'd never wanted to end—these were the happiest times of her life, not having married my father or having me. A six-year world war was her joy. Then, at any mention of the Americans who maybe kinda saved the country, she poofed away in disgust.

"A bunch of womanizing, uncouth boys who just drank, got girls pregnant, and gave out chocolate."

Household administration was way beyond her ability. She didn't know how, and she sure didn't care. Neither did she balance checkbooks or pay bills; she was a housewife (of sorts) and a hostess. The only household decision she made was to banish my father to the spare bedroom on account of his "monstrous snoring." We did have a maid, Mrs. Shields, which was good, as Mother didn't clean, either. In the eight years our maid spent with us, she was just Mrs. Shields, and Mrs. Shields ran the house like a military operation—thank God, as Mother's ineptness with running anything pertaining to real life was a clear and future danger. We had groceries, meals were prepared, bills were paid, and the laundry sat in a clean, immaculate pile every Friday. Sheets were sent to the linen launderers once a week. Every Tuesday, a man in a gray uniform would pick up the bag of sheets and deliver them back five days later, beautifully wrapped in tissue paper, packed in gray boxes with the launderer's name etched in silver lettering. The endless silver and brass was polished every Thursday, and the house was always clean. All was well.

With my father away so much, my mother fell into a kind of single-parent role. Her disciplinary actions were swift and harsh, and I was frequently spanked and sent to my room. That was actually fine, since I cherished being alone. The sting of the slap or twist of an ear was a small price to pay to be exiled to my colorful world of make-believe and my magic flying chair. An old green wicker armchair became the chariot that "flew" me all over the sky; solitude and my little dog, Skiffy—a miniature bull terrier Mother brought home one day—sitting on my lap were all I needed. Skiffy was a precious angel—my precious angel, my world, and my friend.

I look back now, and I get it. What parenting skills could she have acquired, and where from? Who, after all, had been her role model? Crazy lady Grandma? Poor Grandpa, who lived with God? On Lock Me in My Room for Bad Deeds Days, Mother would let me out at some mealtimes, wagging her finger with the tepid threat, "When your father comes home..."

When he did come home, Mother would tell him in detail the nature of my insubordination, the ignoring of explicit instructions to *not* ignore her, and the endless list of just . . . kid stuff. She would then command him to discipline me with a spanking, which he would flatly refuse, then, mumbling something in Turkish, he would go pour himself a gin and tonic and come sit with me and Skiffy. She would sometimes make one more futile attempt but was instantly silenced by The Look. Father sure was a force—even as a kid I knew he had some kind of mighty sovereignty you just didn't question . . . ever.

When I was seven, my father bought a car. Until that point, neither one of my parents had a driver's license, and cars equipped with chauffeurs would appear when transport was needed. Suddenly, appearing outside our house one day, sat a four-door black Humber Super Snipe with a leather and mahogany interior, seating seven in comfort. Driving on the wrong side of the road, my father was a terrifying torpedo, hurtling along at top speed without any awareness of traffic lights, other cars, or, God forbid, crosswalks. I think, on our second or third trip, I heard my mother praying as my father barreled through a red traffic light, shaking his fist out the window and yelling in Turkish to each car he narrowly missed. After three trips, that was it. The Humber Super Snipe went back to the dealer.

Me and my father at a relative's wedding, London, 1955

Then, I got chicken pox. Eventually Mother got tired of reading to me, so television came to the house. Now this was something to be extremely excited about: a small faux-wood box with a tiny black-and-white screen that came alive with enchanted worlds of variety shows, children's puppetry, the news, and eventually horse programs. *My Friend Flicka, Champion the Wonder Horse, Black Beauty*—I'm still recovering—and my favorite, *Fury*, whose introduction depicts the beloved stallion running inside a corral and approaching the camera as the announcer reads: "FURY! The story of a horse and a boy who loves him!"

No one could ride Fury other than the boy—which, of course, was without any saddle or bridle. If anyone was mean to the boy, Fury would come galloping round the corner, leap the fence, and attack them. The show was brilliant. I lived and loved every second of every episode, and my horse passion was solidified right there and then.

Every summer, we would take our yearly August vacation trip to Turkey, always staying at the Istanbul Hilton. Mother loved going there, and she especially loved going back to the Hilton, where my father was treated like royalty. Even the snoring was tolerated, and she would sun herself every day by the shoe-shaped swimming pool, fashioned after Conrad Hilton's footprint. Mother reveled in being waited on hand and foot by the hotel staff, who treated her like a wife of Turkish royalty. I spent most days hanging out at the pool with my cousin Dogan and various American families on vacation. Dogan and I were both experts at self-entertaining, and it was great to have other kids to play with; we also had a ton of Turkish relatives to visit, and they were always feeding us. In Turkey, food is the remedy for every imaginable ailment or illness. My father would come and go on "business trips," but he too was happy—this was his domain where he was king and emperor.

It was in the middle of our 1961 vacation where straightforward and ordinary came to its abrupt and untimely end. I woke up on the morning of August 24 to see an empty bed across the room and, in place of my father, a bunch of mangled white sheets screwed in a knot. A green and gray oxygen cylinder stood at the foot of the bed, standing guard over his slippers, which had been tossed on the floor. A faint odor of vomit hung in the air, and I could hear insistent knocking at the door. I looked to the other bed to see my mother sitting up, gripping her pajamas to her chest. As I was absorbing this abnormal scene, my mother dragged herself to open the door, and the screaming began as four people hurtled in, all speaking Turkish at rock concert decibels. They grabbed her, and the screaming kept going until someone noticed me, sitting on my bed in a heap of bewilderment. They all sort of looked at me like, "Oh, there's the child." No one seemed to know what to do, as my mother was now lying on the floor banging her head on the carpet. I was left sitting on the bed in my pajamas, waiting my turn as my mother's screaming took precedence.

My father had woken up in the middle of the night and gone over to my mother. Shaking her awake, he'd said, "Helen, I'm dying."

She'd replied, "No, you're not; go back to bed."

Then he started coughing and collapsed. Realizing something very bad was happening, she called down to the front desk and, moments later, doctors came and wheeled him out. He died in the ambulance on the way to the hospital at age fifty-one. He'd had a heart attack, and we later found out that he'd had multiple heart attacks over the past few years. I don't remember much else except snippets of being told my father was gone and not coming back, then being grabbed by some aunt and uncle who scooped me up and took me out of the room. A short car ride later, I was led into their home—a big house with cold marble floors. Then all I can remember is the silence and sitting alone in a study, on a green chair, reading American comic books, holding a dog, and warding off the hourly plates of humongous amounts of food that arrived. I waited . . . and waited for whatever comes next when bad things happen. I remember feeling nothing, like a huge, empty hole of . . . nothing. I didn't cry, I didn't ask questions. I just sat, quiet and composed, holding the dog, reading. I knew I had to keep it together. I was only a ten-year-old child, and that feeling of emptiness was all-encompassing. What I didn't know, sitting there on the sofa holding the dog, was that my childhood had just ended.

Eventually, I was taken to the hospital, where that vomit smell was everywhere. They gave my mother the bag of my father's clothes but not his wedding ring, which had somehow disappeared. Some uncle identified the body—Mother said she absolutely couldn't look at dead people. She was in a haze, being led around, following others, doing what had to be done. I was then sent off, back to the green chair with the comic books and the dog, to wait.

My father was given a full military funeral. Apparently it wasn't good for a child to see a funeral, so I stayed put on the green chair, with the comic books and the dog. I have a photograph of Mother at the gravesite, her face white in absolute disbelief. Father was buried overlooking the Bosphorus Strait, where my mother promptly forgot the location of his gravesite.

We returned to London a few days after the funeral. I think the ceaseless crying and endless plates of food had run their course—we needed to go home. During the journey, my mother was a wreck of shock and disbelief. Why had he *done this to us*? My grandfather opened the door to our

My mother at Father's funeral, 1961

house, which was now the scene of misery. He was the only one who put his arm around my shoulders, holding me close. I didn't have a chance to grieve my father because, from then on, I was too busy trying to figure out how to survive a grief-stricken grandfather and two out-of-control, weeping women constantly asking "why?" This was then followed by clanging reverberation of the same ceaseless question.

"What are we going to do?"

"What are we going to do?"

The mantra carried on day after day, and every time my mother said this line, she looked straight at me. Yes, from ten years old and onward, I was supposed to have the answers. Mother was forty-one, yet she'd never written a check, never paid a bill, never had a job of any kind other than helping my father. She could type, speak three languages, and compose a mean shorthand, but knowing how to run a life was not within her limited capabilities, especially life with a small child who was pretty much a stranger to her. My father had not written a will, believing the house would be enough. I don't think he realized the house would have to be sold in order for us to live, as he'd died "in between deals" so our bank account had only enough to pay our bills for a few weeks. Where would we go? I said a silent prayer it wouldn't be to the dreaded Hatch End.

I spent the upcoming days and weeks watching and listening to the desperate colloquies that transpired between panicked adults. Our life had been shattered, and we were in chaos that would soon turn to crisis and . . . no one knew what to do. My life depended on these three adults, and I felt very much alone, as *I* didn't know what to do either.

When the panic reached its boiling point and things felt like they were going to explode, I picked up my little dog, Skiffy, and held her close. What I *did* know, in that moment, was that dogs and horses would always be my peace and solace of mental safety. They were all I had.

Chapter 2

A Horse Called Amber

Every summer since I turned eight, I was sent to spend six weeks on a horse-riding farm owned by Mrs. Ivey in a tiny town in Devon, called Mary Tavy. And so the time passed, with me in school during the year and off to the farm in the summers. Mother had managed to keep the house by taking a quick course in massage therapy and was now qualified to treat clients. She'd set up shop in our spare bedroom, and by good fortune or maybe even The Big Guy, she managed to keep her schedule full. The house became a rotation of men coming and going, which probably raised an eyebrow or two (didn't women get massages too?), but bills were paid, and we had our house plus food on the table. In June of my twelfth year, mother decided it would be a good idea for me to go back to Devon to ride horses and breathe fresh air. London still had those awful pea soup fogs from coal burning all winter, and I'd had more than my fair share of bronchitis and pneumonia.

Mrs. Ivey's was no luxury camp—her true purpose in taking kids in for the summer was to make money. She was a fierce specimen of female force, tough as nails and righteous as an army general. From June until September, we would milk cows, ride horses, look after chickens, clean pens, and pretty much work our butts off. I was in heaven. Alone with horses, myself, and the farm dog, Bella, I never wanted to go home.

One weird thing that started happening around this time was that, at random, I would start to shake violently. The only way I could breathe through the shaking was to quickly sit on the floor and hold the wall with both hands until it passed, usually within a few minutes. The episodes were exhausting and embarrassing and became a frequent occurrence in Devon. Mrs. Ivey would get mad at me, telling me to stop trying to get attention. Believe me, that out-of-control shaking was *not* something I would have chosen in order to be noticed. But the damn attacks went on for months, brought on by random events. I would suddenly be on the floor, my teeth chattering so hard I was afraid they were going to fall out. Sometimes, during these episodes, I would bite my tongue and it would start to bleed. I must have looked pretty scary holding the wall, with blood trickling out of my mouth. Mother thought I was having seizures, so she came down and took me to the doctor, stating almost with pride that *she'd* had epilepsy for more than seven years during the war, so obviously I'd inherited it.

The doctor was baffled. It wasn't epilepsy or any kind of seizure.

"Give her an aspirin once a day, should clear it up," was his professional advice.

I was always cold—we all were. Mother used to curse my father for bringing us back to this damp, wretched country, and obviously it was affecting me—maybe *that* was what was wrong. I lived with the shaking episodes for however many years they lasted, which I honestly don't remember. Many years later, a wise psychiatrist in New York City told me that when the mind has absorbed too much trauma, it shuts it away in a little closet with a big padlock. He explained, "After an animal escapes from a predator or a disaster, it trembles violently, which is an important part of recovery. Don't go trying to open that door. It's full of bad stuff you don't need to remember—that's why our brains bury it away."

The following year, I was again sent back down to Mrs. Ivey, and one afternoon, Mother appeared on an unannounced visit. She'd learned to drive and, just before my father died, they'd bought a Rover. To see this city car roll up to the farm gates was odd. She loved having me out of the house for six weeks as much as I liked going. She'd only ever visited once to take me to the doctor, so maybe someone else had died? Maybe Gaslight Granny? Even more odd was the very thin, wizened man sitting beside her, dressed in milk-stained overalls with a crooked felt hat dragged down on his head.

"This is Mr. Hill," she said, getting out of the car, dressed in a bright blue frock. "Mr. Hill has brought you a nice horse to see, which we can buy, if you want." Mother was beaming as she expected me to leap in the air with joy—which I did without moving.

"Really? A horse?"

"A horse," she nodded, smiling.

I was always slightly suspicious when she had these bouts of kindness, but I figured it was her way of getting me through the loss of my father, and this was a "beyond great" way. Who needed parents when you had a horse? Then logic crept in. We were just scraping by. How could we afford a horse? Where was it going to live? Devon and Mrs. Ivey were two hundred miles away.

Maybe she'd give me to Mrs. Ivey to live here forever? I turned to my mother.

"Am I going to live here now?"

"Good God, no!" That was okay, and I still felt as if I was going to burst with happiness. Mr. Hill's wife had followed, driving a cart and trailer, and they both unloaded Amber, a rather unkempt-looking chestnut gelding, who, in my eyes, was the most beautiful horse I'd ever seen. Mother gave a not too happy Mrs. Ivey £5 for his keep and Mr. Hill £15 for the sale, and off they went. I gripped the rope of Amber's halter and led him into a stall where he would live at the farm with me, until I went home in September.

The sun had just come out again.

When I was seven, I'd a few months of riding lessons, but nevertheless, my experience was limited to the basics. I remember, after my riding lessons had improved, my father bought me a little black pony that was boarded at a local farm. I loved him and called him Blackie. I would bike to the farm almost every day (yes, at seven years old, a child alone could bike three miles in total safety) and ride him around the fields and even on the main road. One day my mother came to pick me and my bike up and I went to give Blackie a cookie. I made the mistake of approaching him from behind and he swung around and bit me hard, taking a large chunk of my shoulder between his teeth. That was that. No matter how much I pleaded that maybe it was just because he was scared and I'd surprised him, in two days he was gone. Where? I have no idea. It broke my heart.

So here I was seven years later with my own pony again. The day after he arrived and my mother had gone home, I led Amber out into a wide-open pasture. I had no saddle or bridle, but Amber was my "*Fury*," and without a thought of safety, I jumped on his back. He just stood there, then turned his head all the way around and bit me hard on the leg. I didn't care. I grabbed some gauze and bandages from the first aid box and told no one. From then on, I rode him every day with a saddle and bridle borrowed from the still "not too happy" Mrs. Ivey. We went all over the moors, watching the sheep and Shetland ponies going about their day. Sometimes I'd just sit on the ground and he would stand still beside me, occasionally reaching his head down to touch my hand. My demands were quite simple: walk, trot, canter, and maybe jump a log. He was gentle and safe, never biting me again, but when I looked into his dark brown eyes, I saw a deep sadness there. It was as if he had given up and become a robot, and I had no idea why or how to change it, so I didn't. I simply accepted him, and we became friends. His life had been as a typical riding horse of those days, sat on by strangers who pulled hard to stop and kicked hard to go, so he'd done what every horse does—shut down to cope and survive. But Amber was mine now, and I loved him. He gave me a reason to be in my changed and somewhat unpredictable world.

We transported him back to London via the train. Completely unfazed, he walked into the trailer at Mrs. Ivey's, rode the three-hour drive to the main train station, steadily backed out, and walked onto the platform surrounded by steam hissing and whistles blowing. People

Me and Amber

ran all around us, throwing suitcases high up into compartments, yelling at each other above the noise, and Amber calmly continued, climbing three *narrow steps* up into a carriage and squeezing himself into the small horse stall. I sat on an equally small bench facing him through the bars. Following more whistles and steam, we stared at each other for the six-hour ride back to London.

I had no idea, then, how incredible this animal was. Normally, horses don't ignore trains whistling and don't readily climb narrow people-steps into metal boxes. Indeed, I had one of the rare ones. We arrived at Waterloo Station, one of the busiest train stations in England, and Amber was equally nonchalant, stepping down those three precarious steps onto the platform and straight into another trailer where he quietly rode another two hours to the boarding stables eight miles from our house.

Now I had a new routine. Every Saturday and Sunday, I would bicycle the eight miles to the stables, ride all day, and bike home. I didn't fit in or make any friends there, but this didn't bother me. I was small and skinny and trying to learn as much as I could, but I had no teachers. I wanted to understand horses, but no one cared about discovering the animal's inner nature and working with that. The prevailing wisdom was that horses had to be *broken* and obedient. The "trainers" all had an idea of how I should "get my horse going because he was obstinate and willfully lazy." They gave me a big stick to "teach him who's boss," and I gave it right back. I rode him, jumped him, and we went to gymkhanas and small horse shows, where I won a few fifth-place ribbons.

For Christmas that first year I had him, I asked for a beautiful cobalt blue blanket with bright yellow piping—the same one Princess Anne had for her horses. We bought it at Moss Bros., a fancy clothing store in London that back in the sixties sold tack, horse blankets, and riding clothes. Eventually the guys at the stables all left me alone—I was "the stupid kid who knew nothing and would learn my lesson one day when I was bucked off by my lazy horse." I tried riding with the paying customers, people who came and spent a few pounds for an hour of horseback riding—whether they knew how to ride or not. One of the stable hands would lead the ride, which was basically a nose-to-tail, single-file, boring plod down the road and around the block. There was the one stable hand who used to think it was great fun to gallop flat out down the grass center of the freeway. People used to fall off, reins and arms flailing, and horses would sometimes run loose down the road, with the stable hand doing his best Western movie impression of a cowboy, whooping and hollering as he tried to catch the terrified animal. It was ridiculous insanity, not to mention incredibly dangerous, so an easy decision was made—no more riding with endangered customers, at least not for me.

That was okay. Being alone was something I was used to. Plus, Amber and I were now pals. I could jump on him bareback and ride everywhere, and for the next two summers, I would take Amber back on the train to Devon, this time to another family, Brenda and Frank Quick, who had a dairy farm a few miles from Mrs. Ivey. I would ride the moors, count sheep, milk cows, put up haystacks, and basically take care of the farm. They were the sweetest people I have ever known, and I would have been happy to have stayed there forever. For those precious six weeks of summer, my horse and I would explore the countryside for hours, sometimes visiting neighbors, who always had tea brewing and an apple for Amber. Those weeks of summer were treasured moments of joy that still live deep within my heart.

Me, age thirteen, riding Amber

Eventually things started to turn, though. Amber's board cost £5 a week, and soon the hints started. I think the novelty of Mother's spontaneous move of loving-kindness had finally worn off and, subtly but consistently, she would remind me.

"Five pounds could pay a bill. Could buy food. Could do anything except pay for that horse."

So, when MGM studios—which had its movie lot down the road from the stables—came calling for stunt riders, I was the first to sign up. I was paid £5 a stunt. I was thrilled—that was Amber's keep, and I'd just solved the monetary problem boarding my horse had presented. Because of the inherent dangers, I never did tell my mother exactly how I was making the money. Instead, I told her people were paying me to ride their horses when they had no time.

The movie folk quickly recognized me for the skinny fourteen-year-old fearless rider that I was, and they capitalized on it, big time. They gave me a tall gray stunt horse, and thus followed many months of flying over impossible jumps, falling into rivers, landing on bushes, jumping into trees, being swiped off by bayonets, getting knocked off by masked bandits, and galloping flat out down a long hill in full medieval armor, all the time waiting for the perpetual command, "HIT THE MARK!" I never said no because I loved every minute. On the rare occasions I did fall off—six feet is a long way down, especially when galloping close to thirty miles per hour—I did get hurt a bit, finally having to confess my new profession to my mother when she came to get me for the third time when I had to get stitched up at Barnet General Hospital after another fun day with MGM but, who cared? She yelled at me and I gave her the money. She stopped yelling. I was paying for Amber and, hey, finally was getting some respect from the people at the stables who'd thought I was just a stupid kid until they saw me ride a big horse in full metal armor, doing some crazy stunts. I was cool, and everyone started treating me with respect. Everything was great. I was happy.

Until the Saturday morning when I got my bike out of the closet and started wheeling it to the front door.

Mother's voice resonated from the kitchen. "You're not going to the stables anymore," she informed me.

My stomach catapulted. "What? Why?"

"I sold him. You're doing too many dangerous things up there. They took him on Thursday. We're going to Grandma's later—you can see Clare."

Those cold words came out of the kitchen, slamming me on the back of my head like ice pellets. I hate that I can still hear the clatter of dishes in the sink and the whistling kettle being turned off. I can still remember that feeling as if someone had just cut out my heart with a rusty knife and thrown it down the drain. My knees gave way and I slid down the wall onto the carpet. My bike toppled down beside me, and I kept holding it as the tears literally gushed out in a burning torrent of pain. I could feel my heart breaking. Amber was gone. Where? Where had he gone to? Who had him? Why?

Then I knew. No one had him. I knew exactly where he'd gone. Down the road from the stables where the Bad Smell came from.

I remember hating my mother.

I remember shaking.

I remember shutting down from the inside out.

I didn't get on a horse again for thirty years.

Chapter 3

Lessons at the Ice Cream Van

Shortly after the disappearance of Amber, my mother abruptly ended her massage enterprise. I never asked why, but money was disappearing quickly, and we needed a new plan before we were back in the hole. Of course, there was no plan, and it didn't take long to go from a respectable, middle-class family, able to pay the bills and live normally, to opening the front door at nine o'clock one night to greet Mr. Pierce, the manager of Barclays Bank, a looming, terrible person dressed in his bank business suit and black hat, informing my mother that she was responsible for a debt of my father for £500.

"We don't have any debt. The mortgage was paid last month."

Mr. Pierce looked tired as he replied. "For the past four years, your husband has had a running business credit . . ."

"My husband died four years ago."

"And the bank has been very patient, but we now have a debt that is past due."

"We don't have £500." She'd started crying. "I have a child." He stood framed under the porch light, his voice flat and cold.

"This house is in your name, correct?"

"Yes." She could barely speak.

"You must sign it over to the bank." From his brown leather briefcase, he brought out three sheets of paper, his eyes narrowed. "Let's avoid any inconvenience or unpleasantries. May I suggest you sign it now?" And my terrified mother signed away our life. By intimidation and an illegal threat, she gave away our beautiful home for a debt belonging to my dead father, a debt for which she had no responsibility. Scribble, scribble, and it was done. "You have eight weeks to vacate. Good evening." Mr. Pierce turned and stepped into the darkness.

The sixties were tough. There were no credit cards, and if you didn't have cash in the bank, you were broke. When you couldn't pay your bills, your gas and electricity were cut off and eventually they "vacated" you. It wouldn't take long to easily end up on the streets, and the fact you had a child meant nothing. It was terribly simple in its awfulness. Two weeks after the bank manager's visit, my grandfather collapsed on Oxford Street and died a few days later. Apparently, he was riddled with cancer from head to toe. No one knew, as he had been to the local quack doctor in Hatch End with bad pain, only to be told he had gas. Personally, I think he died of a broken heart, having never recovered from marrying my grandmother. My father's death was the last thing his fractured heart couldn't handle. I really do hope there's a heaven somewhere because that dear man absolutely belonged there.

Skiffy got cataracts in her eyes, and without a beat—Mother had her put down.

"She was going blind," she said, "and we simply cannot have a blind dog in the house."

This time I made it upstairs to my room. This time the pain was like a dull bat against my chest, and I stopped caring about anything. For the rest of my fourteenth year, I watched my mother stand helplessly as our life cartwheeled down into a ruination that was stunning in its speed and efficiency. We lost our house to the bank, as well as most of the furniture, which had to be sold for basically nothing. She gave away our other little dog, Peki, a four-year-old miniature bull terrier my father had brought home one day, to a family friend, "Uncle" Cyril. She said he was growling

Me and my sweet dog, Peki

at the postman too much. I found out Peki got away from Cyril, ran into the road, and was run over and killed. I never understood why she gave him away. He was just a little guy—he could have easily stayed with us. Mother kept telling me to stop crying—God had taken him; he obviously needed Peki in heaven.

I never had another dog until I was forty-two.

We moved into a cheap two-bedroom apartment a couple miles down the road. I'd been in free public school for the past three years, which was superior to private schools as far as education standards. My school had the coolest chemistry lab, and I'd become fascinated by all the funny-shaped bottles and tubes sitting ready on the shelves to produce scientific wonders. Our teacher, Mr. Evans, was an ingenious guy, making what might have been a dull subject to some students into an innovative and interactive exploration of science. We learned how to make lipstick and antifreeze. We dropped copper pennies into a container of Coca-Cola to watch them transform back to their original gleaming selves. I was the only girl in our chemistry class of thirty-five boys, who were surprisingly friendly. We all had to partner with each other, and I was put with Charlie Lewis, a naturally gifted kid who treated me like a buddy as we often set fire to the lab with our various experiments gone awry. I was totally accepted—until I beat them all in my year-end finals, shooting to the top of the class with 100 percent on my exam. The boys were shocked more than anything—a *girl* had beat them.

Mr. Evans wagged a finger at me, waving my exam results at my nose. "Young lady, you have something!"

To counter my chemistry prowess, I was removed from math class, having been told my hopelessness was beyond help. They were right. Geometry was a boring, unwanted mystery. I couldn't memorize numbers, and I didn't see algebra as anything more than useless and annoying. Our teacher, the evil Mr. Stack, was a fierce representative of math's critical relationship to the world. Math was his life, and as far as he was concerned, it should be the equivalent in ours. He'd painted the entire classroom walls with squiggles of equations and symbols, which he would regularly smack with a long bamboo cane he carried like the sword of Braveheart. Mr. Stack was a WWII veteran, proudly sporting a large blood blob in the middle of his left eye, the result of being poked by a Nazi in a POW camp. The Eye was his weapon, and he would purposely swivel it close to your face during the daily berating of some poor soul's—usually mine—utter laziness and reckless incomprehension of this imperative subject. He would regularly throw hard rubber erasers at us, often bloodying or breaking noses.

One day he called me up to his desk after I'd gotten an F on my test. "*What* are you going to *do* in life?" The bamboo cane rapped my paper, which was covered with angry red crosses. "*This* is a disgrace! How are you going to do your calculations? Your accounts?" More rapping on the paper.

The silence in the room pulsated.

I replied with the only answer I knew. "I'll hire someone."

His face went dark. "Hold out your hand." I obeyed, and the bamboo weapon swished around and whacked my hand three times. His half finger—oh yes, the Nazis got that too—pointed me back to my seat.

Lavinia, my desk mate, whispered, "Did you do it?"

I nodded. The "it" was a trick we all had for times of hand beatings. If you held out your hand and pushed your fingers back as hard as you could, the flatness deferred some of the stinging, razor-sharp pain.

Hillside Secondary Modern was the definition of public school in England in the sixties. Submerged as it was in an arena of rough kids, many often away on remand by police, my life took on a whole new mode of survival. Bullying was part of your existence, and it never crossed your mind to complain to your parents or teacher. There were no school counselors or any helpful resources—you were on your own. During break times, you always sat with your posse facing the playground, near the doors that led back into the building. Your escape route shouldn't be more than a dozen running steps. The principal, Mr. Woolly, was just that—a ball of ineffective, white-haired fluff. The only time I ever had any interaction with him was when he called my mother to the school to inform her—with me sitting in a chair by the door—that I was never going to amount to anything, so I should probably try to learn typing and become a secretary until my pension came due. This wonderfully supportive directive wasn't targeted solely at me—in general, ambition had no place in any public school. Most of the time, kids were pointed toward believing that accepting a menial job was the only direction forward. The boys were told they should be bricklayers or factory workers, and the girls secretaries or housewives.

You dealt with the bullying and abuse as merely standard parts of the day to be conquered. A super fun activity started at three forty-five p.m. every afternoon—combat time commenced as we came through the big iron gates to begin the one-mile walk to the bus stop, home, and safety. The Scary Girl Kids would lie in wait for the unsuspecting Victim Girl Kids, by the ice cream van, holding burning cigarettes and switchblades, all perfectly normal stuff to bring to school in 1965. They would scan the faces scuttling by for The One Going Down Today. Sometimes bad things happened, things involving breakage and blood and hospitals. No one ever said anything to anyone . . . that was the code of survival. Each day, as I came through the gates, I'd be planning my escape and evasion of the viciousness waiting fifty feet ahead, beside the ice cream van. I would ask myself, *How fast can you run?* It's extraordinary what numbing terror can do to your body. So, Monday through Friday, at 3:47, for a few magnificent minutes, I was a gold-medal Olympic runner, a super fucking fast bullet, sprinting the mile to the bus. Reckon I did it in four minutes—okay, maybe eight—a total success... until the day I tripped on a banana skin. Yes, I really did—a yellow fallen torpedo, outside the gate, sending me flying down onto the pavement, right across Head Scary Girl's ankles. I lay on the ground, winded for a second, as her pitted face leaned down, leering at me through a haze of cigarette smoke. The sizzle was seconds away.

And then something happened. A voice came loud and clear in my head. "No, not me. Not today."

And I jumped to my feet, swung my arm back, and smacked her with every bit of smack I had in my hand, right across her spotty, ugly face. The impact sent her spinning, flat on her nose to a squishy thud on the ground. A silence rippled through her troops, and I'd like to think it was the silence of awe and respect—I had just done the unthinkable. A thin trickle of blood ran down the pavement as everyone scattered and her gang dismantled. She stood up holding her bloodied nose and slinked off like a wounded bear. Wow! I felt amazing, and from that day forward I had become The One Who Took Scary Girl Down. The walk to the bus now became a pleasant ritual of girls strolling and chatting together, and I was never bothered again—nor was my small posse of pals. Although, as I think back—big red question—where was the ice cream van driver? Humping Mrs. Waller from biology in the back of the van, or in the lab, wrapped around the Bunsen burners? This shit was going on, and where the hell was any kind of adult supervision?

I learned something on that sunny day, beside the suddenly benign ice cream van—no one was ever going to fuck with me ever again.

And they didn't, and they haven't...

Well, almost.

Chapter 4

Bury My Heart in Rock and Roll

A year later, I left school. I was fifteen. I walked through those iron gates at the beginning of summer break and told my mother I was done—I was learning nothing at this point except good survival skills, and I could get those elsewhere. I did not want to be a chemist, despite the fact that chemistry was all I was good at, and my dream of being a psychiatrist had gone down the drain with my dead father. Oh, yeah—I forgot to mention—when I was eight, I decided I was going to be a psychiatrist. The human brain really interested me, and maybe my family had something to do with it. Yes, I am smiling right now.

We were also running out of money, again. The electric bill was at the end of its month-long grace period, and right in the middle of *Ready Steady Go!*, my favorite pop music television show that aired on Friday evenings, just as the Zombies were halfway through the first verse of "She's Not There"—snap—darkness. All I could hear was the kettle whistling. Thankfully, we had a gas stove, so tea could be made, allowing for thinking time, but we both knew the gas was inevitably going to be the next extinction. From the goodness that seems to occasionally prevail in humans, our exceedingly kind neighbors let us run an extension cord into their place across the hall, and we lived off that one extension cord for months. I remember being cold a lot because our only source of heat was one little electric heater built into the living room wall, a total fire hazard with its exposed glowing elements.

Finally, the neighbor's kindness ran dry, and one afternoon, Mrs. Gitter returned our extension cord. She was very polite. "I'm so sorry. You do understand, don't you? My husband . . ." She trailed off. The Husband ruled the house.

We moved to another apartment a few miles down the street, close to Golders Green subway station. Renting an apartment was easy in those days. There were no credit checks, no first and last month's deposit—you just had to pay your rent at the end of the month. This one was cheaper and smaller but came with a price to pay in the form of Miss Florence Tanner, the crazy woman living upstairs. She enjoyed banging a hammer on her floor—our ceiling—every night, right around two a.m.

The disruption got bad, and I finally went upstairs to have a chat with her. I knocked, and the door flew open, revealing one of the scariest women I have ever seen, holding a large butcher knife.

"Yes? What do you want?"

"Err. Nothing. Just saying 'hello' and maybe, if it's okay, could you not . . . maybe . . . build things at night with a hammer?"

She slammed the door shut in my face. Okay, not exactly what I was hoping for, but we weren't on the streets, so we would have to tolerate Miss Florence Tanner's hammer banging.

Mother got a job in town as a secretary for British Petroleum. The paychecks were tiny, and as her budgeting skills were nonexistent, I began to see an inevitable repeat of the eviction movie coming. It was time to take charge. I picked up the newspaper and found a job at Imhofs Record Store on Tottenham Court Road, London's version of Tower Records. It was nothing short of fab, groovy, and awesome. Alf Lumby was the manager, one of those timeless creatures of the sixties with long gray hair in a ponytail, pulled tight off a face that had lived a hundred lives.

Alf ran Imhofs like a well-oiled rock and roll machine. He knew everyone who walked in and knew which artist was going to crack the big time and which ones were there just for the coffee and cookies. He pushed records for the deserving and threw out the hippies when they lit up their joints. He knew his customers and jazz music as well as he knew himself. Alf was an old-timer—he loved his store and we all loved him. He kept a ledger that looked like the Magna Carta, a huge book in which he meticulously scribed, in perfect tiny handwriting, every sale and every penny that came in and out of the store. You always knew when Alf was *"on the books,"* as a thick plume of his Pall Mall cigarette smoke would glide up from behind the counter and hang like a white cloud below the ceiling.

An old upright piano stood in the corner of the store, beside those wonderful glass-walled listening booths, the favorite and *free* date haunt of every teenager in London. You could take a 45 single or an album—LPs, as they were called—and stay in that booth for as long as you wanted, listening to songs through the headphones. Your date would be tightly squeezed in beside you, sharing the "cans," as there was only one per booth. You could listen to records for hours and not even buy anything!

A lot of the famous pop stars of the day would come by to see how their singles were selling: The Animals, Dusty Springfield, The Kinks, Barry Gibb. On a quick sidenote—I was obsessed with Barry's gorgeousness and of course his hair, which was beyond fabulous. Elton John, Jeff Beck, and Jimi Hendrix used to wander in every now and again just to hang out. The Beatles didn't come by—they were so famous that there would have been a serious mob scene. Nevertheless, we waited and hoped . . . maybe Ringo? Everyone would talk to everyone, and maybe someone would hit the piano keys and a song might get written.

I was paid £7 a week to be a part of this heaven, and the money was handed to me every Friday in a small brown paper pay packet, with the amount written on the outside in Alf's special "pay packet" fountain pen. That first pay packet of seven one-pound notes felt like a million. It was also independence, and that felt pretty great too.

I had been working at Imhofs for about seven months when, one Thursday, Alf called me over to his area of the counter where he used to sit on an extremely high stool. The Observatory Tower, we called it. He

Young and earning my own money. Here I am on holiday in Greece with my mother.

solemnly looked at me, which sent my stomach flipping in circles, then took my hands and said, "If things are tough at home, this isn't the way." I started to speak, but he held my hands tighter, telling me, "I know it's you." I squeezed back tears. "I'm not calling the police, but I have to sack you. Tomorrow's your last day."

The thing was . . . he gave me my pay packet that last day with nothing deducted. I'd thought about leaving this part out. It's the ugly part—not funny or cute or showing me in any light other than crappy, but—it's what happened, and even though it's a hazy, crummy memory . . . well . . . it happened.

I was stealing money from the register. It'd started a few weeks before—a few pounds here and there, and then it grew to more than a few. Twenty, thirty, once I took fifty pounds. I was also stealing records, and the thing was . . . I felt nothing. I was almost in a trance, no feeling of wrong or guilt . . . just . . . well . . . an odd justification, something along the lines of "this will help at home." I had no records of my own, as we couldn't afford them, and I wanted to be able to shut my bedroom door, put a 45 on my little pink turntable, and just switch off. Those were different times, trusting times, when customers all paid in cash and we all had access to the register. Alf loved me because I was pretty and fun, and the customers loved me—thus, I was arrogantly unaware of the fact that eventually, I'd get caught.

What was I thinking? Alf's Magna Carta accounting was never off by a single penny, but things were in a whole heap of shit at home, and I wasn't processing the world around me or my actions very clearly. We'd been in this second apartment a few months, and our heads were nose high above the water of dead broke—again. Mother was working and I was working. Our rent was £7 a month, and my mother made £12 a week, but somehow her earnings all disappeared in the cloud of her imaginary money management. All she talked about was how little we had and how the bailiffs would be at the door any minute—debtor's prison was still a thing—and so it went on. I was scared. I knew nothing about bailiffs and their immense power and authority, but I did understand that having no money was a scary predicament. I was old enough to know that things went bad with no money, and I was *really* scared of being homeless. I felt helpless.

I left Imhofs that Friday. The last thing Alf said to me was, "I'm here if you need me—I'm your friend." With that, he pressed a small piece of paper with his phone number into my hand. He'd met Mother a few times, and I just think he knew. We never spoke of my stealing again, and we stayed friends for the next twenty years.

My next job was at Fortnum & Mason's "The Royal Store," as it was called. The ground floor housed a grocery emporium that sold luxurious items to the royal family—as well as the segment of the general public that could afford it—and thus bore the royal seal on the building's outer wall. A four-ton clock sat above the main entrance where, every hour, four-foot-high models of William Fortnum and Hugh Mason emerged, bowed to each other, and with chimes playing eighteenth-century-style music, declared the top of each hour. I got a sales position in the record department, and I was fired three months later for stealing from the register. This time I was arrested and taken to court. You don't fuck with The Royal Store. I vaguely remember being in a courtroom with my mother, testifying I had stolen money because we were poor, and I didn't want her to go to debtor's prison. I was let off with a warning and had to pay back the money. Now, you'd think I'd have been smart and stopped, but instead I stole from department stores, clothing boutiques, makeup counters, wherever I could. I didn't sell anything but kept it all, because we had nothing. I was a teenager and wanted to look like Twiggy and have her makeup, and . . . I hated living in this constant Being Poor Shit. The last thing I ever stole was a fire-engine red velvet maxi-coat from Biba's, the grooviest, hippest store on Kensington High Street.

And then I stopped. I don't know why, as I never got caught again, but just as I did when I quit cigarettes forty years later, I quit stealing.

Chapter 5

Carnaby Street

Over the following year, I had half a dozen meaningless day jobs, and I hated them all. One that stands out in its monotonous awfulness was as a phone operator in the basement of the Economist Intelligence Unit, downtown in the city. For eight hours a day, I pulled and pushed plugs in and out of a giant switchboard, connecting calls to and from government officials with the same, "*Economist Intelligence Unit, how may I direct your call?*"

I thought I was going mad. The only redeeming factor was the cafeteria, which served an excellent free lunch. I lived for the weekends—London was swinging, and Carnaby Street was my haven. To alleviate my sanity, I'd gotten a coveted Saturday sales job at Carnaby Cavern, dubbed "*The Fashion Legend of Swinging London.*" Colin Wild, the owner, was a colorful character of enormous outrageousness—tall and skinny, he wore "*way out threads*" he'd made himself and stood high and proud with a mane of brilliant red hair. Just before the store opened, Colin had covered the walls and ceiling with scrunched-up aluminum foil and hung a disco ball flashing colored lights in the middle of the room. He told me they'd used nearly a hundred rolls of kitchen foil and fifty thousand staples. Music blared all day—you literally walked into a silver cave that glittered and roared with the greatest music of our time.

Carnaby Cavern made stage wear for all the top pop singers and actors of the day—Jimi Hendrix, Shirley Bassey, the Bay City Rollers, Long John Baldry, the Four Tops, Jeremy Irons, Benny Hill, Alan Price, Barry Gibb, Marc Bolan, The Kinks, The Foundations, Status Quo. Each and every one was Colin's pal and religiously wore Colin's creations. Tight bell-bottom pants with glitter insets, tastefully cascading down into the crease of the bell-bottom flare and worn of course with absurdly high platform boots, satin shirts with long collars, all in one pantsuits with huge Elvis-style rhinestone-encrusted cuffs and collars—these sorts of designs conceived to make the store one marvelous hangout where everyone knew everyone and was guaranteed to look groovy and fab.

Every week, Colin was a regular fixture on *Top of the Pops*, the famous music TV show featuring the artists with their top-ten hits of the day. Colin would be front and center of the camera, dancing like a madman with his weekly "*dolly bird*" of choice, wearing one of his latest creations. I was privileged to be one of his dolly birds one week—I met Marc Bolan and thought if I died at that moment, it would be okay. For those of you unfamiliar with the Briticism, "dolly bird" was a common saying in London in the sixties, a cockney reference to an attractive young woman, especially one whose intellect is rather less in evidence than her good looks. This expression, which would now appear hopelessly dated and offensive to many women, briefly epitomized the ideal gamine of the mid- to-late 1960s.

Sgt. Pepper had been released, and there wasn't a copy to be found anywhere in London. Even Alf had sold out! But I had a pal, Billy Nicholls, who worked at Immediate Records, Andrew Oldham's record company. Andrew was the Rolling Stones' manager, so to be friends with the engineer who worked for The Man inside *the* building where Mick and Keith *might* come by, was to be envied by all. Billy always let me pop over and listen to records that hadn't yet been released. On one particular afternoon, when I had gone over to Immediate to visit him, Billy buzzed me in and stood holding the precious, impossible-to-find vinyl to his chest like a newborn baby. He led me to Andrew's office and plonked me on a stool.

"I'm gonna play it at a TEN! Get ready to be blown to the moon!" He stuck a pair of "cans" on my head and ran over to the turntable. I waited, breath baited, as the first two revolutions of the needle grazed into the opening bars of "Sgt. Pepper's Lonely Hearts Club Band." I had no words. The magnificent ecstasy of musical rapture blasted into my head and threw open the door to paradise. If I had dropped dead there and then, on the floor, in that small white room, it would have been totally fine by me. (Marc Bolan was now a heavy second in the drop-dead category.) *Sgt. Pepper* was the gateway to the rock and roll angels, and I realized I could well be the *only* person in London, at that precise moment, to be in Andrew Oldham's office listening to "Lucy in the Sky with Diamonds." It was pure magic.

Going home at the end of that day, I was in a haze of amazingness as I opened the door to the dark and always chilly apartment. Immediately the haze of amazingness collapsed with the first words out of my mother's mouth, some doom and gloom about a nasty letter that had come from the gas company, or the electric company, or the landlord, or the bank. Of course, as always, mother elicited the daily dire prediction, "Maybe they'll come tonight and then we'll be homeless."

I didn't care. I'd just *experienced Sgt Pepper*. I went to my room at the end of the hall, with its creaky wooden floor and blue wallpaper that continually peeled near the water pipes. A small gas heater sat in the corner beside a solitary chair, on which I threw my clothes. I'd hung a picture of my father in one corner, a pull-out poster of The Monkees inside the door, and a large poster of Cat Stevens, my heartthrob, above my bed. I used to stare at that beautiful face and daydream of falling in love. I had one window with a view of a weedy, overgrown backyard. I used to sit on the floor, close my eyes, and if I focused hard enough, I could see a chestnut horse, mane and tail flowing, running toward me through tall green grass. Then, like a glass mirror shattering, the image would vanish as the door opened, and Mother would be standing there, dry mouthed in anxiety and panic, holding yet another brown envelope. All bad news came in government-issued brown envelopes.

"They're going to call the bailiffs. What are we going to do?"

She sat on my bed, pulling at her sleeve and shaking her head, as I said the same sentence I was to say for the next forty years.

"I'll take care of it."

I simply had to get another job, but having left school so early, my skills were pretty limited. Working in another store probably wasn't going to happen since my murky past ruled out any references. I decided I was going to get a fun job, one that didn't require much education and that would make the most money. My darling friend Pete Thompson said I could come and work with him and make lots of cash—he drove part time for the Kray twins, Ronnie and Reggie Kray, the famed, most notorious gangsters of the London "Mob" of the sixties. Pete wasn't sure what I could do, but "The Twins" would find me something. They were good boys who loved their mother and were always ready to help a "friend." How bad could it be? The promise of lots of cash clinched the deal.

I joined Pete for one of the drives. We met at Charing Cross subway station at nine p.m.—I'd told Mother I was going to see Pink Floyd at the Roundhouse—and we drove south of the city, slowly driving up and down through a couple of pretty rough neighborhoods, casing the streets. We were on the lookout for someone called Scotty "The Scuzz" Jones, who'd been nicking cash from The Twins and had to be sorted. Thankfully, we didn't find Scotty that night—yes, I was relieved because I am a "gang coward." Also, I wasn't quite sure what our "sorting" mission entailed and what would have constituted a successful sorted conclusion. I do know Scotty was found very dead a few weeks later, tied to the bottom of a concrete pillar holding up Battersea Bridge, his mouth taped to a floating buoy in the Thames. Those Kray lads had quite the imagination.

Since working for The Twins was obviously not going to be a sensible career choice, I had to get resourceful. Mother still had her secretarial job, and by someone's good grace, we were holding our chins above eviction

Me, age sixteen, and my fabulous Sixties look

water, although she had developed this creepy habit of staring at me. I was doing the dishes one evening and I could feel her eyes.

"What?"

She shook her head. "You look hard, not like my little girl anymore."

There were a couple of options as to a valid explanation. One could be the thick-black-eyeliner-and-white-lipstick "Mary Quant" look I was wearing that was all the rage—I thought I looked just fab. Or else I was simply exhausted from trying to save our asses from the damn bailiffs. She said my education was ruined. What education? Making lipstick in chemistry class and surviving almost being beaten up at a school had been a dead loss any way you looked at it. She then ended with, "It's all your father's fault for dying and leaving us."

I had given up trying to explain that he probably hadn't wanted to die and leave us in this mess—although you never know, right? I was a little kid when he died. Surrounded by all the madness as he was, he might have been really unhappy and perhaps welcomed the journey upward to wherever. I tried explaining to Mother that all the weeping and falling into dark holes of depression weren't helping pay the bills. "How dare you blame me! After all I've sacrificed!" she objected.

I felt the sting of her hand as it made direct contact with my cheek.

Chapter 6

The Playboy Club

Gambling had been legalized in Britain and, one evening, I saw a news story about the Playboy Club, which had opened in London a year earlier. Playboy was said to offer the highest paying job in town, as £35 a week was the basic wage. Nobody made that kind of money! An executive secretary who spoke two languages, typed a hundred words a minute, and took shorthand at the lightning speed of a hundred and twenty words a minute made a top salary of £12 a week.

The TV news guy said they were interviewing for Bunnies starting the following afternoon, and you could walk in without an appointment. Well, I was absolutely going to walk in—straight to fame and wealth. Hey, even Mother was a bit excited—Playboy Bunny girls were tantamount to movie stars in their shiny satin corsets, bunny ears, three-inch high-heel shoes, white collar and cuffs, and fluffy cottontails pinned on the back. This was London's "Swinging Sixties," and even though we were swinging full tilt, this Bunny thing was a real enigma for the British. I read the newspaper article again and caught a small paragraph, sinking my heart into my shoes. You had to be eighteen years old. I was sixteen, born in 1951, and I needed to have been born in 1949. My hopes cracked and crumbled until . . .

A very odd thing happened—Mother became the crusader.

"Don't worry, I know what to do," she said with mission authority in her best front line "WWII" voice. She marched into the living room and pulled my birth certificate out of one of the mystery drawers of our old credenza, went over to the window, and studied it through her strong glasses. In those days, UK birth certificates were large pieces of pink paper with all your information typewritten on an Olivetti typewriter. She pulled out our typewriter, which happened to be an Olivetti, and rolled in a piece of paper. After a moment of clacking keys, she pulled out the paper, pushing it under my nose.

"What do you think? I think that's good enough, don't you?" I looked at the type on the paper then on my birth certificate—they were the same. I mean, they were *exactly* the same.

"That looks identical," I said. "What are you . . . ?"

She put the typewriter onto the coffee table and went into the bathroom, coming back with an open razor blade.

"Go and make tea," she said, waving me away.

An hour or so passed with my mother bent over the table. Finally she handed me my birth certificate; it was a miraculous piece of work. By slightly diluting some Wite-Out, she'd carefully erased the date, scraped off the excess liquid, and retyped the date to read 1949. It all lined up perfectly. I told her she'd totally missed her calling, that she should have been a master forger.

"I was, during the war. They'd called me one of their best. I also drew the secret location maps for the RAF's bombing sites in Germany." I waited for The Story, which of course never came and which of course was typical. More secrets never to be divulged. "We'll go to the paper shop in the morning and get it photocopied. You'll take that with you to Playboy." She was actually grinning.

The next afternoon, I did my makeup extra carefully—I looked like a cross between Cher and Yvonne De Carlo from *The Munsters*. You had to get that black eyeliner dead right, in that perfect winged line. Mother handed me my now criminal birth certificate, and I promised her I was going to save the day and get the best and most fabulous job in town. I grabbed a bikini—required interview wear—and took myself off to 45 Park Lane, an entire city block housing the most glamorous building in the world. With great confidence, I walked into the Playboy Club and handed them my Document of Crime, then stood in line with around seventy-five bikini-clad, winged-black-eyeliner-adorned gals for my trip to gorgeous salvation. This would certainly be better than the damn Economist Unit, answering phones for damn politicians.

Victor Lownes, a dapper and genius yet supremely arrogant American, was president of Playboy. Victor was a close friend of Hugh Hefner—another genius—and together they were building the Playboy Empire. Hef, as he was known, had started the magazine in the late fifties, and now clubs were starting to pop up everywhere. This one in London was Victor's brainchild, and he was lord and leader combined. Stepping onto the stage in the Playboy Cabaret room, we went before Victor one by one. He told us to turn around, then asked a couple of questions, and that was that. You left the room, sat in the hall, and waited. By the end of the afternoon, all but ten of us were gone. I was getting chilly in my bikini and thought, *If I get this job, I'll probably be cold all the time.*

At five thirty p.m., the Bunny Mother came out of Victor's office with a clipboard holding The List. I was one of four hired as Croupier Bunnies, and I would deal roulette and blackjack. Trying to be cool as I silently screamed in joy, I was ushered into the executive office, and Victor gave me a big hug.

"Welcome to Playboy." Not a word about my birth certificate or age or anything. I was in my fabulous job—and not being escorted to prison.

At that moment I think I thanked God . . . and baby Jesus.

I raced home and blew through our front door like a happy hurricane. Mother was drying a teacup . . . smiling.

"You got it, didn't you?"

In triumph I stood up straight. "Yes, I did."

And then she hugged me and gave me a big kiss on my cheek. "I'm very proud of you. Let's make tea."

And that was the one and only time she ever uttered those words.

Beginning my life as a Bunny at the London Playboy Club's roulette table.
Photo courtesy of Getty Images

For the next week, I was immersed in a flurry of activity that included Bunny costume fittings and meeting the casino director, Derek Barnard, who was also our gaming instructor and head honcho—the Pit Boss. Derek gave us our schedule for the month-long casino training. Monday through Friday, the day would begin at nine a.m. and end at five p.m. We would be starting the following Monday.

By the end of the first week of training, everyone was sailing along, learning how to flip the little ball around the wheel, cut chips into stacks of perfect twenties, and lay out a hand of blackjack so that each card was mathematically against the next in a fan of precise alignment. Everyone got more proficient every day.

Everyone except me.

Math was my worst subject. In fact, it didn't even qualify as a subject for me, just an unpleasant memory of bamboo canes and Mr. Stack's blood-clotted eyeball. Dealing roulette and blackjack was all numbers—fast numbers played and counted with speed and precision. Playboy had extremely strict rules about how you dealt roulette—the more games you spun, the more money the house made. You had to "*feel*" a stack of twenty chips, then take that stack and snappily cut it down into fives, tens, threes, fours, whatever the payout needed. When the number came up and the table was covered, you had to carefully clear it with two swoops of your hand, without disturbing any of the chips around the winning number, then quickly work out each bet and payout. Then you had to deftly pick up the scooped chips and stack them neatly back against the wheel, in their respective colored towers of twenties. The faster you stacked, the more money for the house. Sometimes Derek covered the table with multiple bets, simulating ten to fifteen punters, all with different colored chips representing different payouts. A single number payout was 35 to 1. A two-number bet, called a split, paid 17 to 1. A three-number bet, called a street bet, paid 11 to 1. A four-number bet, called corner, paid 8 to 1. A six-number bet paid 5 to 1. A bet on the outside, even money bets, paid 2 to 1. A bet on the outside, even money bets, paid 1 to 1. If you hit on the red or black box, it was 1 to 1.

Now, work all this out in different quantities at lightning speed, and *do not* make a mistake and give the wrong person the wrong payout. At one point, I sat on the floor and started crying. I couldn't do it—couldn't count, couldn't add, couldn't see two double-digit numbers and put them together *immediately*! My brain wasn't wired to calculate these impossibly large equations of multiplication, subtraction, and all the rest. Still now I have to count with my fingers—slowly. The first week turned into the second week, then the third, and I was still unable to master this insane task. Occasionally Victor would come and stand in the back of the room watching us . . . me?

I felt sick.

I saw it all ending. I heard Derek Barnard's voice, kindly telling me he was so sorry I didn't make it. I saw my mother crying, disappointed.

"What happened? You used to be so clever," she'd probably say.

I saw the bailiffs coming and taking her to prison, and . . . I saw us homeless. On Wednesday of the third week—eight days before the end of training and the test, everyone had left for the day and I was putting on my coat. Derek came up, took my arm, and led me to a roulette table. He then picked up stacks of different colored chips and covered the numbers with various bets in different combinations.

"Spin," he said, and with arms folded, he watched as I spun the wheel. The ball clattered into the little square slot of number 4. I stood there staring blankly into nowhere.

"You can't do this, can you?" he said.

"No, I can't," I replied with the voice of despair.

"Why not?"

"I see the numbers and I can't . . . don't know . . ."

He led me over to a stool. "You know you've got to be able to deal a game in five minutes for the test?" he said.

That was the criteria to pass. At the end of the four weeks of training, the executives would come in, headed by Victor Lownes, and watch us deal a game. The table would be saturated with multiple bets, carpeting all the numbers, and you had to be able to spin the ball, make the payouts, clear the table, and spin again, all within five minutes. "You're not going to make it through the test."

I nodded.

"What's wrong? Why can't you do this? You're smart."

I was in despair. "I can't add at this speed. I can't . . . I can't do it."

"How did you do in school?"

"In math? Terrible. They moved me to the sewing class."

I can still see Derek now, looking at me long and hard. Oh crap . . . did I look sixteen?

"All right, come here." Grabbing my hand, he walked me back to the roulette table. He took one chip and put it on the line, and asked, "What's that?"

"Seventeen." One chip in one place—I knew that.

He took another and put it on the opposite line, finishing with one in the middle. He tipped down his black-rimmed glasses and said, "Look at the picture. That's sixty-nine." He went on, putting chips in patterns around the number. Thump, thump, thump. "That's sixty-seven." Again thump, thump, thump. "That's a hundred and three. Can you add a hundred and three and sixty-seven? Put the two pictures together."

"A hundred and seventy!" Wow! I actually saw a picture.

"All right. Good."

And for the next three hours, he made pictures of every single payout. He multiplied and mixed colors, on and on. "Count the pictures, Juliette, not the numbers." There was silence. He stared into my eyes and must have seen a glimmer of light. "Yes?" he asked tentatively.

"Yes!" I nodded frantically.

"Good. We've got three days—let's make some magic happen." He was smiling when he said that.

I will never forget Mr. Derek Barnard—he changed my life forever by giving me faith in myself. He was my first mentor and real teacher. He was the first person who gave a shit—who cared. He'd been watching me, and he'd figured out *why* and *how* I wasn't learning. He taught me.

"There's always another way *and* you can do *anything* if you find that way. Laser focus, Juliette. You can do anything."

"Yes . . . I can." I truly believed him.

What I accomplished in those following three days was astonishing. I flew past the test and eventually became the fastest dealer in the club—the one they called on to take over a heavy-hitting table that was losing money. Peter Ryan, the manager, would come down from his office, survey the situation of some Greek tycoon sitting in front of foot-high piles of chips, and say, "Go get the kid."

I loved it. That's how they spoke. I think it was the Sinatra influence—he was a regular VIP patron and thereby, *"a great friend of the show."*

I still hear Derek's voice in my head telling me I can do anything. I still see that roulette table covered in brilliantly colored chips and my hands flying over the numbers, cutting down the stacks and expertly making the payouts.

And . . . to this day I still feel I can make magic happen.

Chapter 7

The Bunny Costume, Mr. Bojangles, and the Chairman

I passed the test, and now the serious business of working began. Playboy was a twenty-four-hour operation. There were three shifts: eight a.m. to four p.m., four p.m. to midnight, and then the graveyard shift from midnight to eight a.m. You rotated one shift a week, so you lived with constant jet lag. The first order of business was the fitting of the Bunny costume. We had two, both of which were individually made for each girl. I feel I would not be doing this part of Playboy history justice if I didn't spend a few minutes on said Bunny costume, the wearing of this extraordinary apparatus, and what you went through to be allowed "on the floor" to serve the esteemed Playboy guests.

First, you applied full stage makeup. You literally obliterated your skin under a thick coat of beige plaster—Max Factor Pan-Cake base. False eyelashes resembling thick, dead spiders were compulsory, along with the red lipstick that matched the red chipless nail polish. Then you squeezed into two pairs of thick black pantyhose and stepped into a bodice/corset contraption called the Bunny costume. Holding it close against your breasts, you went to be zipped up by Martha the seamstress, a determined, dry, humorless woman who I swear enjoyed performing this evil act multiple times a day. You leaned forward, grimly holding on to whatever solid object was available and pressing the costume tight against your breasts, sucked in all your breath, and held as Martha took a kind of extended crochet hook and attached it to the end of the zipper. Digging her heels into the ground, she then heaved her full weight and gusto into the operation of "zipping you up," sometimes leaning forty-five degrees against gravity until that sucker reached the top. A tape measure was produced, and your waist was measured—the goal of twenty-four inches had to be achieved. Master rule from the Bunny Manual: twenty-four inches, no matter what it took. If you gained an inch—well, you were sent home until that inch was gone.

Yes, really.

You made sure your rosette name was pinned correctly to the bottom right of your costume, then, either handfuls of Kleenex or the more popular choice of a pulled-apart sanitary pad was stuffed under each breast to "accentuate" perfect cleavage. The one problem with this particular master rule was that if you were a "big girl," you ended up looking like you had two pendulous watermelons that were just about ready to topple out and over. Sometimes exposure was imminent, so we were all on "nip brigade" for each other. Glue was your friend—until later when you had to un-glue. You then donned a white collar with the little black bow tie and matching white cuffs with Bunny cuff links, making sure they faced toward each other. You teased your hair in that oh so fab sixties bouff, clouded the room with Aqua Net extra-hold hairspray, and wedged on the five-inch-tall Bunny ears with as many hair pins as it took, as the bouff *must* puff up at least three inches behind the ears. You fluffed your tail until it looked like white cotton candy, and the finishing touch was to hang a cigarette lighter on the bottom of your costume, to light ciggies for guests.

Your last and final piece of attire was a pair of three-inch satin stilettos, dyed to match the color of your costume. Upon donning these objects of torture, you teetered on your toes into the Bunny Mother's office for inspection. If deemed perfect—an accomplishment rarely achieved, as more than often you were sent back to re-fluff the tail or adjust your cuff links because they weren't "kissing"—you were allowed onto the floor where you breathed shallow breaths (you had no choice) and stood or walked (if you were a cocktail Bunny) for your eight-hour shift.

"It hurts to be beautiful." Did someone say that? Maybe Joan Crawford, 'cause she did weird shit to herself. I don't know if I was beautiful. I *do* know I was in pain, a sharp, searing agony that burned up and through my feet and legs like hot razor blades rising up from those motherfucking shoes. Your toes would eventually begin to bleed, usually around hour four or five of your shift. You couldn't afford to stain your shoes, so on breaks you'd go to the bathroom and plunge your feet into the toilet bowl, flushing as many times as it took to remove the blood and take down the swelling. Then you'd wrap tape around your toes to stem the inevitable future bleed because if you damaged your satin shoes—you had to pay to replace them. On breaks, we used to sit in a chair in the Bunny room with our legs propped up a wall at a straight vertical angle to stop the throbbing pain and send the blood back to where it belonged.

I smoked my first cigarette on day three of my first week's shift, but it was all good. I didn't complain—I was working at The Place to Go and Be Seen, and I was making more money than university scholars with degrees in biophysics. Every Friday, I would hand Mother my £35 paycheck, and I was grateful. Playboy had given me a new identity—I was special. I had a purpose and a pride in my work. I made friends with some of the most wonderful women I have ever known, women who worked their butts off every single night, and also with a multitude of celebrities who made me laugh and cry and who put a little glitter in my life.

When in town, Sinatra would strut in accompanied by his "boys"— two or three guys who looked like the Blues Brothers, complete with dark suits, sunglasses, and fedora hats. Hilarious, but of course you couldn't laugh. One night, the Chairman sat at my blackjack table playing heavy money, and behind him stood the "Blues Brothers," making sure no one else sat at the table. As I flipped the cards down, he looked up once to give me a cursory inspection—I didn't make the grade, so eyes back to the cards. There were a few short weeks where Sinatra was in every night, and for some odd reason he always ended up on *my* blackjack table, which of course we had to clear of patrons—the Chairman sat alone. I usually dealt roulette, but we were short on girls, so I was going between the two. He never once looked at or spoke to me—I didn't care. It was Sinatra—yes, a legend, but not a very pleasant legend.

One night, we had a "situation." Sinatra wanted to drink bourbon at the table, but you couldn't. Consuming alcohol while gaming was illegal. Period. Sinatra ordered his bourbon, a worried-looking Bunny brought it, and he started drinking—at the table. No one stopped him, but I lifted my hands from the cards and refused to deal the hand. This time, he raised his head slowly and looked at me.

"Deal the fucking cards."

"No, I can't, Mr. Sinatra. You're drinking alcohol and it's against the—"

His face filled with anger. "DEAL THE FUCKING CARDS!" He stood up, and the "boys" stepped closer. The entire room had been silenced. Determined he wasn't going to ruffle me, I kept my hands held high. I was not going to commit a crime because of some not-so-very-nice legend.

"I'm sorry, Mr. Sinatra. It's illegal and—" I didn't get to finish my sentence, as another Bunny appeared, and the Pit Boss whisked me off the table.

"Mr. Lownes wants to see you upstairs."

Standing in the elevator, I was sure Victor was going to applaud my courage and dedication to the Playboy rules. Instead, his words were brief and to the point.

"You will go back down and apologize to Mr. Sinatra. He can do whatever he wants—whenever he wants. Playboy is his club. He is the Chairman."

"But . . ."

Victor held up his hand and delivered the winning punch. "He'll tell me to fire you. And we will." I was aghast.

"Really? *Really?*" I was genuinely surprised. Okay, so here was a choice. Righteousness versus eating.

I dutifully apologized to Mr. Sinatra, and he stared at me for way too long. I stared right back. He said, "Y'know, for a pretty broad, you sure are a mouthy one. Now get out of my fucking sight, in case I change my mind." I presumed that meant to tell Victor to fire me. I don't believe we ever spoke again, but I did learn one important life lesson that night: pick the hill you're going to die on carefully.

When in town, Clement Freud, Jerry Lewis, Sammy Davis Jr., and pretty much the entire cast of the show business world would pass through those doors at one time or another. There was a large board by the front door, just inside the entrance, where the Door Bunny would put up the names of all the famous people in the club that night. We were encouraged to socialize but not fraternize, which basically meant "don't date anyone." Oh, right—sure.

The sad sights were the casino punters who arrived early in the evening and were still there at six a.m., heads down to either cards or chips, unwavering in their intense concentration. We could have all been butt naked and it wouldn't have mattered; rarely did they look up from their supreme focus—the table. Occasionally, another box of chips would be brought as they gambled away thousands, sometimes their lives.

One night, I was on the graveyard shift, dealing roulette. A Greek businessman had been sitting at my table since five p.m.—it was now around four a.m. His wife appeared and stood by his side, but he didn't acknowledge her, and I saw the tears in her eyes as she put a hand on his shoulder, whispering to him that it was time to go. Without looking up, he brushed her hand off and laid more chips on number seven, *his* number, which had kicked him in the ass for the past ten hours. Down about £100,000—the equivalent of at least $1 million today—he signaled for more chips from the cage. This time, nothing arrived except the cage boss, who quietly told him his cash limit had run out. The guy stood up, downed the last of his coffee, walked to the front door, collected his overcoat, and left, his poor wife following behind.

I had been at Playboy almost a year when one night I was again on a roulette table and heard my name. I looked up to see Sammy Davis Jr., glittering in all his diamonds and gold rings and huge gold chains, with Peter

Lawford, looking a bit sleepy and not quite sure where he was. With them was another guy I didn't know. They were all staring at me. The guy I didn't know was movie director Richard Donner, who was appropriately dressed in movie director gear—customary tight satin/silk shirt unbuttoned way down to reveal enormous gold chains front and center, tight pants flaring just right over snakeskin boots, and the largest, goldest Rolex watch I have ever seen. Oh, and everyone had sunglasses on. They were all smiling at me from across the table.

Sammy called out, "Hey, kid! You wanna be in pictures?" (God, I miss that wonderful language!) Hell, yes! And so I was chosen, along with a couple of other girls, to be in *Salt and Pepper*, a fun "Rat Pack" romp, typical of many movies of the sixties. It was being shot at Shepperton Studios in London, and the club gave me the time off to be a *Salt and Pepper* girl. Richard (Dick) Donner later went on to become one of the biggest movie directors in Hollywood, with films including *The Omen*, *Superman*, and all the *Lethal Weapon* pictures.

It was about a week's shoot. Our first scenes in the cemetery were done and we were moving to the casino set, when Dick said to the three Bunnies they'd hired that the picture would pop if we all went topless while dealing our various games, and of course, we would earn more money. The other girls didn't hesitate, agreeing unanimously.

I said no. I was asked again, being politely informed how much more exciting the picture would be. Didn't I want to "pop"?

"No. Thank you."

"C'mon, kid, no way can you be the only one wearing a [bikini] top. We'll give you a close-up."

I shook my head.

"You're being difficult. Not cool."

"Sorry. I can't."

"Why not?" He barely covered his anger.

"My mother might see it."

I was exiled from the casino scene and sent to the crafts table for the rest of the day. That evening, Dick invited me over to his rented apartment in

Belgravia (super posh) for drinks and to "talk about my role." I was slightly puzzled, as I really didn't have a "role." I never said a word throughout the entire movie, being just one of the silent mourners at a gravesite and a *Salt and Pepper* girl in a casino scene—where I'd been banished from the set for not wanting to "pop."

I remember considering possible reasons for the invitation. Maybe he had applauded my courage for saying no and was going to offer me a different role? In another movie! Something with speaking! Maybe I was going to get some lines in *this* movie! Dick greeted me at the door dressed in a white fluffy bathrobe.

"God, you're beautiful," he said in his best movie director voice as he led me to the sofa. He offered me a drink. I declined. He laughed.

"How about a nice glass of lemonade?" he said in an atrocious British accent.

"That would be lovely," I said as he slid in beside me, confirming no lemonade would be forthcoming. A knot started to form in my stomach. Oh shit—I could see in his eyes he was about to kick it up a notch. He leaned in closer.

"Do you know you look exactly like Judy Garland? Only prettier." He was drooling . . . slightly. "You wanna be a star? I could make you a star if you want." He moved closer. "Can't you see your name in lights? C'mon, kid, do the scene. We won't shoot your breasts . . ."

"Then I can have a bikini on with the straps down." Gotcha.

"Kid. You're being . . ." He stopped, smartly knowing that angering me would only kill any chances of a successful score. He leaned in, his voice soft and enticing. "Don't you want to be a star? I can put you in my next picture. If you're gonna be in this business, you have to learn how to be . . . accessible."

Yes, he said that—he did—but that's what they all said. That's how they were, and that's what they did. He waited patiently for my reply, and since he was as close as he could get, he leaned in further, now mere inches from my face.

"Thank you, Mr. Donner, but . . ."

Suddenly I was overwhelmed and smothered by Aramis cologne and Scotch whiskey as this large man landed on top of me, gold chains hitting my chin like ice cubes. He planted a sloppy wet kiss right on my lips, forcing my mouth open. He didn't scare me, and I really wasn't that mad and my life wasn't ruined. He was just doing what all guys did in those days, and you just had to take care of yourself, whatever it took. I pushed him off, telling him he was just fabulous but I couldn't.

So he came back in—another angle. "C'mon, kid, don't be dumb. I can make you—" I slid out from under him onto the floor and stood up.

"I am a virgin. I don't take the pill, and I *know* you don't want that potential obstruction in your life, right?" If he hadn't gone for that, I had "time of the month" up my sleeve. He backed off and told me to let him know when I changed my mind.

With stardom off the table, he stood up, became a total gentleman, and called me a cab. We said good night, he handed me a few pounds for the ride home, and I left. I do remember thinking, *If this is the deal to star making—I'm going to fail miserably.*

I do believe—to this day—that it's all about perspective. That encounter could have gone bad—I mean ugly bad. He could have dropped something in the lemonade that never arrived, and that would have been a different situation. But he didn't, and "bad" didn't happen. I was lucky. I'd flatly rejected him, and he didn't get angry. Now, I certainly wasn't worldly or, hell, I certainly wasn't experienced in men's sexual behaviors, but I knew Dick Donner meant no harm. I knew he was just being a typical horny, chauvinist guy, and I also knew it was my responsibility to stop him dead in his tracks from what could and would have happened. Something learned by the ice cream van. I wasn't wounded and I wasn't damaged for life. I didn't hate men from that day on—I was just wiser and a lot less gullible and certainly not as eager to make late-night visits to famous men's apartments, especially when they greeted you at the door in a fluffy bathrobe.

My time on the movie was great. Dick and I came to an understanding, and along with Sammy and Peter Lawford, we became good friends. Not long after we wrapped, Sammy opened in *Golden Boy*, starring as Joe

Wellington at the London Palladium in the West End. He took one of the Playboy apartments above the club for the run of the show. A few weeks into the run, Sammy came down with a bad cold and had to stay home for a couple days. I don't quite remember why, but he called and asked me to come over for tea, and could I bring him some good British cough candy? Okay. Tea was good. Tea was safe.

I arrived, armed with a bag of lemon sherbet candy, just as Sinatra was leaving—we did have a moment of acknowledgment as we politely nodded to one another in the lobby. Sinatra stared at me as the elevator doors closed, his face disappearing behind the steel curtains. I had to chuckle, as this was pretty funny—Frank Sinatra and I weren't talking. We'd had a tiff.

Sammy greeted me at the door, cocooned in a huge white toweling robe. Tea had been served and a tray was on the table, complete with a lilac-patterned Wedgwood tea set. We sat, almost disappearing in the large overstuffed sofa, and for the next three hours, Sammy talked about the assassination of Dr. Martin Luther King, Vietnam, apartheid in South Africa, Nelson Mandela's unjust imprisonment, as well as his car accident and how he nearly died, but because of the Jewish mezuzah he had around his neck (given to him by the singer Eddie Cantor) his life was saved. Hence, he had converted to Judaism. He roared with laughter.

"Black and Jewish! Now that's funny!" (His Jack Benny reference.)

He told stories of playing the Sands Hotel in Las Vegas and how Sinatra refused to go on until Sammy could walk into the hotel from the *front* door and not the kitchen. I asked him why he had to go in through the kitchen. For a second, he looked at me as if I was trying to be insulting, or a wise ass. He popped a lemon sherbet in his mouth.

"C'mon, kid. Really?"

I nodded. I truly didn't know. I knew there was a lot of rioting in the US from the odd news items on TV, and I knew Black people were being treated badly, but as both my parents had thought Black people were a scourge on the world, I was confused. Even though it kind of made sense, as my parents probably represented many racist people of those days, why were Black people treated so badly because of the color of their skin? It honestly didn't make sense . . . and to this day, it still doesn't. Sammy explained to me how going in through the kitchen rather than through the front door was an insult—and this somewhat redeemed the Chairman in my eyes.

He took both my hands and covered them with his own. I became very aware of how tiny his fingers were inside those huge gold rings, how small and vulnerable he was sitting in the corner of the overstuffed sofa in his huge fluffy robe. He was a megastar—at that time, the biggest in the world—but here he was sitting beside me, just being Sammy, a Black man who continued to suffer every day from the continual and rampant racism back home. He knew I had no clue.

"You are young, unique, and so innocent. One day you'll know much more than you want, maybe even more than you need to know. Stay young for as long as you can."

And in that second, *I knew* this man was a gentleman. In those last few hours, we'd become good friends, and he really *had* just wanted to have tea and talk. He wasn't married, and though he had his Rat Pack family and the world adored him, he was pretty much alone. I knew I was experiencing something important, and this was a moment of time *I knew* I should never forget. I realized how unaware I was of anything outside my own personal world, my endless day-to-day struggle to get by, to fit in, to make friends and learn—maybe—to do something more meaningful than look after my mother and be a world-class survivor. That afternoon, sitting on that overstuffed sofa, Sammy Davis in his white fluffy robe taught me there were people who had real problems—people out there actually *dying* for a cause.

As I left that evening, I made a vow. I would pay attention. I would never get to my death bed with one single regret or feeling of bitterness, and I would never judge anyone by the color of their skin. I had seen the pain in Sammy's eyes as he talked about the awful segregation in the States, the unrelenting violence and humiliation of people, good people who just happened to be Black. Megastar he might have been, but his life still hurt. He had a lot of bitterness, and with just cause. I pledged to myself—I

Sammy Davis singing "Mr. Bojangles"
Photo courtesy of Evening Standard Ltd.

would do everything I could to live out loud. To be authentic, and to hell with the consequences.

Sammy Davis Jr. came in and out of my life for many more years to come. When I eventually moved to New York, he asked me if I would visit his mother, as he didn't get to see her much. So, every Thursday afternoon I'd pick up butter cookies and spend an hour with Elvera, one of the most elegant women I've ever met—and funny. Sammy was an extraordinary talent and a unique human being, and there will never be another. I am honored to have known him and to have called him my friend for the length of time I did. To this day, when I feel down, I'll find his "Mr. Bojangles" on YouTube, and for a few minutes I'm back in the Playboy apartment on Park Lane, drinking tea out of a lilac-patterned Wedgwood china teacup, listening to my friend talk about life.

Chapter 8

Helter Skelter

It was the end of my fifth week of a midnight to eight a.m. shift. I walked out of the club so tired I could barely stand. Ahead of me, I had three bus rides to take me the long two-hour journey home. I decided I had to buy transport, but having little money and no driving license, my options were limited to a bicycle or motor scooter, neither of which required any type of license. The bicycle option wasn't going to work, as I was exhausted when I left work, and the thought of pedaling twenty miles home was . . . well . . . not going to happen. When I was on the four p.m. to midnight shift, the trains and buses ran on a night schedule, which meant fewer buses and no trains, and sometimes it would take three hours to get home.

Finally, I decided a scooter was the answer. I bought a used Vespa from one of the bartenders. Its top speed was a whopping 35 mph, but it was cheap and convenient—a full five-gallon tank of gas lasted two weeks, and parking meant nothing more than propping it up beside the back door of the club and chain locking the wheels. Cold weather and rain were my biggest challenges. Quite often, I would have to get to work early just to thaw out from driving twenty miles in freezing weather, sometimes with ice pellets hitting my face. Damn, I do remember that cold.

As I think about those days . . . it's weird—I braved the elements daily, but it was a special time. We all felt so safe. Girls, alone and in full stage makeup, out and about at all hours of the night . . . that seemed perfectly normal then. I lived way out in the suburbs and rode my scooter back and forth during the middle of the night and early mornings, never bothered by anyone and never stopped by the police. Regular folks, movie stars, and politicians all walked the streets day and night in total safety. Restaurants and nightclubs were the same. No one had a gun, and *no one* was trying to blow up anything or steal kids. The only people who had bodyguards or security detail were the royal family and visiting dignitaries—oh, and the London version of the Brinks money van. I learned who to trust and who not to.

At the club, I had friends who were beyond awesome, friends who covered for me if I messed up under the Playboy crown, friends who lied for me on the phone to my mother when I was dating so I could stay out late, or maybe not even come home. Friends whom I laughed with until my sides hurt, sending the pain in my feet miraculously away for a few moments. We had no cell phones, no social media, no instant anything. If you wanted to make a phone call, you found a pay phone and hoped it wasn't broken. I always liken my tenure at Playboy to being in a glamorous, hard-core military unit like the Navy SEALs, with all of us carrying the big log into the ocean together on three-inch stiletto heels. I miss those gals a lot.

My best friend was another Bunny by the name of Cassidy. She lived in Kensington in her own apartment and became my finest and best excuse not to have to go home at night. She was Academy Award brilliant on the phone to Mother, carefully explaining in her most articulate British why I was needed in Kensington. Sharon Tate was also a dear friend of ours. At the time, she was pregnant and would come over to the apartment to smoke cigarettes so her husband, Roman Polanski, wouldn't find out. Roman was in London scouting film locations, which kept him busy, though he did find time to join us on occasions, making a point of telling us how much he trusted us to take care of his beautiful wife. He was very polite, but he was a weird little man. You had to keep reminding yourself of his tremendous talent in order to take him seriously. One evening, I was also reminded that this "funny little man" was anything but funny.

Sharon hadn't been feeling well and Cassidy was working her four p.m. to midnight shift at the club, leaving me at her apartment, as we'd thought we might go out later. Around nine p.m., the phone rang—it was Roman inviting me to his rented home in Belgravia to have drinks and look at some preliminary footage of his next movie—for my opinion. I was flattered—and also stunningly ignorant—and jumped in a cab. We were upstairs in his office, and I don't think I was halfway through a glass of wine (with obviously no film footage forthcoming), when he grabbed my waist and started kissing me with a sloppy ferociousness, pushing me backward onto the couch. As his hand went up my dress and literally ripped my underwear down, I punched him in the chest, then face—hard. He fell to the floor, cursing in Polish, and walked out, *locking the door behind him*! Are you fucking kidding me? How the hell did I get myself locked in Roman Polanski's fucking office? This was not a pinch of the butt or a suggestive whisper in the ear, and this wasn't merely a harmless guy following the whims of arousal—this was an abusive attack by a man with violent sexual intentions. Seeing a telephone on the desk, I picked it up and yelled through the door, "Hey, Roman! I'm holding the phone, and I'm two seconds away from calling the police to report an abduction and attempted rape, and then I'm calling your wife with all the details!"

The door opened and, taking the stairs two at a time, I was out of the house, only to find myself somewhat stranded in the silent residential streets of Belgravia at midnight. I walked the four miles back to Cassidy's. She came home just after I got there. I never said a word. Roman Polanski may have been a great filmmaker, but he was one sick, perverse little guy. He and I used to see each other often at various get-togethers, never speaking, never acknowledging one another, just letting our reptilian brains tick away between us.

I didn't want to upset Sharon, so I kept the incident to myself. At this point in time, Sharon, Cassidy, and I had become best friends, spending many crazy good evenings together, rolling far into the night at all the different trendy clubs in town. We'd start at the Revolution and hang out with The Animals, Manfred Mann, or whoever was playing that night. Then it was on to Tiles on Oxford Street to catch the Bee Gees and maybe finish up at the Scotch to have a couple drinks with Hendrix and Jeff Beck. I have a deep and fond nostalgia for those days, even though you sometimes had to dart around the "bottom pinching" and seduction attempts, and everyone told you they had fallen madly in love with you right then and there. We laughed—we knew it was bullshit, but we also knew it was all good-hearted fun. Guys did what guys do, but there was no question, we were always treated like ladies. We never paid for a thing, and we always got home safely at the end of the night. I suppose it was a kind of honor code. They tried, and we said no. It was accepted, and respect prevailed.

Two weeks before she was to give birth, Sharon went home to the States to have the baby. I had transitioned over to be a cocktail Bunny, and I was working the disco the fateful night of August 8, 1969. Roman and Victor Lownes were sitting at my station, having dinner. I'd just served their drinks when the room director hurriedly brought a phone to the table. Roman took the call—his face stopped moving. He hung up and said something in Victor's ear. They both stood up and hurried out of the room. The DJ stopped the music and stepped out of his booth to make the announcement.

My friend had just been cut to pieces by a posse of demons, under the manipulation of their crazed, malevolent leader, Charles Manson.

I learned something that night that I honestly had not known.

There are some seriously evil people out there.

Chapter 9

Cat Stevens

One day, Cassidy announced she had a new boyfriend, Barry Ryan, and we were going over to hang out with him and his twin brother, Paul. I was excited. Barry and Paul were famous pop singers who'd just had the hit single "Don't Bring Me Your Heartaches" come out. Their mother was Marion Ryan, who'd been a fifties icon dubbed "The Marilyn Monroe of Popular Song." Their stepfather was Harold Davison, one of the impresarios of the day, who'd introduced Sinatra to the UK. Harold, along with Lew Grade, also introduced The Muppets to British TV. I was a huge fan of Paul and Barry but tried not to look even a bit impressed—you know, you had to look faintly bored with everything, according to teenage rules.

We went over to Paul and Barry's parents' place, a gorgeous Georgian apartment in Grosvenor Square, *the* desirable address of the rich and famous. When we arrived, Paul opened the front door, and a waft of familiar music trickled out into the hallway, probably from a record playing. We went in, and he gave Cassidy and me both a hello hug. My eyes traveled over his shoulder to a chair in the middle of the room, the origin of the wafting music.

And my heart stopped beating.

Cat Stevens was sitting in that chair, playing the guitar. Yes, there he was, head down, wearing a pair of thin, wire-framed glasses, playing the guitar—the most beautiful man I had ever seen and the idol of my dreams. I closed my eyes then opened them—he was still there, ten feet away, playing the guitar. Barry Ryan came out of another room and said hi, but I couldn't move. He introduced Steven—his actual name was Steven Georgiou—who put the guitar down and stood up. I was really trying to take a breath—one gasp would have worked—just so as not to look uncool. *Be casual*, I told myself. Steven stood in front of me, holding out his hand, and I faintly heard him say, "Hello." I shook it, inwardly cursing this weird shivering thing that was happening, damn it. He released my hand, went back to his chair, and picked up the guitar. I sat too, right beside him on the carpet, where I stayed for the next two hours.

At the end of our visit (of which I have little recollection, other than if I'd died that day, it would have been okay—way more okay than *Sgt. Pepper* or Marc Bolan), we were getting ready to leave, and Steven asked me if I wanted to go for a walk. Now, I'd had lots of dates with "kinda" boyfriends, a few famous pop stars, all of which involved lots of teenage smooch kissing and clumsy gropes under the sweater, but that was as far as I'd gotten; I had never "done it." Cramped in phone booths, squeezed into doorways, secreted in someone's tiny bedroom in a flat they shared with five other guys, or while sitting in the tried-and-true back row of the movie theater were pretty much your only options for making out, as most everyone lived at home with their parents. I suppose there were lots of kids who could have afforded their own place, but why do all your own cleaning, cooking, and laundry, when Mom could do it? Parents, except for my mother, who was not *ever* included in any of these parental equations, were mostly good natured and trusting, never worrying where their kids were going or who they were with. The world was safe. Right now, I'd been asked to go for a walk with a man whom I'd worshipped and adored from afar, whose four-foot-high poster hung above my bed—this man who was my dream come true.

The walk turned into coffee. He asked to see me again. I tried not to cry. Then phone calls and dinners. Then Princess Mariam of Johor's engagement party at the Grosvenor House Hotel, and more phone calls, and hanging out a lot with Paul and Barry and everyone's pal, Pete Thompson. Then more dinners and hanging out at Steven's flat. He lived above his dad's café—the Moulin Rouge (yes, my grandfather's old lunch spot)—on Shaftesbury Avenue right across from the Shaftesbury Theater. His mom, Ingrid, was Swedish, and his dad, Stavros, was Greek. Together they owned the restaurant on the ground floor; they were divorced but still living together.

It was a tiny apartment, and I can still see the piano taking up most of the living room. I can still see and hear him playing those songs . . . I was in love, you know, that blind, agonizing, brutal, tear-your-guts-out love that teenagers can feel better than anyone? Yup, that one. Extra strong because I had never felt love for anything in my life, other than a dog and a horse. Now, here was this beautiful man who was gentle and talented and thought I was perfect. We would talk for hours on the phone and see each other almost every day. We would go to dinner at the Coq Au Vin and Mr. Chow's and hold hands and plan things. He would tell me he loved me and how happy he was, and I would melt.

For the first time, I felt I belonged somewhere.

He was my first love, the real one, the one you remember for the rest of your life. As time went on, we talked about which day we would *do it*, as *it* had to be done and must be planned. I was terrified. I thought I would go home, and Mother would know I had "done it."

I remember the afternoon it happened: there, on his mom's sofa in the living room, above the restaurant. "Hey Jude" was playing on the record player, and it was clumsy, awkward, and hurt a bit. I didn't hear fat sparrows singing and the earth did not move, but I was with the only person I could have ever imagined it to be with, and so it was magical. I can remember every moment of that afternoon—it was and still is one of my most precious memories. I loved him so much it terrified me. I used to sit on the floor as he wrote his music and remember thinking that thought again, *I must never forget this moment—these days, this time—ever*. I had this weird and awful feeling it wasn't going to last long, so I had to keep it close.

Steven's career was in a lull. He'd had some success with a couple of singles ("I Love My Dog" and "Matthew and Son") and an album, but he'd also recently recovered from tuberculosis, where he'd lain in a hospital bed for months with just a guitar and time, giving him the wherewithal to change the direction of his music and his life. He wanted to get away from the pop singer thing and be his own person. A few years later, he rose to the top of the music echelon, becoming one of the most well-known and beloved singer-songwriters of our time. To this day I meet men and women of all ages who "grew up" on Cat Stevens's music: "Peace Train," "Father & Son," and so much more of his music were and still are the anthems to many people's lives. But for now, he was still just Steven, the man I loved.

I look back and see it all so clearly. This young man was wiser than his years. I wish I'd had a little more courage to talk to him and a lot more wisdom to have listened and really heard what he was saying. If so, maybe I would have understood his anguish and confusion about who he was and where he needed to go. I wish I could have appreciated and been proud of how he stuck so solid to his quest of being authentic and not changing for other people, or the business. But I was young and thought I knew a lot (everything), with no idea how fragile and damaged I really was and how fast I was running from my own darkness and pain.

I had no awareness of what I was becoming. I became so scared of losing him that I lost myself. Many times, I tried to remember how I felt leaving Sammy Davis's apartment that day, when I vowed and pledged all these wonderful things I would and wouldn't do—and who I would and wouldn't be. I couldn't remember anything—my life and very existence had become a hazy, distant fog. One day, Steven proudly showed me his latest acquisition—an Arp machine, a revolutionary synthesizer capable of creating sounds from a keyboard no one had ever experienced before. We sat on the floor listening to the record *Switched-On Bach* by Wendy Carlos, one of the original albums to use the synthesizer. Despite the underlying dread that I was losing myself, I was happier than I'd ever been—I was in love and it would be forever and ever . . . and ever.

Needless to say, Mother hated him. One day, I invited Steve over for tea where, for two miserable hours, she interrogated him on politics, his philosophies, all to which he had nothing to say. He was a gentle man, a musician, certainly not mentally equipped to go head-to-head with a woman on a mission of character destruction. She lifted her cup. She wasn't done.

"Did you go to school in Greece?" she said, knowing full well it was a bullshit question.

"I was born here. I went to school here." He didn't look at her. I could feel him folding up on the couch beside me.

Finally she grilled him on his family—his Greek father and Swedish mother.

"Of course, Juliette's father hated the Greeks," she added when he had answered her questions. "He knew they could never be trusted." An intentional, piercing stab at a man she knew I deeply cared about. Steve's face clouded in anger, but he still said nothing, just continued to drink his by now cold tea. My embarrassment was profound. I wanted to cry and strangle her at the same time. This is what she did when she saw I was happy with someone. She had no one and so would constantly remind me how she was alone because of me. "I never met anyone who was good enough for you." Another accusatory sentence usually accompanied by tears. She hated everyone I liked or loved, and I spent way too many years trying to convince her of people's goodness.

There was another eight months of pure joy with Steven, then it ended. I did something stupid and thoughtless—I had a brief thing with Paul Ryan, one of our closest friends. Why? I thought Steven had had a brief thing with Cassidy when I was on holiday, so I did what every dumb teenager does—retaliated. I don't know exactly what was going through my head, and it doesn't matter. I was eighteen and trying to fill the hole with so many missing pieces, and so I jumped in headfirst with anyone who showed me the slightest affection or more.

For many years after, I slept with guys way too fast, thinking that was the way to make them stay. Maybe I was trying to see a light at the end of a tunnel that had nothing but oncoming trucks hurtling at me. Perhaps I wanted to create a brief feeling of happiness, of being loved and accepted. I used to manipulate circumstances and cause drama, gossip . . . anything that created chaos. It gave me a rush—a high of adrenaline that made me feel something, as most of the time I felt nothing. When a teenage girl has no solid fatherly guidance in her life, as in my case, odds are she may run adrift. I also had a mother who was grabbing at me daily in her neediness, and it was awful. I couldn't handle this massive burden of another human being hanging around my neck, but it was there. Her pain became my pain, and I didn't want it, so I grabbed at any and all emotional contact—didn't matter the source—just to feel something.

Our love affair faded day by day, as Steven became cold and distant. I was the one calling him now, and suddenly there was nothing to say. Finally, he told me I'd betrayed him with Paul, and he simply didn't love me anymore.

It was over. Done. I wanted to die. He'd just signed with Barry Krost, a well-known entrepreneur, and would soon be going to America. Suddenly he was gone, and my heart broke in shredded pieces. Life was over, and the pain was unbearable. I actually thought I was going to die of a broken heart. I stopped sleeping and eating, and I went through the motions at work, staring at the pay phone on the Bunny room wall, thinking of how to call him with some deep, enlightening insight that would bring him running back. I didn't know how to get through the day—there was a committee squabbling in my head that wouldn't shut up. *It was all my fault*, I told myself. *Why did I do it? Obviously, I wasn't lovable enough for him to forgive me. Maybe not pretty enough. Maybe I wasn't talented enough at anything and he was amazing, so what kind of girlfriend could I be as a nothing, a nobody, and a cheat? Maybe my mother drove him off with her insults. Maybe he saw me for who I really was . . . maybe . . . maybe . . .*

My head was filled with the rantings of a teenager's suffering. He was gone, and I genuinely believed there would *never* be another—never, never, ever. I wanted to close my eyes and disappear—end the pain. Recently, I found the letter I wrote him the day after we broke up. It was difficult to read the tragic sadness that young me felt, and it reminded me of how alone we all were back then, living in a time when, if you were in any kind of emotional trouble or trauma, you just needed to figure stuff out. Yes, you had your friends, but we didn't talk about feelings and emotions—you broke up with a boyfriend, you cried a bit, then it was on to the next party. There were no therapists, no psychologists, no Oprah, no Dr. Phil, no one. There wasn't even a damn self-help book. You were on your own.

I was gutted, smothered in a pain I had never known, and . . . I had to keep it from Mother. She'd recently asked me why I wasn't seeing him anymore. Of course she knew. She watched me like a hawk and never missed any phone calls I tried to have in private. I told her we'd broken up and didn't let myself cry—not in front of her.

Patting my shoulder, she smiled the benevolent smile of the devil. "He was never good enough for you." And the damn kettle whistled in the kitchen.

I was mentally shattered. For the first time, I felt I was losing hold of life, and there was nowhere to go for help. If you really went bat-shitty, they would put you in a mental hospital or a care home where a psychiatrist would give you drugs to numb you out, or electroshock therapy. The sixties may have been swinging, but they were pretty bleak on the help-me-figure-out-why-I'm-in-agony front.

Notwithstanding all this, I went through the motions of life, gathering with and around my friends, getting it together and slowly trying to glue my heart back together. Pete Thompson made me laugh every day. His wife Chrissie was an angel, and Paul and Barry Ryan were my rocks. I recovered . . . well . . . kind of.

I did have one dear, unexpected friend. Since the time Steve had taken me to her engagement party—now broken off—Princess Mariam of Johor and I had become close. She was the sweetest, most generous person I have ever known. She helped me cope with my mother by inviting me out to everything with all our friends, including Paul and Barry, Pete and Chrissie, and of course sometimes Steven, which was difficult, but I knew why she did it. I had to get past him—he was gone—and she led me

Clive managed to capture me in the perfect light for my "breakup photo."
Photo by Clive McLean

through all the awkward moments, standing right there beside me. She was also extremely efficient and creative in lying to Mother when we went out to the clubs and I stayed over at her gorgeous home in Chelsea. She gave me clothes that I could never afford and a new television when ours blew up—literally. Of course my mother disliked her intensely.

"She's insincere. I don't trust her. All she has is money."

"Which she spends on us! The television we just got? Where did that come from?" Surely that would convince her of Mariam's sincerity.

"She's just trying to buy your friendship. I really wish you would stop seeing her."

I was ready to go full-in on an argument that would have gone ugly, but I didn't. It wasn't worth it, and . . . I actually didn't care. Fuck what my mother thought. I owe a huge part of my survival during those painful times to Mariam and her love and kindness.

Included among my new friends was the incomparable Clive McClean, who was hilarious, as well as an outstanding photographer. Later he was to become the leading photographer for *Hustler* magazine—he made naked look gorgeous. I was at his apartment one afternoon when he told me to go sit on the window ledge. Moving me around the room, he snapped his

My precious friends, Paul and Barry Ryan
Photo courtesy of Shutterstock

camera for an hour, producing photographs so beautiful I hardly recognized myself in them.

Steven became crazy famous in America while my friends turned me around and helped me begin again. I remember how much and how often we laughed. One day I was over at Paul and Barry's apartment in Eaton Square. Paul had just been to Carnaby Street and bought himself some platform boots. Everyone knew they were the *only* kind of boots you should own! He tipped up the bag and out fell four pairs of these ridiculous sixties inventions. Increasing your height by at least four inches, they were almost knee-high, with "layers" of platforms on the soles and heels. Paul had bought a white pair with alternate white and gold platforms, a black pair with alternating red and black platforms, and finally a piercing blue with gold stars all over the three layers of platforms. Lovingly, he held a blue and gold star boot to his chest. He chuckled as he said in his perfect John Lennon voice, "What'dya think, love? Pretty bloody smashing, aren't they?"

I fell off the couch laughing, then Paul and Barry started laughing, and we laughed together until our sides hurt. The wonderful, innocent absurdity of it all crackled something back to life inside me, and I will forever love those guys for the hilarity that was just who they were. Life was so simple back then. No one took anything too seriously, especially not themselves. I miss my friends every single day.

But . . . I used to do something a bit strange. Every time Franco Zeffirelli's film *Romeo & Juliet* was playing, I would go and watch the movie by myself and, by myself, I saw that film over forty times, crying in the same place, forty times.

No, I didn't understand why. That took another thirty years.

Chapter 10

Eviction to Misery

It was one of those weather anomalies that occasionally occur in England—an arctic blast of misery, where the snow piled so high people couldn't get out their front doors and the buses couldn't run. The underground trains were barely working, and cars were half buried in walls of snow on the sides of the road while the ones that could move crept along, spinning in circles over thick black ice. The temperature plummeted to below freezing, which, in England, is tantamount to torture. Mother and I had managed to put our ancient car around the corner on a side street and had thrown old blankets over it in an attempt to keep it from freezing. Most of the vehicle was covered, and we had tucked my Vespa under the blankets against the door. The snow kept falling, adding a thick cloak of invisibility to the world around us. Darkness came around four p.m., and it was eerie seeing people walking down the middle of the main road, their cold, shadowy silhouettes bowed against the blowing snow, lit only by the dim streetlights. We were accustomed to forty degrees and rain this time of year, and not this ferocious cold and wind that belonged on some Alaskan mountain.

It was Friday night. The wind was howling and the snow blowing, and the cold was wet and bone chilling. It was just six days after Andy

Stewart had dragged us into the New Year with his *Next Year Tonight* TV show. Mother had our three portable electric heaters all going at the same time, and just to clarify, back in those days, these heaters were dynamically dangerous. The elements were uncovered, glowing bare and white hot—no front protective coverings or bars and absolutely *no* safety/emergency shut-off feature. She also had all four burners going on the gas stove, plus the oven blasting at 450 degrees with the door wide open. Fuck any fire hazard—this was survival. We were wearing four layers of clothing, and hot tea and brandy had been our dinner. The lights flickered, threatening darkness at any moment. Even the crazy lady upstairs was quiet.

Now, I have since learned, if you believe something strongly enough, you can will that sucker right to you—it'll arrive grinning, with a shrill wail of "I'm here!" Well, someone in our house must have been believing the bailiffs would arrive, and they did—promptly at ten o'clock that bitter cold January night. There was a loud rapping on the front door. Mother let out a shriek and ran into the kitchen. I opened the door to two men dressed by code of the local magistrate's court bailiffs, in black suits under large gray overcoats flecked with snow, with black hats and black lace-up shoes. They introduced themselves as Mr. Fletcher and Mr. Brown and produced written authorization to act on behalf of the creditor—our landlord—to take an inventory of goods to be seized. Mr. Brown waved a large roll of yellow tape to be wrapped around everything we owned. He carried on, saying, "An inventory of goods will be left with the debtor or at the premises, along with any documents required by regulations or statute."

Mr. Brown was brief and to the point. We could take one suitcase apiece, but everything else—furniture, appliances . . . everything—now belonged to the court. I honestly didn't believe what I was seeing and hearing. Mother had crept out of the kitchen, holding the teakettle, and stood trembling behind me. Mr. Brown solemnly took the kettle from her hand and told us since we no longer owned any of "said" belongings, we could not use them anymore. They would box up all personal items like photographs and extra clothing, and we would be notified when to pick them up from an appointed location. I tried to speak, and a large leather gloved hand went up to silence me. We had one hour to pack.

"Pack for what?" I was trying to grasp the truth.

"You must vacate the premises immediately," said Mr. Brown.

"Really? Now? It's ten thirty! At night! In this weather?" I was horrified. There was no answer.

Mother was paralyzed in place as they started taping, and I can still hear the *swish* of that big yellow roll as it wrapped like a snake around everything we owned. I grabbed her, and we randomly threw clothing in a couple of suitcases. Her face was white. She wasn't crying, but I was.

I was terrified. My world was being sucked up into a tornado of horror I had no control over. On the outside, I may have been a tough, get-things-done person, but inside I was still a kid, and that kid was scared shitless. The rent hadn't been paid in five months—I don't know why. I had been bringing home a paycheck for two years, so . . . who knew? It was gone—but where? Nowhere; just gone from my mother's incapable hand. By the time we'd finished packing, it was almost midnight.

Mr. Fletcher said we could make a phone call. Mother called her mother in Hatch End, and I could hear yelling on the other end. We'd woken her up, which was apparently more inconvenient than being evicted in the middle of the night in an epic blizzard. We had no choice—that's where we were going. Mr. Fletcher opened the front door and asked if we wanted a ride to the train station? Oh, sure, the train station that was buried in snow . . . *with no fucking trains running*!

"We're fine," she said, unnaturally calm.

"No, we're not. We're *not* fine." I was sobbing.

She put a hand on my arm. "We'll manage. We'll catch a bus."

I looked at her and explained, even though she knew already, that all the buses were stuck down the middle of the main road, in seven feet of snow. Mr. Brown and Mr. Fletcher handed us a bunch of official documents and opened the front door. Wrapping coats and scarves around us, we walked out of our home into the blowing snow. They closed the door behind us, taping a large yellow X across the glass. All I could think of was how they used to tape people's front doors with a red X when someone had the bubonic plague back in the 1700s. A padlock and a bolt on the door handle completed Mr. Fletcher and Mr. Brown's work for the night. Without a word, they turned on their heels and left, skidding away in a big black car. A door slammed, and I looked up and saw Crazy Lady standing on her porch, holding the hammer . . . grinning.

It was almost Dickensian. These guys had just dumped two women out of their home, at midnight, in the middle of the worst winter London had seen in fifty years, without a care about where we were going or how we would get there. I did wonder, in silence, why they hadn't arrested my mother. Debtor's prison was still welcoming everyone who was obliged to enter. We'd just been put out on the street for a debt of £35. Yes, it had finally happened.

The Men in the Dark Suits had come and gotten us.

Mother and I stood on the sidewalk and looked at each other. We were holding the only things we now owned—as much winter clothing we could layer our bodies with and two suitcases. It was eleven degrees outside, and the wind was blowing harder. Mother started walking.

"Where on earth are you going?"

"To see if the car will start."

Oh, right! They hadn't found our car or my Vespa scooter, parked fifty feet down the side street.

They hadn't even asked.

The blankets over the car and scooter were covered in snow and ice. We managed to drag them off, and I climbed onto the frozen seat of the Vespa as mother wrestled the car door open. This really shouldn't have happened, but—by the unbelievable good grace of Someone Up There—the car and my Vespa started. I was already frozen to the seat as we carefully drove through the blizzard, to Hatch End. I ended up with pneumonia that lasted two weeks.

Honestly, at that point, dying would have been a welcome option.

Chapter 11

Why Can't I Fly for the USAF?

Life at my crazy granny's wasn't that bad—eventually. She now respected me and was pointedly nice. Of course, the newly turned leaf was partially a result of my grandmother and I having a come-to-Jesus "understanding" of sorts.

It was a Saturday afternoon, two weeks since we'd been evicted. Mother wasn't home and I'd been chatting to Cassidy on the phone in the hallway. The kitchen door flew open and Grandma stood there fuming in rage.

"You've been on that phone for half an hour!" she screamed.

I said goodbye and hung up. She went back in the kitchen, slamming the door so hard the hat stand wobbled. I followed her, not quite knowing what her next move would be. As I opened the kitchen door, she picked up a pan of scalding milk and threw it at my head. Apparently, I'd been on the phone too long. In her house, the phone was a demon, only to be used to call the doctor if you were dying. It wasn't a toy for children to frivolously chitchat on. The milk flew past my ear. I paused for a second or two, and then I was across the floor, pinning her up against the wall by her scraggly neck. Her eyes bulged in fear.

I was brief and calm. "I'm not my mother, and if you ever try to hurt me again, I will strangle you dead."

My grandparents in 1918.
My grandfather's serious expression predicted the unhappy marriage to come.

She dropped to the floor and put her head in her hands, but I didn't care—that's what you do to bullies, and I meant every word. I remembered Mother's kitty, which she'd murdered without a grain of feeling in her frozen heart.

Now that she was scared of me, she treated me with a cloying sweetness that was quite disturbing. Nevertheless, for the rest of her life, she still remained to me . . . an unforgivable human.

Mother still had a secretarial job in the city. Half her paycheck went to the magistrate's court to pay down the debt that got us kicked out, and the other half (including my salary—always) paid for food, gas for my Vespa, and her ticket to London every day. She took the train to the city, and I scootered to the Playboy Club every day—or night, depending on when my shift started. I seemed to be on the four p.m. to midnight shift a lot more than once a month, but I didn't care—it was an escape from what was now home. The journey to Park Lane was a grueling three-hour round trip, which I willingly did during that famous winter. I will remember the cold for the rest of my life. Sometimes, when I got home, I almost couldn't get off the scooter's seat because my butt had frozen to the plastic. How I didn't die of a second pneumonia or get frostbite everywhere, or something much worse, is a miracle.

I'd taken the train to town one Friday afternoon to meet Cassidy for coffee. I was on my way back to the subway when I saw a large booth had been erected on the sidewalk, in the middle of Piccadilly. Across the front was a huge American flag, and a US soldier was standing at the door. Intrigued, I crossed the street to check it out, and learned that it was a US recruitment center for UK citizens to sign up to join the military for the Vietnam War. By now there had been protest riots, and we were all very aware of a war, though we didn't understand it well. Vanessa Redgrave was usually at the forefront, but again, most families didn't take it too seriously. I walked into the booth and saw Colonel William Marshal—I knew this by the gold nameplate—sitting at a desk.

"Hi there, little lady. Can I help you?" He looked a bit like John Wayne.

"I was just wondering what this was . . . about."

"Becoming a part of our fine USA military and supporting our forces in Vietnam."

I was confused. "But this is England."

"We need everyone we can get. If you join us, you'll receive US citizenship and everything the military has to offer. Training, health care—"

I stopped him, saying, "I'd like to join the Air Force." I have no idea where that came from—but it suddenly sounded exactly like what I wanted to do.

"And we'd love to have you!" He stood up and started gathering application papers. "How's your typing?"

"I can't type. I'd like to be a pilot. A fighter pilot." His smile became the smile of a benevolent uncle.

"Well now, little lady, our fighter pilots are men. We have important positions for you ladies back in the States, in our offices, helping our boys, or in the factories, making—"

"But I want to fly." The colonel was doing his best, but I wasn't buying it.

"Ma'am, that will not be possible."

"Why not?"

"There are no women pilots."

"Would I be sent there? To Vietnam?"

"Yes, ma'am. Er, no, ma'am. Our boys fly, but our gals are doing important work back in the States—many of them are serving as village patrol guards, intelligence agents, propagandists, and military recruiters." And the next sentence came with great gravitas. "Some of our gals are also serving the South Vietnamese and Viet Cong intelligence services."

"I just want to fly."

"No." His patience was wearing thin. "You can't."

"Is there a rule? In some book? A rule written down that says I can't be a pilot and go to Vietnam? Show me the book with that rule."

I folded my arms and was politely escorted out of the booth by a nice army soldier.

I got home late. Mother was standing on the doorstep, watching me walk down the street from the train station.

"Where on earth have you been? I've been worried sick!"

"I was . . . I thought I'd try to join the American Air Force."

"What?"

"They have a recruitment booth in Piccadilly. They need people for the war in Vietnam." Her mouth literally dropped open in horror.

"And what am I supposed to do when you go to war and probably die?"

"It's okay, I'm not going. They only want secretaries or factory workers or something about patrol guards and intelligence. I wanted to fly airplanes." We were still standing on the doorstep.

"Your father was a pilot."

"Yes, I know."

"He taught Gary Powers how to fly the U2."

I knew that was unlikely since Powers learned to fly the airplane in Nevada, but ignored the comment.

"Maybe that's why I want to fly, because I love airplanes. Probably got it from Dad."

She pursed her lips, opened the front door, and spoke with her back toward me.

"You are *always* so hurtful."

Two weeks later, I left Playboy—actually, they asked me to leave. Victor called me into his office and said they had to let me go. He shuffled around for some reason about overhiring and too many girls. After a few more minutes of shuffling, he finally told me they'd found out I'd been underage when Playboy hired me. I have no idea how they found out, but it was Playboy. They had "contacts."

Victor spoke very quietly. "If the police had known, this would have closed Playboy down, and we would have been criminally liable. As would you too."

I nodded, feeling sick. "I'm so . . ." I had no words. Tears fell down my face onto the polished wood floor.

"Give your costume back to the Bunny Mother and clean out your locker." He started moving toward the door.

I was stuck to the floor. My heart hammered in my chest. Were the police out there waiting for me? "Victor?" He stopped and turned. "Am I being arrested?"

He shook his head and guided me to the door. As he opened it, he again spoke very quietly. "Sometimes you gotta do what you gotta do. Be careful, okay?" And he closed the door behind me.

I can't tell you why he did what he did. I had committed a significant crime, but somehow he did nothing.

I went to the club, and all the girls were shocked. I quickly said my goodbyes, gave my Bunny costumes back, and left, grateful I wasn't going to jail.

And now what? This was the worst time to be out of work—those two paychecks every Friday had been critical.

Chapter 12

Behind the Iron Curtain

The Penthouse Club—which doubled as a casino—had opened in London. It was owned and operated by the infamous Bob Guccione, an American photographer, painter, and founder of the adult magazine *Penthouse*, created in 1965.

Guccione was an enigma. He'd taken $1,700 and turned it into $150 million and, in the space of a few short years, had managed to topple Hef's *Playboy* magazine from the throne atop the kingdom of the American men's lifestyle. *Penthouse* was now outselling *Playboy*'s 5.6 million circulation, and a minor war had ensued between these two erotic tycoons. In order to have accomplished this extraordinary feat, Guccione had stretched the limits of legality by showing everything you ever wanted to see on the naked female body—albeit shrouded in misty elegance. It was all there, veiled beneath fluffy organza or carefully draped lace. Without professional training, Guccione applied his knowledge of painting to his photography, establishing the diffused, soft-focus look—never seen before—that would become one of the trademarks of the magazine's pictorials. Guccione would sometimes take several days to complete a shoot. His editorial content was constantly rivaling *Playboy*'s, which was well known for its fiction and in-depth interviews. Still, *Penthouse* outdid *Playboy* in that arena, offering content more sensational and far more investigative, with stories of government cover-ups and high-up scandals.

Sounded cool. Might be the job for me.

I called Guccione's assistant, Kathy Keeton, and the minute I mentioned I'd been a dealer at Playboy, I had a time and day to arrive for an interview.

Meeting Guccione was not what I expected. Entering his office, I was greeted by a slick, good-looking man wearing an unbuttoned silk shirt and enough wrist and neck jewelry to fill a Vatican vault. He resembled a high-class pornographer, or maybe the director, possibly the star. Looking around, I felt like I'd just entered the Roman Empire, complete with silk carpets and everything you'd need to furnish an Italian emperor's palace. He stood up and greeted me like a gentleman.

"Welcome to Penthouse. I've ordered tea."

His voice was a cross between a good old-fashioned mobster and Tony Robbins after a hard week of Date with Destiny. He was well spoken, articulate, and made sure I understood that, along with the magazine, Penthouse was a class operation. He took great pride in his photography, calling it "art in its purest form." He believed every part of a woman was beautiful, even the parts that shouldn't be seen. *Penthouse* was breaking through boundaries that *Playboy* magazine couldn't.

"Hef doesn't have that kind of courage," he rumbled.

I didn't feel like I was coming to work at a pornographically driven establishment. He really wanted me to feel comfortable, and I immediately liked him, instinctively knowing there was a good man beneath the radiating and bizarre erotic magnetism. We had tea and, within an hour, I'd gotten the job. Two days later, I was fitted for the Penthouse Pet costume, a tramped-up version of a French maid's outfit, with a short dress, frilly underskirt, low-cut corset, fishnet stockings, and a lacy maid's hat pinned into my hair. Oh . . . and of course, the customary three-inch stilettos.

Unfortunately, I lasted only four short months. I hated it. Don't get me wrong, the staff was great, and Guccione was the best person to ever work for, but . . . I was burned out on guys who wanted to touch and grope me. Also, I was tired of my mother berating me about working for a pornographer.

"After the classiness of Playboy, how could you?"

At this point, I was beyond explaining myself. Often respite came when Bob would invite some of us to his house for dinner. I found out his full name was Robert Charles Joseph Edward Sabatini Guccione. He was an Italian boy from Brooklyn who adored his mother and revered women equally. The evenings were delightful, the food was amazing, and the conversations intellectual and fascinating. A rotation of interesting guests showed up—movie stars, rock stars, and the odd politician trying desperately to be groovy, hanging with the "in" crowd.

Again, Sammy Davis was often in town and a frequent guest at the dinner table. We would always sit together since we were old friends, but Sammy had changed, and I became pretty much the only one who would listen to his endless tirade on the plight of the Black man back in the States. I tried hard to converse intelligently on the topic but simply didn't have enough information available to me and, naturally, I failed. Mother's deep biases—like her thinking all Black men were perverse murderers that should be sent back to Africa—had greatly thwarted my education on one of the most important times in American history. When I eventually came to the US, I learned all of it. I learned about Vietnam, which I also knew nothing about, no thanks to the general in Piccadilly. I learned about Korea, about slavery, Thanksgiving . . . and of course July 4, when they kicked us all out. England had stayed out of everything and made sure we good British folk did the same. Great Britain did not give any education about American history at that time—and it was embarrassing how much I didn't know.

Another frequent guest at Bob's soirees was my pal Roman Polanski, usually showing up with some tall blonde model on his arm. We ignored each other, although every now and again I'd just stare at him. A movie was always shown and, at the end of the night, Bob would escort you to the door, where a cab would be waiting to take you home. Never once was he inappropriate; never once did he make me feel uncomfortable.

Bob Guccione was a cool dude.

I often wonder if my "pornographic" career choice was what prompted my mother to make probably the worst decision she ever made in her life. I'd left Penthouse and been gone about a month, wondering what on earth I was going to do, when, on a Friday, she came home and announced she'd given her two-week notice at BP and we were moving to Turkey—Istanbul, to be precise. She hauled me into the bedroom and told me life with my grandma was hell, so we were going to pack up the car and *drive* to Turkey. She got all sentimental and weepy, at one point saying, "It's Daddy's country, and we need to go home." No, it *wasn't*! It was our *vacation* place! She continued jauntily, "I speak enough Turkish for us to get by. I was happy there, Juliette. Don't I deserve to be happy again?" Sure, but let's get this right—not as happy as during the war, right? Maybe a healthy second? "We have all the relatives. We'll be fine."

"You're serious?"

"Yes, I am."

"And we're driving?"

"Yes, we are. Please don't be difficult and argue. We're going."

The sheer insanity of this ridiculous, unprepared-for expedition only crossed my mind a tiny bit. Our car was a mechanical wreck, ominously rattling from years of neglect, and Istanbul was over 1,800 miles away, but—hey—whatever. This was what we were doing now.

We had Fred the mechanic look at the car, a 1961 Ford Consul. With his head under the hood, Fred uttered the words of doom.

"Don't know if this'll get y'er there, Mrs. B, to that rag-head place you're going. Lots wrong, and the big end looks dicey."

"Then make it right," Mother said. She hated being called Mrs. B. She said only common people who wore caps called you by your initial and that I should never associate with "people of that caliber. You'll always know them—look at the kind of hat they're wearing."

The car went to Fred's garage, and he did his best with the big end—the bottom end of a connecting rod that engages with a crankshaft—that kind of holds the engine together.

When he had made the repair and we picked the car up, he proclaimed, "I've done what I could do, and if the good Lord sees fit, you might make it."

Well, the good Lord hadn't seemed to be too pleased with us lately, so he might not see fit to give us any chance to make it anywhere. Still, we were going. I wish I had a picture of that car when we were done packing it up. It was a joke. Loaded so high, it was at least a foot closer to the ground—I could literally hear it groaning. We had no business driving to the store in that thing, let alone an 1,837-mile journey, across possibly hostile lands. After crossing Austria, you entered Hungary, and then, until you got through Bulgaria, you were basically behind the Iron Curtain, going through countries where officials were just rubbing their shiny, leather-gloved hands, waiting to catch two stupid women in a near-broken car, driving through their country with the "wrong papers." You rarely ever had the right papers—that was their thing. Once you crossed over and away from the safety of capitalistic Europe, you were on your own in the grayness of the 1970s Eastern Bloc.

On a rainy Thursday, with this joyous journey ahead and against all common sense, off we went, creaking and groaning down the road, armed only with six Shell touring maps and the AA petrol guide to Europe. Oh, we did have a plug-in teakettle that worked off the cigarette adapter. No self-serving Brit would ever leave home without the ability to make a cup of tea. Grandma had locked herself in the bedroom, and no one said goodbye.

We managed to get to Liezen, a small town in Austria, when black smoke started pouring out from under the hood. I was surprised we'd made it that far, since the engine had been making awful sounds since Paris, but somehow, right there in the hipster town of Liezen, we sputtered into a funky little garage blasting Led Zeppelin's "Whole Lotta Love" into the street. There was a half-empty bottle of some mystery alcohol sitting on a plastic chair, and we pulled in, hoping as usual that someone spoke English. Then God walked out, rubbing his hands on a rag: a tall, dark-haired guy built like a linebacker, in blue jeans and a "Ban the Bomb" T-shirt with a USA flag bandana tied around his head. He coughed, waving the smoke away.

"Shit, ladies! You look like you're in a whole heapa' trouble there!"

I was so happy I almost cried. An American! His name was Aceman. He told us he flew F16s during Korea, and in 1965 he'd had a *situation* and left the US of A, ending up here in this obscure little town. We didn't care if he was an axe murderer on the run—he was a mechanic! We were saved! In less than three hours, we were back on the road. Something had broken, and Aceman had jimmy-rigged it enough to get us moving.

"If you don't drive over forty-five miles per hour, you might make it," he said, rubbing his oily hands on an equally oily rag.

We had some thousand miles to go, no faster than forty-five miles per hour. I carefully suggested that we might want to go home since it wasn't a good idea to drive into communist countries in our crappy car.

But my mother's mind was made up. "We're going to Istanbul," she said.

Automobile gas in communist countries was weird-smelling stuff, and I'm almost sure it contributed to the massive disaster that occurred fifty miles out of Belgrade, Yugoslavia (now Serbia), on the road to Nis. We were on the cobblestoned "highway" bumping along at forty-five miles per hour, our teeth rattling, when Mother decided it would be a good idea to drive through the night and get through this godforsaken country quickly. There was nothing around but empty fields and barbed wire buried in the pitch dark, broken only by the odd truck headlights flashing by at a hundred miles per hour.

Then the car exploded.

This time it wasn't just black smoke but a thunderous scream of cracking metal and blue flames shooting out of the engine. The force of the blast sent the hood up and off the car, flapping onto the grass beside us. We skidded off the road, onto the verge, and came to a bumpy stop. The flames popped a couple more times, firing out sparks and more black smoke. The engine emitted a couple more cracks and, with a shudder, died its final, painful death. Then silence and the smell of burnt everything filled the air. This was not good. Foreigners driving behind the Iron Curtain had to obey the extensive, never-to-be-broken rules, and one Very Serious Rule was you could not under *any* circumstances stop your vehicle on the side of the road at *any time*. If you did, you had to exit the vehicle immediately and walk to the nearest assistance station, which was almost funny since there were no assistance stations. We were basically fucked. We made the choice to stay in our vehicle—oh, and did I mention it was pouring with freezing cold rain—and wait to be found by the police. Not good. This was a very bad place to break down and be found by anyone. You could disappear. Literally. Maybe, if you had a ton of cash—in dollars, of course—maybe you might get out. Back then, Communist Europe was one scary place with some very scary, non-English-speaking communist cops that could do whatever they wanted to you, and *there was nothing you could do*.

It was two thirty in the morning and so dark and rainy you couldn't even see the grass, but I have to say, I was impressed with my mother. She was totally calm. Here we were again, in a situation entailing something she understood and thrived on—crisis. It was 1940 all over again, and the Nazis were around the corner. We had plenty of water, so we filled the teakettle, plugged it into the adapter (a miracle it worked), and, like all good Brits do in times of crisis, we made a cup of tea and pulled out the brandy. We had absolutely no idea what to do, so we drank our tea and brandy and waited for morning.

It was way too dangerous to fall asleep, so when the rainy daylight arrived, I was so exhausted I thought I was hallucinating—there, not a hundred yards away, parked in the grass, sat a Volkswagen Beetle. For a second, I thought it might be police, but it was beige and old and had a roof rack, which didn't look like "authority" to me. Mother had dropped off to sleep, so I poked her and pointed to the car.

"Look!"

"Is there someone in it?" She was terrified.

"Don't know."

She pushed me. "Off you go. See if there is." Of course, I'd been selected as the designated examiner. I walked, very purposefully, up to the Beetle, convinced a gun could and *would* appear out of the window, attached to a Russian Politzi. I had no choice, having nothing to lose except my life—we were in deep trouble, and caution had to be thrown to the rain and wind; this was a job needing to be done. Looking in the side window, I saw a tall man sound asleep in the driver's seat. I tentatively knocked on the window, and his eyes flew open. He wound down the window and stuck his head out.

"Yah?"

I remembered that German was a second language for many in this part of the world, but my German was painfully limited, so I pointed to our wreck and said all I knew.

"*Automobil kaputt.*" He jumped out of the car, thrust out his hand, and shook mine.

"Hans."

Our savior. Hans grabbed an umbrella out of his car, held it over my head, and in a few strides was helping Mother out of her seat as if he were escorting her to an elegant soiree. He spoke a couple words in German and she answered back. Mother spoke German. Who knew?

"How come you speak German?" I asked, to which she replied airily, "A man I was in love with during the war—he was a German lieutenant on the run from the Nazis. Long time ago."

Really? Great. This secret was good to know since it might come in handy here in Scary Land. Hans sat us and *all* our belongings in and on top of his car. We drove away from our now burnt, empty vehicle.

Between my mother's German, picky English, and a lot of hand gestures, we were able to understand he was taking us to breakfast to make a plan. It was about seven a.m. when we arrived at a café in Belgrade. Hans ordered coffee and Slivovitz, a potent fruit brandy made from damson plums that would take away your troubles—and part of your mind—in one mouthful. The place was hopping with men in dark blue suits (not a woman in sight), and we learned this was the morning ritual for every businessman in Belgrade—probably the country, too. The coffee came on a tray, with a bottle of Slivovitz beside the cups. An hour later we were roaring with laughter, and life was good. Mother and I were stone cold drunk, and I think we were singing, "Tie a yellow ribbon 'round the old oak tree." Hans gathered us up and drove to his house, where we had eggs and more coffee, and he gave us the phone, explaining that because he was a government worker he was "allowed" a telephone. His wife—who was just adorable—spoke some English, and she told us that we must call our consulate to get help.

Mother, still tipsy, grabbed Hans's arm. "What about our car? It's still on the side of the road, fifty miles down the highway."

Hans shrugged his shoulders. "Is gone. They take it."

This man from heaven did not leave our side for three days as we tried to navigate and negotiate our way out of this potentially dangerous mess. At one point, my mother said something about paying him for all his time, but he shook his head. "You do not pay friends."

The car did disappear—confiscated by the government as an abandoned vehicle—and the British consulate was useless, being staffed solely by non-English-speaking locals. You had no idea where you were, as all the letters were Cyrillic, which to us was merely a long line of jumbled nothing. Hans basically saved our life. This kind and good man took us everywhere, including a cheap but "safe" hotel. Our money situation was pretty dire, so we took what we could get. We told him we needed to store our belongings, as we had no way of getting to Istanbul with a carload of stuff and no car. Hans took us to the train station, where we rented a storage locker and filled it to the top. Hans handed us the key and took both our hands as we weaved in and out of goats and donkeys, back to the car. Now we had to get to Istanbul and, without enough money for a plane ticket (Aceman's car fix had been expensive), we were stumped. Of course, Hans had a solution.

"I have friend."

We drove to the outskirts of the city to meet this "friend," who turned out to be a round, jolly person called Rodavan. Over tea and Slivovitz, the two men had a rapid conversation, occasionally punctuated by fists smacking the table as some hilarious anecdote was shared. Finally, Rodavan stood up, downed the last of his Slivovitz, and we all walked out, heading toward a vehicle parked behind the house. And what a vehicle it was. Rodavan declared with pride, "American! Jeep!"

That it was. Originally introduced in 1956, this was a Jeep FC-150, FC standing for forward control. Before us stood a round, rusty orange little thing with a small, squatty cab up front and what looked like a six-foot truck bed behind. Rodavan had sold the passenger seat so he could carry more stuff. The front of the cab displayed a center grille panel, with two little headlights on either side, looking like someone had tried to imitate the classic seven-slot Jeep design but instead had unwittingly created what looked like a talking cartoon car that whizzed around solving crimes. Hans, beaming, took our hands and pointed to the Jeep, which I firmly believed would start twirling on its wheels, laughing and chattering.

"Istanbul. Rodavan drive." And before we could say anything, Rodavan came bounding out of a small shed carrying two fold-out lawn chairs. He squeezed them side by side in the back of the little truck.

"Limousine!" He was certainly having a good time.

It was agreed that, the following morning, Rodavan would pick us up from the hotel and drive us to Istanbul. We again offered to pay. He waved his hands.

"Hans, friend. You, my friends."

The next morning, Hans came with Rodavan to the hotel carrying food, water, and blankets for the lawn chairs. Of course, we had to leave all our belongings at the train station, but we'd cross that problem when we got to Turkey. Hans hugged us goodbye, and we wanted to exchange addresses and write, but he shook his head. He would never receive the letters—seeing us safe with his friend was enough.

"Goodbye, and many lucks."

I must admit, as we got into the truck, we were crying. It was a humbling moment to acknowledge this extraordinary man's kindness and the kindness of Rodavan driving us. We perched on the two lawn chairs as best we could, covered ourselves in blankets, and tried not to freeze during the ten-hour outdoor ride to Istanbul. The last we ever saw of Hans was his hand, vigorously waving as we pulled out of the parking lot.

Chapter 13

Istanbul

"You can stay for as long as you need. Take your time. No payment is necessary. You are Sureyya Bora's wife and child, always welcome." Mr. Sayed, the manager of the Istanbul Hilton, sat across from us in his office. "Your husband was a very important man and a great friend to Turkey—this is our small token of thanks."

Mother and I finished our coffee, and Mr. Sayed tipped a short bow and escorted us up to our room. We never questioned this unbelievable generosity, nor did we question how my dead father—from the grave—could still have the kind of influence he'd always had. Yet, here we were, walking down the familiar yellow and green corridor, to room 351. Mr. Sayed opened the door and we walked in—I could still see the oxygen cylinder, propped in its metal holder at the bottom of the third bed, now a sofa. We thanked Mr. Sayed, and with another bow, he closed the door gently behind him.

I went to the big picture window and my throat tightened. I could see Dogan and myself running around the edge of the shoe-shaped swimming pool. I saw my father patiently explaining how I could be brave and pull out my loose, hanging tooth by myself. And I saw the past—I saw happiness. Turning away, I saw my mother sitting on the edge of the bed staring at the floor. I snapped back to the present and realized "stay as long as you need" had not been spelled out.

"How long does 'as long as you need' mean? Why didn't they want any money?"

She waved her hand dismissively. "Your father was a great man."

Okay, so was Churchill and a whole host of other great men, but I'm pretty sure that even they had to specify how long they would be staying in a busy five-star hotel. I started to ask again.

"But—"

The hand went up. "You don't need to know."

Yes, I *did* need to know, damn it! What if, suddenly, the time of generosity ran out? Were we going to be looking for somewhere to live—now? Or wait to be on the street—*again*. These strange, unanswered secrets prevailed. It was as if my mother "*knew things*," about my father, our life, her life, and I was only permitted to receive the odd snippets of information.

We stayed at the Hilton for three months. I was getting nervous until finally, we found a cheap—about seven dollars a month—two-bedroom apartment in a building directly across the main road on Uftade Sokak, the *steepest* street known to man. We left the hotel, being told by Mr. Sayed that there was no bill. Three months at a five-star hotel and . . . no bill. I still have no words.

Living on Uftade Sokak was quite the challenge. On the impossible climb from the bread store to the apartment, you had to lean forward as far as gravity would allow and breathe like a marathon runner to make it to the door. Our apartment was in the dark basement, next to the hot water heater and Mustapha's apartment—Mustapha served as the building's concierge.

The inside of our apartment was quite a contrast to the hotel room we had just left behind. You opened our front door only to enter a dark, narrow hallway that abruptly turned right, down another hallway to a kitchen and a bathroom on the right side. At the back of the apartment, there were two adjoining rooms side by side, with the only two windows in the place giving limited light, as both looked out onto the brick wall of the next-door building. I took the small bedroom on the left, and mother took the larger one on the right. We had no money for furniture, so the Hilton gave us two bed frames, mattresses, bedding, and a bunch of fruit boxes to use as tables and seats—again—the generosity never stopped. Everything we owned in the world was still sitting in a locker at the Belgrade train station near the goat pens. Trying to find a way to retrieve it was posing a problem since we didn't have a car or any other means to get the stuff. Mother used to sit and cry on a fruit box, obsessing about her lost things.

"They're not lost," I said. "They're just in another place. I'll take care of it."

I had no plan, but I knew I'd have to come up with one or we'd never see our things again and the crying would go on and on. Meanwhile, as I tried to figure out this dilemma, we still had to pay our rent and eat. Fortunately, since we were both Turkish citizens, we were allowed to work. Mother got herself a part-time job teaching English at the French consulate, and I got a gig singing with the band at the Hilton in the fancy supper club. I was not good, but I honestly think they felt sorry for me—I was, after all, the daughter of Sureyya Bora, the great man, and our family had fallen on hard times.

I was immensely grateful for the job—I loved singing and it was an easy gig. We only played Bob Dylan and Beatles songs, as well as a smattering of famous foreign songs. It could have been worse, but once again, Mother was in her element—and we were in survival mode. All hands on deck! She seemed convinced I was going to be a famous pop singer, which was highly improbable, as I *really* wasn't very good. Crisis seemed to always bring out the best in her, which should have worried me, but I honestly did not know then that my mother was dangerously mentally ill.

Istanbul in 1969 was trippy. An old and deeply historic city, it stands on both sides of the Bosphorus, half in Europe and the other half in Asia, making for a truly diverse culture. There was a lot of wealth and a lot of extreme poverty. People were kind, friendly, and always helpful, and it was as affordable as a country could be. I learned as much of the language as I could, and made a ton of wonderful friends.

Mom in Istanbul in the early sixties

Melding into the daily ritual among the Istanbul teenagers was hilarious—all of them had cars, and every evening they would pull up outside, underneath a friend's apartment window, and honk their horn—the sign to come out and party. I became one of those friends, and they worked out how to park a little way down my street, beside the building next door, where I could hear them from our basement living room. Every evening, I opened the living room windows and waited for the honk, then I'd bolt out of the apartment to go have baked cheese sandwiches from the street vendors and hit the various disco hot spots. We danced to Santana; Blood, Sweat & Tears; Chicago; and of course always lots of smooch dancing to James Taylor. Sometimes we went to clubs with a live Turkish band playing the same American music, and I was always amazed at how they all managed to replicate the original band's sound.

I had a boyfriend, Bulent, who worked at the Hilton's reception. He was very romantic, writing me love notes, which he stuck on our front door. Mother adored him—after all, he was Turkish and could do no wrong. Bulent and I were out to dinner one evening at a fabulous restaurant on the Bosphorus waterfront when he took my hand and stared at me . . . for a long time. Oh, no—I knew what was coming.

"Juliette . . . you are the most beautiful girl in the world and so very wise." I was nineteen—kinda shaky on the "wise" side—and we'd only been dating three weeks. "I love you more than life . . ." Actually, that was ridiculous, as he didn't, but that's what Turkish men said to swoop you along in their wonderful romantic illusion. "We will get married and make babies, yes?"

"No."

And the evening ended with polite goodbyes and no hard feelings. I had a few more boyfriends, and the loving narrative was always the same. Get married and have babies. It was funny, as they were all great guys, but in those days, that's what women did in Turkey. Got married and had babies. Anything else, like a career, was not even in the realm of discussion.

I stayed out of the house as much as I could—pokey wire beds and fruit boxes did not make for a comfortable home . . . though having the building's hot water heater right outside the front door did make for a *very* appealing home to Turkey's national insect, the huge, massive cockroach. These critters were about four to five inches long with hard shells, and they "scuttled" into the shadows when you turned on the light, clacking like mini high-heeled shoes across the concrete floor. Sometimes there were as many as fifty running free at any given time. They only crawled over my bed (with me in it) twice in the two years we were there, but I will remember that "clacking" sound forever.

Also, we had a family of healthy-sized scorpions who folded themselves into corners and . . . waited. You'd be sitting, and a movement would catch the corner of your eye, which was the cue for one of us to grab the broom (always by a chair) and cover said arachnid. The object of the mission was to push the broom, with the scorpion pinned underneath, along the hallway toward the front door. I suppose it was somewhat of an absurd sight, seeing these two screaming women pushing a broom, opening the door, and throwing the broom outside then slamming the door shut. The next day it was always, "Who's going to check to see if it's gone?" No surprise there— Mother would push me out the front door. We needed the broom back in its place by the chair for when the rest of the "relatives" came to visit.

Aside from cockroach or scorpion dramas, sitting at home with Mother was generally pretty dull. Sometimes we'd go out with relatives, but usually we'd sit, and she'd talk about how bad it was. She wondered how long our money would last or how we'd get our damn stuff from Belgrade. How . . . how and how? Eventually, I'd hear the "honk" of a car horn outside the window. Being out with happy people gave me space to breathe, and unlike back home, my mother didn't seem to care who I was with or where I went. After all, this was Turkey, my father's country, and (most) everyone could do no wrong. Looking back, I could have gotten into some sizable trouble partying and drinking and whatever, but I didn't—I knew I had to keep it together. Even though I had friends, I was alone and totally responsible for the preservation of our lives. It was that simple.

I had started dating Salim, one of the Turkish band members from the group I sang with. He was the drummer and looked like Andy Gibb. We'd been going out for just over a month, when one morning I woke up and ran, heaving, to the bathroom. I vomited about four times that day and felt very strange. I reckoned I'd probably eaten something odd because the street vendors offered some questionable food items—that was, until it didn't stop. Mother thought I had a bug and took me to a local doctor. He gave me some evil-tasting medicine and I waited to be cured. Then my breasts started hurting and I kept throwing up every morning—which I learned to do in silence. What the hell was happening? (No, I honestly didn't know.)

Mother spent three days a week teaching at the consulate, so on one of those days, I took myself to a clinic downtown, explaining to the nurse how I felt. She gave me a cup to pee in, and I waited until she returned with the deafening information—I was pregnant. Seeing the stricken look on my face, she discreetly handed me a piece of paper with a phone number.

"If you don't want . . . but be quick and be careful. It's illegal."

I was terrified. What if my mother found out? How had I gotten myself in this awful predicament? I didn't know about birth control—was there even any to be had? No one had told me—and Mother had never had "the talk" with me, other than the basics on how to wear a bra and the time when she handed me a packet of sanitary napkins, telling me that, once a month, I would bleed for a few days and it was perfectly normal.

I hid the phone number from the nurse in my Bee Gees album cover and paced through the days ahead, throwing up and thinking. There was no choice—babies were not in the picture of my life. I went to a pay phone at the Hilton and called the number, and they instructed me to come the following evening at seven p.m. I told my mother I was going out with friends and walked to the address, which was about a mile away. Once there, I entered a small green building in a back street, then down to the basement of someone's house. No one asked me my name or address, and I was taken into a dubious but clean room where a green plastic hospital cot stood in the corner. A nurse-type woman covered it with another green plastic sheet, gave me a couple of Valiums, and wheeled in the stirrups, accompanied by a man in a white-ish jacket. He said nothing and began . . .

It was excruciating.

The pain went up into my teeth and back through the top of my head.

My fingernails started breaking as I gripped the sides of the bed.

I could feel warm blood running out of me and remember thinking, *This would be a dreadful place to die.*

When it was over, they handed me more Valium and a bunch of thick cotton napkins. I called a cab while debating what to tell my mother, as I had no idea how I looked. Food poisoning maybe? I got home, she asked me where I'd been—no car honk that night—I mumbled something about dinner with the band and that I didn't feel great and was going straight to bed. I did bleed onto the sheets, but when she saw it, ironically, she was convinced that I was fine.

"*That's* what was the matter with you. Your period was coming. That's why you felt sick. You're going to be one of those who suffer every month—like me."

It took a week of pain and more blood, but I did recover and miraculously, I didn't end up with any infection.

I was damn lucky.

Chapter 14

1969 Cabaret in Cairo

I had become good pals with Saad, the Lebanese manager of Saudi Arabian Airlines. Usually once a day, Mother and I would drop by for coffee, brought in by a young boy swinging a tray loaded with small glasses of tea and coffee for his "rounds" of stores along the street. Saad was fond of Mother and kind of also knew our crummy situation. When I used to visit him by myself, he would constantly pester me to get out of town and leave Istanbul behind.

"Go to Beirut, have much fun, drink, and make love!"

I must say he had me considering it. I had a couple of English girlfriends working in Beirut, but I couldn't fathom how I would tell my mother I was leaving her, so Beirut was filed to the back of my mind.

The band I had been singing with at the Hilton had taken off for a month to make room for a traditional Mexican band, here to do their four-week stint in Istanbul with their lead singer, Enrique Gonzalez. Enrique asked if I could do background and play a tambourine, and I said, "Of course!" with supreme confidence. He then invited me to officially join the band for the Istanbul run, and I accepted gratefully, knowing that now we didn't have to worry about food or bills for the next month.

Enrique and I started dating, and it was a passionate and intense love affair. He fell madly in love with me within a week and I didn't quite reciprocate—but I did adore being with a terrific guy who treated me like gold and made me laugh. About two weeks into the run, Enrique told me they'd been booked to play New Year's Eve at the Hilton Hotel Supper Club in Cairo. He said he couldn't imagine being without me—and asked if I would like to stay with the band for the gig. Apparently, my tambourine talents were good enough to be needed—plus, the leader of the band was my boyfriend. Also, I'd been singing a little background, so absolutely, I was in! Mother was fine with me going—she liked Enrique—but unfortunately, those of us with no interest in politics were unaware of what was going on in Egypt and totally naive to the volcano of brewing trouble.

Since earlier that year, the Middle East had been turning and twisting into a red-hot boil.

Egypt's prime minister had recently been assassinated, which put an end to the country's cease-fire with Israel. Egypt, with renewed attacks on Israel, had fully enforced what was now called the War of Attrition. Golda Meir had just become Israel's new prime minister, and she was in full retaliation mode, sending troops that successfully annihilated the Egyptian air defense system.

I knew almost none of this because we had no television and I couldn't read the newspapers since they were all in Turkish or Arabic. Turkey was a peaceful country, not at odds with any other nation, so there was little reason for us to know or care about Israel or the Arabs and their troubles. It's not that people didn't care, but these were such different times. Problems in the Middle East were foreign and extremely far away from our own personal existence. Wars, cease-fires, commando uprisings, political assassinations—all of these were happening but in another world entirely, not in our backyard.

That December in Cairo, we'd involuntarily walked into a critical situation. The year ahead would bring civil war to Jordan, created by a movement known as "Black September," an uprising by the Palestine Liberation Organization (PLO) led by Yasser Arafat, in an attempt to topple King Hussein and take control of his country. They failed, resulting in

King Hussein expelling Yasser Arafat and his PLO from Jordan. In 1971, Arafat took his band of merry men to Lebanon, where they were allowed into the country as "refugee guests." Arafat then proceeded to create another tyrannical state-within-a-state, weaponizing a dozen Palestinian refugee camps around Beirut and South Lebanon. It was the beginning of the end of any kind of peace in the Middle East. In 1972, the PLO orchestrated the horrible Munich Massacre during the Summer Olympic Games and eventually, in 1975, civil war came to Lebanon.

But here, back in the December of '69, not being able to foresee the future, we innocently arrived for our New Year's Eve gig to a town steeped in ancient history and truly lovely people. We were greeted at the Hilton Hotel by Cairo's chief of police, a huge, smiling teddy bear of a man who informed us we were his guests and he would be at the party after the show. He also told us he was our personal escort for the next two days in Cairo—we never knew his name, he was just "Chief."

The next two days were a blast. We went to the museums and saw the history of thousands of years, then the Giza Pyramids, which for the life of me I do not know how they were built, despite the explanations. Each side of the Great Pyramid rises at a perfect angle of 51.5 degrees to the top, and not only that, but each of the sides are aligned almost exactly with true north, south, east, and west, and—they built these things by dragging two-and-a-half-ton blocks one by one across the hand-watered desert sand, then stacking them 481 feet high to form a perfect triangle.

Our show that night was a big hit, and the after-party was fabulous fun. We were instantly booked for the following year. New Year's Day was spent sightseeing and eating, but we turned in early, as the boys were due to leave the next morning for Germany, and I was going back to Istanbul that same afternoon. During the evening and into the night, I'd heard gunfire and explosions off in the distance. Chief said it was normal and the Egyptians' way of arguing with each other, but I was fairly sure there wasn't supposed to be gunfire *this* close.

As the sun rose the next morning, dozens of police in armored vans roared up the hotel driveway and began frantically evacuating everyone.

Enrique Gonzales (center) at our New Year's Eve gig at the Cairo Hilton, 1969. Me (far right) and the chief of police (far left) who saved me.

Chief found me carrying my half-filled bags down the steps and ran up and took my arm.

"You must come with me, now!" he told me.

Before I could ask, he grabbed my hand and we ran down the street to his car. Opening the door, he practically threw me and my bags into the back seat, and off we screeched in a cloud of dust. Chief explained that Israel had initiated "*deep penetration*" air raids on Cairo, and war had been declared. The only bit I understood was "War had been declared." He went on to explain that Israel had launched an air raid and the city was no longer safe.

"What about the band?" I asked.

"They left the hotel early this morning. Their flight was the last to leave Cairo. The airport is now closed."

"I can't go back to Istanbul?"

He shook his head. "You will come and stay with my family where it is safe . . . for now."

I was an absolute stranger, yet this man (albeit a highly ranked police officer) had immediately invited me into his home . . . but now I had another concern. What could I say to my mother? And how? It's not as if I could pop over the street to the nearest pay phone and call another country. What would I say? "Sorry, mum, can't come home right now—kind of in the middle of a war."

She'd probably be fine. In her mind, being trapped within a war zone was a lot more respectable than me dating Cat Stevens.

By now the city had suddenly turned from happy-go-lucky to a smoke-filled battle zone. Mortars were firing, bombs were dropping, and RPG-7s (Russian-made, portable, unguided, shoulder-launched, rocket-propelled grenades) were all firing in full force. The chief drove about as fast as a Fiat could go, winding through suburban back streets to a small house five miles from the hotel. Home was a tiny apartment on the ground floor of a corner building that housed the entire family. His wife, two young children, Grandma and Auntie and Uncle, all living under the same roof.

I took in the cramped living room, which appeared to be less than five hundred square feet. A tiny kitchen area was squeezed in at the end of the space, wafting out the constant aroma of cooking. There were chairs and old velvet sofas in every corner—I guessed that most likely one would be my bed. The floor was covered with a multitude of Middle Eastern carpets, and the walls were crammed with old photographs of family and friends. Dressers and cabinets and side tables were all jam-packed with knickknacks, mementos, and plastic flowers in various vases. Everyone slept in the two tiny bedrooms off the main room. On the large dresser in the middle of the room, an ancient television sat perched on a phone book, aluminum foil wrapped around its antenna. Mrs. Chief was wiggling it, trying to get a picture out of the "snow" to listen to a reporter trying to talk amid the roar and boom of shells dropping outside.

As we came into the room, everyone started shouting at the same time, Arabic flying with the odd smattering of English, as Chief explained who I was and why I was staying with them. They all hugged me and said, "Welcome" about twenty times, and of course Grandma brought out a plate of baklava, assuming I was hungry.

The city was now in a full-scale battle. Day and night, all you heard were machine guns, mortar shells, and Israeli low-flying airplanes. There was no phone and no way of communicating with the outside world. I hoped Mother had heard the news, somehow, and understood I was stuck.

Life at the chief's house was highly organized—it had to be with seven people living in those five hundred square feet. Everyone had their duties. Mrs. Chief oversaw the household, which included looking after the kids and taking care of Big Chief. Grandma cooked all day, and the kids hung out with me. Auntie sat in her chair, staring at the snow on the TV, shaking her head, cursing Israel and every soldier that had invaded her home country.

The main problem was getting food, and as head of the household, it had fallen to Uncle to be the sole member of the home-supply excursion team. As the fighting got worse, Chief had organized sandbag barriers to be stacked along the sides of the sidewalks around the apartment building. Therefore, in order to go and buy food (which was disappearing by the day), Uncle had to crawl on his stomach, staying close to the sandbags, until he got to the cross street. Then he would run as fast as he could, in between mortar and gunshots, across said street to the one and only store that was miraculously somehow still in operation. Then he would buy bread and tea and whatever else was available, only to repeat the perilous journey back to the apartment, dragging the paper shopping bag beside him.

With seven mouths to feed, this outing was a necessary daily event. One day, Chief's wife decided this was too much for poor Uncle on his own, and that the whole family would all have to begin taking turns to accompany him in braving the shopping trip. Grandma was the first to protest. She was the cook. Who would eat if she left and never came back, shot dead? A little dramatic, but it did make sense in an awful way.

"And I cannot walk without my stick. I am NOT crawling! I will never get up again," Auntie declared loudly in very fast Arabic. Chief was out of the equation; he could not be a dependable team member, as he was frequently absent for days at a time, trying to save his disintegrating police force, so . . . it would still just have to be Uncle out there on his own and, as they all proclaimed, he was, after all, the head of the household, so it was the right thing.

"I'll go with him!" I announced. The room burst into chatter as they vehemently said I was their guest and they would *not* let me put myself in such danger. I thanked them and replied, in fairly respectable Arabic, "I may be the guest, but I'm young. I can run fast. And we're in this together, so please, no more discussion—I will be Uncle's second on the shopping mission."

I was then hugged and blessed in the name of Allah many times. It'd never crossed my mind not to go, although when the day came and it was my turn, I must admit I was moving toward accepting the "guest" exemption. This was a real war, and not the movies. If I died, would Mother even know?

Uncle and I left the house, dropped to the ground, and started crawling. We made it to the cross street and decided I would run to the store, as I was probably faster than Uncle. I was about to stand when Uncle nudged me to stay down. We were about fifteen feet in front of an apartment building. The front door opened and, simultaneously, a movement above caught my eye. A soldier was kneeling on the roof of the building across the street, his machine gun aimed down to the pavement beside us, watching an old man who had just come out of the front door behind us. He started shuffling toward the corner to cross the street.

I jumped to my feet and shouted for him to stop. "*Tawaquf!*" I cried.

Uncle pulled me back down, pointing to the soldier on the roof, but I pointed to the man who was now about five feet away. Uncle shrugged and said, "He knows what is war."

The next ten seconds went by fast. The old man took another step and was next to me. The soldier's eye shifted. He readied his gun and aimed. I couldn't help but shout to the old man again as I rolled against the sandbags.

"*La! La! Tawaquf! Tawaquf!*"

Following a brief and monstrous rattle of gunfire, the old man exploded in a hundred pieces, spewing blood and bits of his body all over me. A part of his brain landed in my hair and was dripping down my neck. I was paralyzed in shock. Uncle started pulling me back along the pavement, toward the apartment. I could feel the concrete bite into my pants, ripping them open as the remainder of the old man's brains slid out of my hair, landing under my scraped knees. I turned my head, and the last thing I saw was the soldier on the roof, tipping back on his heels, lighting a cigarette.

As we rushed into the apartment, everyone stared at us, me primarily, as I looked pretty nasty covered in blood and body bits. Uncle said in Arabic, "That's not her blood, but we can't get food today." Then Grandma took me into the bathroom to clean up.

When you're young, you don't know what you're learning—especially when you've learned it. A man had been blown up all over me and, as Grandma cleaned me up, she asked if I was okay.

I was fine. It'd been part of the mission—I was just relieved it wasn't me in pieces on the sidewalk.

I stayed with the chief's family for almost three weeks. I dutifully did my store runs with Uncle. In my mind, I still saw that soldier on the roof, who by now was no longer at his post. You'd think it would have been the old man and his sticky brains that filled my dreams, but it was that soldier, tipping back on his heels, smoking a cigarette.

Chapter 15

Werewolf Eyes

A cease-fire was called, and the airport opened for two days. I said my goodbyes to this wonderful family, and Chief drove me to the airport, thanking me over and over for risking my life every day for his family. He put his hand on my shoulder.

"*Allah sayakun dayimaan hunak min 'ajlik.*" Meaning, "God will always be there for you"—a hopeful thought.

I got back to Istanbul and dealt with a silent, brooding Mother for days. Apparently, I *should* have found a way to get word to her—after all, there'd been telephones during *her* war.

"I was out of my mind with worry! You're so good at *that kind of thing* [being in a war?]. Why didn't you get a message to me?" I had to smile at the somewhat apt oxymoron.

"Mum, I was in the middle of a pretty bad situation. There were no phones—nothing was working."

I never told her about staying with the chief's family and the old man in the street. She never asked where I was, or who I was with. It wasn't about her, so she didn't really care. Life resumed, and I went back to the house band at the Hilton.

One day, I walked up our road to stop into Saad's for tea, and I realized I could hardly make it to the top of the street. I felt ill and needed to sit down—immediately. As I walked in, Saad leapt to his feet, ordered tea, and started talking. He loved to talk and always had a story.

"*Habiti!* You will not believe what I am hearing today! Prince Mubah Al bin Fashru, fifteenth brother in line to Saudi throne, has shot the moon!"

"Ah. Moon shooting, not good," was all I was able to utter—my brain felt like my body.

"VERY bad! This time could be very serious!" he emphasized, with a finger to the ceiling. "He is in hotel room with American girls partying and . . . and . . . there was too much alcohol, and one of girls is now in the hospital!" I wish I cared, but I was feeling nauseous. Saad waved his arms. "His father will send his peoples to bring him home! *Tama aliantiha' min!* He is finished! No more holidays with—" Suddenly he stopped and peered at me closely. "What is wrong with your eyes?"

"What do you mean?" Did I look dizzy?

"They're yellow."

"What? What yellow?"

I ran into the bathroom and looked in the mirror, and a pair of fluorescent werewolf eyes glared back at me. The whites were the color of British mustard, and my normally brown eyes had turned bright green. There had been a countrywide cholera epidemic, and Mother and I had gotten shots, but apparently I must have gotten sick from dirty needles. Saad told me to go home, get Mother, and get to the hospital.

"*Hemen!*" Meaning . . . "Now!"

When I got home, Mother was sick too—she wasn't yellow, but she felt equally shitty. The only medical facility we knew that was remotely clean and safe was the Italian hospital downtown. We took a Dolmuş—this was a fascinating system of communal taxis, old Chevys or Buicks (and I do mean old) driving around the city twenty-four hours a day, picking up as many people as would fit in five seats, to be dropped off anywhere they needed around town. The cost was about ten cents, and it didn't matter how far you went. I don't remember much of that ride—I'd taken my temperature, which was hovering around about 103, and I was seeing purple dancing fairies across the backs of people's heads. Mother sat beside me trying not to throw up.

The hospital was full with hundreds of really sick people. I could barely stand, and we were throwing up in every garbage can we passed. Miraculously, we managed to see Dr. Mousalli, who said Mother was sick but I was very ill (no shit!).

I had hepatitis B—the bad one—and mother had hep A, which was not a potential death threat. Dr. Mousalli said I might not make it without serious organ damage, but I could get lucky since I was young. He gave us a large box of fifty glass syringes and fifty bottles of concentrated vitamin B. He said I should get two shots a day and Mother one and say a prayer to Allah that we would live. Mother would have to administer both injections, as there was no room at the hospital—which no sane person would have stayed in anyway—so we needed to go home. We thanked him and that was that, and we got back into another Dolmuş. By now the purple dancing fairies had become coal black goblins.

I was at death's door for about three months. I was so weak, I couldn't walk, not even a step. It took me about thirty minutes to fall out of bed and crawl to the bathroom, ten yards down the hall. I had lost forty pounds. *I'm going to die here among the cockroaches and fruit boxes*, I thought.

My mother fared a little better, as she wasn't so sick. She daily administered two of the most painful injections I have *ever* had and was merciless as she handed me a rolled-up washcloth.

"Bite down and roll over," she would tell me.

The pain of that vitamin B injection was incredible, and when we ran out of shots, Mother used to go to the local drug store with Dr. Mousalli's prescription—they gave us whatever we needed and didn't charge a penny. Yes, it was that kind of town. After about two and a half months, the only thing I could eat was tiny amounts of plain yogurt and mashed potatoes. Bulent, my ex-date receptionist from the Hilton, came over every three or four days with beautifully wrapped dishes of food, each with Mr. Ahmed's gold-embossed business card attached with a white satin ribbon. This was so kind and thoughtful, but I don't think it was the norm. I concluded that my father wasn't just some ordinary guy—he had been a Very Big Fucking Deal around here. I silently thanked him up there in heaven, as the Hilton was basically saving our lives—again.

Chapter 16

Bifocals and Very Big Guns

Around the beginning of March, I had recovered, but I was a sad, scary-looking human. I was skeletal thin and had a ghostly white face, but thankfully no organs were lost or damaged.

We went to see Dr. Mousalli, who checked us out. He patted me on the shoulder. "You have good Turkish genes. Strong like bull!"

Hardly—I felt more like a crippled spider.

Mother went back to teaching at the consulate and instructed me to find a way to get our stuff back from Belgrade. Through friends, I'd met Berat, a swarthy, handsome fellow who owned numerous businesses all over the city, many sporting the ever-famous title of "import and export." One of his local enterprises was a mechanic shop on Istiklal Avenue in Beyoğlu, which was a couple miles down from where we lived.

One afternoon, I was at Berat's shop having coffee, shooting the breeze (the Turks do a lot of coffee drinking and shooting breezes to preclude work whenever possible), and we got to talking about what I now termed as the "Belgrade Situation." It sounded a lot more interesting than "our stuff is in a locker with goats and chickens in a communist country." Berat knew my mother, as his cousin was a friend of another friend's brother, who knew one of her English students.

"Ah, yes. I have heard about this problem, and now we make it no problem!" With that he threw me a set of car keys, pointing to a white-paneled minivan sitting out on the street. "Take it! It's very roomy. Go to Belgrade and get your things. Stop your mother crying." He smiled. Oh, dear God! Did she cry to *everyone*?

Suddenly I had a thought. "Berat, Belgrade is over nine hundred kilometers away. One way."

He shrugged. "My sister lives in Germany, many more kilometers."

And so it came to pass, once again through the unmitigating kindness of strangers, that a couple of weeks later, with little preparation, Mother and I set off for Yugoslavia. We were totally unprepared for the weather we were about to encounter; it was the end of February and promised to be Russia Badass Cold. With just enough money to get gas, food, and a night in a hotel in Belgrade, off we went, armed with sandwiches and coffee from Berat's family.

The 605-mile drive would take just over ten hours. Knowing we had to do it without making any stops, we started out early. The scary part would be crossing the borders. Rodavan, being Yugoslavian, had negotiated them easily, speaking the language and knowing the rules. We triple-checked and made sure we had the right paperwork, but you never knew—tomorrow it could be the wrong paperwork. The crossing from Turkey into Bulgaria was the tricky one. You crossed from west to east—Europe to Russia—from freedom to fear. Any reasonable state of law and order ended at that Turkish line of demarcation. We drove into the Turkish checkpoint and were waved through in minutes. We then had to cross a small stretch of no-man's land—about a hundred-yard-sized square of sand that divided the two countries—a square of nowhere within which so many tried—and inevitably failed—to escape the rigid gray of communism.

Arriving at the next checkpoint, we were swiftly stopped by the Bulgarian border guards, who pointed machine guns at the windshield, motioning for us to get out. They escorted us into a hut where a fierce-looking female with bionic bifocals sat in a small cubicle below the level of the barred counter. She looked up at us, extending a beefy hand.

"Passports and papers," she demanded.

We pushed them under the bars knowing there was always the chance we might never get them back. We didn't speak and instead stood motionless, praying to whoever was listening with the desperate hope that this wasn't going to go bad—this was the kind of shit that got you religion in a big way. There was then the relieving clunk of the rubber stamp hitting the various documents—hope—which was then dashed as she left the room with our passports.

We waited fifteen anxiety-riddled minutes until she came back.

"*Versicherungsvertrag!*" she screeched. Mother muttered that we were English, and the woman scribbled something down and showed it to a guard behind her who said, "Insurance. You must pay insurance. One hundred American dollars. For border crossing."

Without a word, Mother opened her purse and took out our precious hotel and food money. She handed it through the bars. Bifocals took it and once again left the room. Mother and I didn't speak or even dare look at each other. Visions of the Gulag were flashing, but the woman came back, slid our passports and stamped "*insurance*" papers under the bars, and silently dismissed us. The guards were finishing up checking our vehicle, machine guns at the ready. They then arranged themselves in a semicircle around our van. We showed the stamped papers and passports, and they waved us on.

We drove in silence for about an hour. There was nothing to say.

We were about seventy-five miles out of Sofia, in Bulgaria, and it was seven a.m. when sirens and lights came speeding up behind us from a large black motorcycle. We instantly stopped. A tall politizi with dark glasses and a gun strapped to his belt demanded we show our papers and passports—which we dutifully did. After leafing through the pages for what felt like an eternity, he said, "You must go back to town to verify papers. Follow me." We turned around and drove twenty-five miles back to the small town of Tran and waited on a metal bench outside the town hall building until it opened at nine a.m. Papers were inspected and, mercifully, they only asked for another twenty dollars (more "insurance"). The money was disappearing, but we just didn't think about it. At least we were back on our way again and not in the town jail.

It's difficult to explain the kind of choking terror that being there—in that place—felt like. It's such a terrible, foreboding fear of the unknown. Anything could happen. You could disappear, just because. You could be shot, just because. When you leave behind the freedom and security of a law-abiding capitalist country, you leave behind rules you know and trust—everything true and ethical. Your identity becomes meaningless. Your money could, maybe, get you out of trouble (who knows what would have happened had we not paid "insurance"), but aside from the money, it doesn't matter who you are. You are in their domain, subject to laws that can be made on the spot. Now and forever, every time I have to show my passport and I get it back, I am grateful and thankful and my heart beats back to normal. I can still smell the odor of that hut, and I can still see that woman's bifocals. I can still picture the gun hanging from the politizi's belt and my terrified reflection in his dark glasses.

We drove into Belgrade at eleven p.m. It was so unbearably cold, and we were in trouble. We had enough money for gas back to Turkey and maybe some food, but we knew we had to spend the night in the van, where we could easily freeze to death. We drove to the hotel where we'd stayed last time and I tried to call Hans, but his number had been disconnected. I then had a mad thought—maybe they would give us a room and we could send them the money? I went in and asked. They said no but we could park in their parking lot. At about one a.m., just when I was contemplating what I would look like frozen dead, a handsome young blond bellboy ran out of the hotel and said he would get us blankets. We had also brought the blessed teakettle (and plug) so at least we could make a hot drink—if we had water. The young man came back with blankets and bottles of water.

"My name is Nebojsa." He gave a big smile. "Why are you here?"

Pretty fair question. Why *were* two English women sleeping in a van in this bitter cold with no money for a hotel? We explained what had happened and that we were here to pick up our belongings from storage at the train station. His English was good. He told us he was a physicist engineer but was now working as a bellboy because he could only get a job as an engineer if he worked for the KGB. He desperately wanted to escape (that was the only option) and go to the West.

"Tomorrow is my day off," he told us. "I promise to help you." He then went back into the hotel and got us a comforter.

With the blankets and comforter, we took turns sleeping, rubbing each other's hands and feet every few minutes so as not to freeze to death. It was so cold I can't even describe that eternal night. I don't know how we survived, but we did, and at seven a.m., there was Nebojsa at the window with a pot of hot coffee and a bottle of Slivovitz.

"You're alive!" he said with a big smile. I think he was trying to make light of a potentially terrible outcome. He pulled two bread rolls out of his pocket and we started the engine. After we had downed the coffee and a couple of good slugs of the magic Slivovitz, he jumped in the back seat. "Let's go! I direct!"

The Belgrade train station was pretty much an open-air affair, buzzing with dozens of people running and carrying bags and boxes. Men were pushing farm animals onto trains and wheeling large containers of stuff around on pallets. It was a veritable zoo of hurried madness. Nebojsa held my hand, and Mother held me as we weaved in and out along platforms and corridors, until finally we reached the long bank of storage lockers. We opened our extra-large locker, and my heart sank as I saw the two huge suitcases, shopping bags, and all our crap—the thought of carrying this load back to the van was daunting.

"Nebojsa, how will we . . . ?"

"No problem!" He flipped up a suitcase that must have weighed at least eighty pounds, then the other equally hefty suitcase, and planted one on each shoulder. Loaded like no human I have ever seen, he *jogged* back through the station. We followed, carrying all the shopping bags, scurrying behind this Amazonian human, never breaking stride all the way to the van. Locked and loaded, we were ready to go. We turned to say goodbye, when suddenly Nebojsa grabbed my arm. The desperation on his face made my heart jump. His whisper was frantic. "Take me with you? *Please? Please!*" My face must have given away my next words, as he held my arm even more tightly. "Please! I cannot be here. I am engineer and I want to do my work. I want to be free. I am not bellboy. Please?" The pain in his voice was almost too much to bear.

"You have no passport . . . no travel papers, right?" I asked.

He shook his head, and Mother was at my side. "Are you allowed to leave for a . . . holiday?" she asked him.

He shook his head and quickly glanced around.

"I have plan. We go to my house and I have rope. I can tie myself underneath"—he pointed to the van—"between the wheels."

Mother was very calm. "It's over nine hundred kilometers to Turkey," she stated.

He shrugged off her doubt. "It's easy. I hold on strong."

Mother put her arm around him. "We have to go through checkpoints. If they find you . . ." She didn't finish.

I was trying hard not to cry. Of course, I knew we couldn't take him the minute he asked. I knew what was waiting for us at the Bulgarian border; machine guns and bifocals were still a clear and present danger. Nebojsa would have been shot on sight if they found him underneath the van. Every day, these folks were searching each and every border crossing for someone or something contraband. I couldn't even imagine the punishment we would have faced for smuggling a Yugoslav citizen out of the country. Nebojsa dropped his head and nodded.

"Yes, I understand." He put two sandwiches in my hand. "You will be hungry."

I have never seen my mother so kind and caring—she wrapped her arms around him and held him like a precious child.

"You are young. One day this will end. One day you will be free. Here is our address in Turkey. You will always be welcome." She gave him a piece of paper. He held it tightly and nodded again. "We will never be able to thank you for what you've done for us." She squeezed his hands tighter. "Remember, you are always welcome, any time."

"I understand. Thank you for being my friend." And without a word, he turned and walked away.

The drive back was somber and quiet, and at the Bulgarian/Turkish border checkpoint, as predicted, the guards, with their machine guns drawn, surrounded us. We went into the hut, but there was a different person at the counter behind the bars. As the stamp was clunking on our passports, I looked out the window to the three guards. They were lying on the ground. One of them had a mirror on a long pole, and he was slowly running it along the underside of the van, the other following the mirror with his weapon. Mother and I walked out of the hut as the guards were lightly tapping the sides of the van with their guns.

I whispered, "What? Do they think we have someone in the doors?"

Her response was harsh. "Ssshh!" As we drove off, she said, "They were looking for illegal contraband in the panels."

We drove for some time in silence. "They would have found him," I finally said. She didn't look at me.

"Yes, they would have." And we never spoke of it again.

Many years later, when we'd moved back to England, a letter arrived at my grandmother's house, from Nebojsa's mother. She said he had been shot trying to escape under the barbed-wire border fence into Turkey. She thanked us for our kindness, as he had talked for many years about visiting his dear English friends in Istanbul.

Chapter 17

The Driving License

In June 1972, Grandma demanded my mother come home, so she got herself a ticket and left Istanbul, saying she'd be gone for at least a month. This was good news and bad news. The good news was that Mother was gone. The bad news was I was terrified of our apartment and left alone to battle its demons. The cockroaches were now living under and in the fruit boxes and had tripled in numbers. The scorpions had all had babies, who were perfectly content living at home with Mom and Dad. And I think the place was haunted; I swore my father walked into my bedroom one night and sat on the bed, shaking his head in helplessness. And the seventy-five-year-old creepy landlord kept showing up to take me to dinner. I stayed out as much as I could, but I had to sleep there, and did I mention that I am also deathly afraid of the dark as well as The Thing That Lives under the Bed? Yes, it really does. It's there. It's always been there . . . waiting.

I spent many days having coffee with Saad at his Saudi Arabian Airlines office or waiting for the "honk" of the car horn outside the window. One morning, Saad was listening intently to my long and painful lament of the apartment, embellished slightly with extra awful cockroach stories. He poured more tea and went to his desk and came back, handing me a ticket.

"Go to Beirut." He planted it in my hand and waved me over to his desk, smiling from ear to ear. "Let's make reservation for you to go to the Big Party!"

I never questioned why he suddenly decided to give me a ticket, but I took it with gratitude and, not giving a hoot what Mother would think, I decided I was going. I knew I had learned my lesson, and I sure as hell wasn't going to show up in another country knowing no one, with nowhere to go. I managed to write to my English friend Dilys, who was working at the Crazy Horse Nightclub in Beirut. She wrote me back immediately and said I could stay with her. Two weeks later, I wrote Mother telling her I had gone to Beirut to visit my friend, then I packed two bags, put ten dollars in my purse—all the money I had—and left Istanbul behind.

And . . . arrived in paradise.

I quickly discovered that Beirut was not deemed to be the "Paris of the East" for nothing. The oldest and largest city in Lebanon, Beirut was party central for everything and everyone east of Switzerland. In 1972, Lebanon's precarious geographical position, bordered to the east by Syria and to the south by Israel, was of no real concern to anyone since the Lebanese had lived with everyone in relative peace and harmony for many years. Everyone traveled in and out of Syria daily with no thought or worry. Damascus was a great place to buy all kinds of things, including cheap cigarettes, and many young men took their dates on the short two-hour drive for dinner. Israel, a respected and slightly feared nation, was basically to be left alone. The Lebanese were a nation of happy-go-lucky people who had few worries beyond tomorrow's dinner plans, shopping, or which club to frequent.

The Beirut I arrived in was an enigma to me. It was easy and cheap, modernized enough to be more comfortable than any Middle Eastern country and inhabited by some of the happiest and richest people I have ever known. Business was booming, and all the top designer stores were there, making a fortune. Everyone spoke Arabic, English, and French at the same time, creating a colorful mélange of the three languages. I knew French and a respectable amount of Arabic, but this crazy method of conversation sure got you fluent fast. Saad was right—the Lebanese were a people who thrived in close-knit groups, and making friends was a breeze. These groups of friends did everything together, never forgetting to take you, the stranger, along to meet more friends to do more fun things. The Lebanese were much like the Turks in this regard.

At the beginning of the previous year, Yasser Arafat had arrived unexpectedly in Beirut, announcing he was going to "stay for a while." By the time I arrived, he'd secretly created a tyrannical state-within-a-state, weaponizing a dozen Palestinian refugee camps around the city and in South Lebanon. These refugees lived in the slums, buried out of sight in gated communes, and the ones who worked had the most menial jobs. Beirut citizens were aware Arafat was there, but no one paid much attention—he certainly wasn't perceived as a threat to the country. The rich, upper-class women at their various tea parties and soirees used to refer to him as "just some funny little brown man, completely illiterate, with a silly tea towel wrapped around his head." Such descriptions were always followed by titters of laughter. Everyone knew Arafat was on a mission to get Palestine back from the Israelis, but as long as his quest didn't interfere with the fun and frivolity of day-to-day lives, all was well.

At that time, Lebanon was headed by President Suleiman Frangieh, a slightly corrupt Christian and a bit of a warlord. His cabinet was 60 percent Christian and 40 percent Muslim, and he'd given the Palestinian refugees sanctuary in Lebanon after the 1948 Arab-Israeli war. President Frangieh kept them under his strict control and very much out of sight.

Upon my arrival in the city, I jumped into a cab at the airport, instructing the driver to take me to the Saint Georges hotel, where I was meeting Dilys by the pool. The Saint Georges was one of the most famous hotels in the world, situated on the Rue Corniche along the ocean's edge, known as the favorite haunt and hiding place of the infamous spy Kim Philby. Within minutes of my stepping into the beach club, I was greeted by Serge. He stood up very straight and royally introduced himself,

"Bonjour, mademoiselle! I am Serge, head manager!"

A short, rotund fellow, Serge ruled his eight hundred square feet of paver-stone patio on the beach with the intent and commitment of a marine general. He was excited to show me his table under the canopy, which was heavily laden with all sorts of periodicals.

"See! *New York Times, English Times, Francais Le Monde.* Everything I am reading every day! I am watching this Yasser Arafat and his PLO interlopers! You know of this man?"

"Um. Kind of." I honestly didn't care. It was boring politics. I started to take a step toward the pool area to find Dilys. But Serge was on a roll. Deeply insulted that this heathen peasant Arafat had had the audacity to set up shop and home in *his* country, his voice rose in conviction.

"He is making his home here! In my country! He is UP to something! I DO NOT trust him!" And to demonstrate with purpose, he spit vehemently on the ground. He then took my hand and led me to the front of his desk. "But . . . no one will worry, I am a man prepared!" he said, dramatically opening a drawer underneath his desk.

I took a sharp breath. Inside the drawer, hidden underneath stacks of clean towels, was a veritable artillery of guns, automatic weapons, and a couple of grenades for *bonne chance.* Just in case one of those PLO undesirables arrived at *his* beach with criminal intent, Serge was ready to blow those sons of bitches back to the desert they'd come from. I think he even had a couple Russian Kalashnikov machine guns stashed under the rubber floaties for a real *situation de crise!*

I met Dilys on her chaise and, catching up, we were soon joined by a dozen other friends, both English and Lebanese, and I got a healthy debrief on my new home. Oh yes, I'd decided I was staying. Within half an hour, Halim Khoury (who looked like Peter Frampton) had made two phone calls and gotten me a furnished studio apartment in his father's building across the street for ten dollars a month. No need to stay with Dilys—I'd just moved to Beirut! As Dilys and I were leaving to see my new apartment, we passed Serge, who leapt to his feet and grabbed my hand.

"Welcome to Beirut! Come every day! You are always safe here at the Saint Georges Beach Club!" And with a flourish, he gestured to the closed towel drawer and winked. "We are always prepared!"

At that time, Serge was probably the wisest man in Beirut. Lebanon was on the brink of a catastrophic shift—and life as it had been known for all these years was heading toward a fast and furious end. On the surface, you saw the "Paris of the East"—wealthy citizens in their prosperous businesses, hop-popping nightlife, and busy restaurants—but behind the shiny curtain was the dark underworld of the Palestine backstreet ghettos where families lived on the other side of electrified barbed-wire fences in an unfathomable state of poverty. President Frangieh made damn sure it was all hidden from view and that no tourist or money-spending individual would see the awful situation he'd allowed to exist. I look back, and it's astonishing how no one, including me, was even slightly disturbed that the town was surrounded by ghettos of enraged, heavily armed Palestinians.

In order to work, I had to get prior approval from the Ministry of Labor, bringing a letter proving you could get a job, which I obtained in an afternoon from Dilys's boyfriend, Edwaard, who owned a nightclub. Then I needed to apply for a work permit at the ministry within the maximum ten-day period after my entry into Lebanon. I'd had three days left when I was issued a three-month permit, which did concern me until I found out that one simply had to go back to the ministry and get another three-month permit . . . and another . . . and another.

Surprisingly, it was tough getting a job. Lots of promises of "I have a friend who has a friend who owns a club" disappeared into a lot of nothing, and soon I was out of money. My friends had lent me a few bucks, so rent was paid, but time was running out on my visa. I figured if this didn't work, I'd pop over to Tehran in Persia (Iran) for a while. I'd met a cool disc jockey in Beirut on his vacation who said I could come and sing at his club. Then, Edwaard, who'd given me the letter but couldn't give me a job, miraculously found me a gig singing with the house band at the Hotel Phoenicia. I was off and running, securing another gig at a big club down the Rue de Corniche, owned and subsequently named after the famous singer Farid El Atrache. Finally, the show biz gods must have woken up, because I secured a third and fourth gig, first at the Venus Club, then joining a group called *The Dark Eyes*, Lebanon's top six-piece band, who sounded remarkably like Blood, Sweat & Tears and were led by the ever handsome Vahe. I was hired just as the band had been booked to play at the famous UNESCO Convention, a week away. We rehearsed like mad people—the band was covering Chicago; Blood, Sweat & Tears; Santana; and many others. My tambourine was going to be busy.

One of our Kuwaiti customers at the Venus, Farouk, had just gifted me a bottle of Christian Dior's "Joy" perfume, which cost more per ounce than I made in three months. I was thrilled and tried it out a week before my UNESCO evening. The next day, it started to itch, then burn like a hundred bee stings, and that evening, when I looked in the mirror, my entire neck was covered in oozing red sores that were starting to blister. I immediately went to the doctor, who just shook his head and told me, "This is a very serious allergy, and you will most likely be scarred for life."

He handed me a bottle of Calamine lotion, and that was that. I went to work that night wearing a silk scarf wrapped carefully around my intolerable, injured neck. My last set was at Farid El Atrache, and I couldn't sing the last two songs—the pain was unbearable. Halfway through "American Pie," I apologized to the band and stumbled off the stage, running right into Adnan, the club's manager.

"What's wrong?" he asked me.

I showed him my neck. "I think it's perfume that doesn't like me. The doctor said it was bad. The pain is terrible, and I'm going to be scarred for life."

Adnan chuckled. "Ah, doctors . . . come with me." He led me downstairs to the basement, where they held weddings and banquets, and pulled out a stool in front of the bar. "Sit," he said with the authority of knowledge. He went behind the bar and pulled out a large, fluted vase. Then he took a small wad of newspaper, rolled it into a taper, set it on fire with his cigarette lighter, and tipped it inside the vase.

Trying not to sound a teeny bit terrified, I asked tentatively, "What . . . are you doing?"

He smiled. "We will fix it tonight. This—gone, two days." And with that, he took the newspaper out of the vase, simultaneously covering the opening with a small dish. "Okay, sit tight." Humming his favorite

Lebanese song, he took the dish off the smoking vase and tipped the smoke on and around my neck. I screamed—there was no doubt my neck was on fire—and then I screamed louder as Adnan patted my shoulder. When he was done, he draped my scarf back around my neck and patted me again. "Go home and rest; take off scarf in one hour to let air breathe."

What had I done? What had I *let* be done? I was sure I was now definitely scarred for life—burn scarred. I went home and cried the rest of the night. I couldn't see straight the pain was so bad. But then, the next afternoon, strange things started to happen. The sores began to dry out and eventually, by the next evening, they'd become flaky gray scabs, which literally started dropping off my neck. By the end of the third day, my neck was totally healed. Not a mark anywhere. Someone later told me the smoke had cauterized the sores and burnt them off. The doctor said it was Allah.

Beirut came alive around nine p.m. each night, with music pouring out of bars and restaurants. I was dating Varouche, the Armenian lead guitarist of the band at Les Caves du Roy nightclub—in between working three to four gigs a night and paying only ten dollars a month rent for my studio apartment. Life was good. Dilys had introduced me to some of the other English girls: Carol, who worked as a stewardess for Middle East Airways; Susy, who worked in another bar; and Lizzie, who worked . . . somewhere—we were never quite sure but we adored each other. Every night after work, we'd meet up and go out in groups to other clubs. We all double dated with lots of adoring guys—they loved English girls—who fell in love with each and every one of us usually a couple of hours after we'd met. And oh my God did we have fun. Like Saad had promised, this was Beirut, a town like no other, although every now and again we'd be driving somewhere and we'd pass ominously darkened side streets leading to one of the many well-hidden Palestinian ghettos. To us, they just weren't there— we didn't *see* them. We laughed at how nasty they looked and how could people live that way? Yes—we were the privileged, ignorant foreigners who didn't give a flying . . .

I worked seven nights a week, from nine in the evening until whenever the work ended—sometimes five in the morning. I stayed employed, so I figured my singing had gotten better—or no one was bothered. You didn't have to be Streisand, you just had to be pretty, chat with the customers so they'd buy more champagne (a mixture of wine and seven up), and be able to carry a tune. I made friends with the guys who were the traditional Lebanese Dabke dancers, as well as all the DJs and other performers.

Everyone literally knew everyone—it was that kind of town. Once established as a cool, fun English girl, then whatever you needed and whenever you needed it, well . . . everyone had a friend, who had a friend, who had a cousin, who had a friend who would get it for you, no questions asked. You could buy opium, Dexedrine, morphine, antibiotics—whatever was required, all across the counter at the local pharmacies; they also delivered! I managed to acquire a small 125 hp Honda dirt bike—I say "acquired" because I can't remember who I got it from. I was just happy I could finally stop sitting on the back of other people's motor scooters, praying for my life at every ninety-degree, full-speed turn! As cheap as it was to live in Beirut, we were paid very little, and none of us ever had much money. Sometimes we ran out, but it was okay because everyone took care of each other.

I had a friend, Tony (it was cool for guys to give themselves American names), who was a champion Dabke dancer and the local motorcycle-car-everything mechanic. His shop was on Hamra Street, the main drag. One day I needed a quick fix on my bike and took it over to his shop.

As he was pulling off my back wheel he said, "You want to make some money?"

It took me a minute. I wasn't dumb.

"Doing . . . ?"

He shrugged. "Small deliveries, up and down the mountain. Easy."

"What deliveries and where?"

He explained there were "patriotic soldiers" living with their families just outside of Zahlé, a town known to harbor the famous Lebanese Red Beret, political assassins who needed deliveries of ammunition every week. My face went white.

"To protect their families from thieves," he reassured me.

And then I really had to bite my cheek not to laugh—oh, okay, it was just your regular mom, dad, and kids of serious assassins worried about the bogeyman stealing their goats and guns. Got it. Tony went on to explain—as if I'd already said yes to his request—that twice a week he would retrofit my gas tank to accommodate about four hundred bullets. All I had to do was drive to the "compound," where someone would meet me at the gate and take the bullets, and Tony would pay me when he got the phone call. Each trip was worth a hundred bucks. Quick math—one trip was almost a year's rent.

"What if I get caught? They'll put me in a nasty Lebanese prison." (The movie *Midnight Express* was not made up, folks.) I was only sort of joking. Prison in this part of the world was a Very Bad Place.

Tony put his arm around me. "I can fix everything . . . do you have a driving license?" I shook my head. "I don't need one for a motor bike."

"Okay. You need it for identification. Good. No problem. I have good friend—come back in five days."

It didn't take five days for me to decide. Crazy, but why not? Didn't Zorba the Greek say, "If you don't have a little madness in your life, what the hell have you got?" Even still, I don't think he meant running bullets to assassins. Yet—here I was, five days later, pulling up to Tony's shop, ready to go to work up the hill. He greeted me with a big hug and handed over a 4X6, two-page laminated document.

"This is your driving license."

"What is this? I haven't taken any test for a driving license."

"Not necessary." He was grinning from ear to ear. "Look. See?"

I looked again, and it was indeed a driving license—in my name, printed and stamped from . . .

The country of *Palestine signed by Yasser Arafat*! I couldn't believe it.

"Oh my God! Is that 'his' signature? Really?"

"Of course."

"Tony, this is brilliant! Where did you get this? It looks so real!"

He gave me a withering look. "It is real. I just came from *him*," he said, pointing to the infamous signature.

And so it was. A totally legal, authentic Palestinian driving license which Yasser Arafat had signed that morning.

"You will have big respect on the mountain and with every Freedom Fighter," Tony said with great confidence. *That was comforting*, I thought.

"But Tony—there is no Palestine," I told him.

He poked at the laminate page.

"Yes, there is. *He* says so."

And then I had the realization—of course, Tony was Palestinian.

Chapter 18

Gun Running and Spiders

Zahlé was a picturesque town halfway to Damascus, about thirty-four miles east of Beirut. Sitting three thousand feet up Lebanon Mountain, Zahlé could easily fit the bill for an afternoon picnic or a scenic drive—but this picturesque place was actually home to some of the most dangerous people in the country, loosely known as the Lebanese Political Militia. These were Muslim civilians who had banded together in an assortment of military-style factions to "right the wrong." Recognized by their dark red berets, black shirts, and combat pants, their sole purpose in life was to basically go around assassinating whomever they deemed "political dissidents."

On my first journey up the mountain, Tony hadn't given me any directions other than to "follow the road to the top." I wasn't going to a real address, but rather, I would be met at "the gate," deliver the precious cargo that had been expertly and tightly packed into a blocked-off section of my gas tank, then turn around and return. I was starting my climb along the narrow dirt road, when I hit the first checkpoint: four heavily armed guards dressed in military uniforms, their faces two-thirds covered by the traditional *keffiyeh*—a black-and-white checkered scarf worn around the neck or head, usually pulled up, exposing only the eyes. The guards stood across the road, weapons drawn and crossed, a definitive sign that I must stop. Now, let me just paint you a quick picture of the absurdity of what these guards saw as I pulled up. A young, dark-haired girl, riding a motorcycle, wearing a Carlos Santana T-shirt and a pair of cut-off shorts. I was the only girl in Beirut who drove a motorcycle and certainly the only foreigner daring to drive into such a forbidden area. Thank God I wasn't blonde, as it might have been a vastly different story. I stopped the bike and waited.

Should I have been worried? Hell, yes! It was obvious these guys were the real deal and I might have had only a few minutes more to live, but I was on a really cool, dangerous adventure, and worry isn't your primary *go-to* when you're twenty-two.

The main guard walked over, and the rest followed. He stared at me for what felt like a week, then he pulled down his keffiyeh and asked, "*Illaa 'ayn tadhhab?*" which meant "Where are you going?"

I replied with the name of the family in Zahlé that I had been instructed to mention. He asked for my identification papers. The other guards walked up and stood behind him. I did have my Turkish passport, but I had a feeling the PLO driving license would be a better option. I pulled the laminated card out of my pocket and handed it over. He opened it, and his face contorted into a peculiar expression. It took a minute for him to stand bolt-up straight, and holding The License high for the others to see, he crisply saluted, shouting, "*Allah' Akbar. Fatah!*" Then, with a flourishing gesture, the small sea of soldiers parted, and I was reverently waved on my way.

The next four checkpoints garnered the same results. Energetic salutes and many cries of "Allah Akbar!"

As I drove up to the iron gates of the compound in Zahlé, more guards halted me. They looked at The License and stepped back with a salute. A soldier came out of a house and took my bike away for a few minutes, then brought it back and asked me if I wanted tea or coffee.

"Yes, please," I answered, knowing to never refuse libations from friendly assassins. Propped up against my bike, next to the smiling soldier, I drank my tea out of a tiny glass. There was lots of smiling and nodding, then another soldier escorted me back to the gate, and home I went. This time as I passed the guards on the highway, they waved as if I were their best buddy on my way home from work. At the last checkpoint, before I reentered the city, the guard whom I'd first encountered motioned me to stop. *Oh shit. Was my license a forgery?*

He smiled a huge smile and said in broken English, "American Hershey chocolate?"

I smiled and nodded. *You betcha*, I thought. *I'll have two kilos of the stuff if it keeps you guys happy and me death free.*

I drove the mountain to Zahlé for about five months. The guards became my pals, and I provided abundant bars of chocolate to all of them, on each trip. I had also become a favorite of the families who received my "deliveries," and, in turn, they became dear friends of mine. Yes, I was *dear* friends with serious Lebanese assassins who invited me into their homes and showed me utmost hospitality.

"These are Very Bad People. Politicians, making bad things for Lebanon," they assured me. I nodded. Got it. Made total sense and, besides, it wasn't my business, and I know this may sound terrible and heartless, but—I honestly didn't care. They were kind and funny and took good care of me. I never had a problem and I never got caught. I was one of the safest people in Beirut, although I'm pretty sure all the guards on the mountain absolutely knew where I was going and what I was doing, but hey—chocolate was a precious commodity, and in their eyes, I was their friend, and you didn't fuck with your friends.

I was dating—in between delivery assignments—one of Zahlé's top soldiers, known as the head political assassin. His name was Najid, and he looked *exactly* like Che Guevara. (By the way, it always helps when a man looks like another gorgeous man you've had a massive crush on.) He was dressed head to toe in black combat gear, which was embellished with a red beret and gold badge, authenticating his status as the leader of the highest militia group in the country. We'd met at the UNESCO event. I'd noticed him across the room, dressed in all his black combat gear. He saw me and strode over.

"What time you are finished?"

"In an hour." God, he was gorgeous and fast!

"I will come. Here. To take you." He stroked my hair and walked away.

Our first date was memorable. We went to Les Caves du Roy and sat at the bar. Najid ordered a bottle of tequila—the one with the worm at the bottom. The strong shit. I have absolutely no recollection of what we talked about, as he didn't speak but a few words of English, but we managed. We also managed to drink the entire bottle of tequila, with Najid dramatically downing the worm at the end. The bartenders applauded. He stroked my face and stood up.

"I will telephone." And he was gone. I sat at the bar marveling at how okay I felt. Wow! Tequila was fabulous! Then I stood up and the room flipped upside down. Shit. Where was the door? Where was the wall? I stumbled through the whizzy room and somehow got to the door and onto my motorcycle. The Big Guy must have taken a minute to watch over me on that drive along the coast to my now new apartment. I don't remember the rest of the night—not that there was much left of it to remember.

In the morning I telephoned Dilys. My head was breaking, my stomach was burning, and my body had stopped working.

"Please come and take me to the hospital. I'm dying," I pleaded. I heard her laughing.

"What did you drink?"

"A bottle of tequila," I said quietly.

"You have a hangover—a *terrible* hangover. The worst kind. Give it a few hours and drink lots of water. You'll be fine. I'll be over soon and we'll go for coffee." She hung up still laughing.

I recovered, and Najid soon became my official boyfriend. Each night, we'd hit the rounds of clubs, ready at any minute to drop our glasses and leave, as police were constantly searching for these guys. When that happened, someone would call out—you never heard sirens—and the police would storm the building. Before they came through the door, there was always somebody, a different "somebody" each time, who'd grab my hand and drag me out the back to the street. Then I'd run by myself around the corner to The Speakeasy Club, looking back always to see Najid holding up his fist in what I think was a wave "goodbye" as he screeched out of town on or in whatever transport he'd brought that evening. The police would run around the club shouting their frustration at having missed him, yet again.

Why did I always seem to not care about putting myself in dangerous situations? Running bullets up to assassins on the mountain, dating basically a murderer—let's face it, these guys were notorious criminals, wanted by every law enforcer in the country, all instructed to shoot Najid and his cohorts on sight! Well, to be truthful . . . it was exciting, and Najid was a gorgeous, wild, and passionate man who did scare the crap out of me, but it was worth it. He always carried his gun in his two-hundred-round bullet belt, which dug into my hip every time he grabbed me close. I didn't care. I also didn't care he was a criminal—I was in love. It was like dating a very intense rock star, who just happened to kill people. Najid and I would spend long evenings at Les Caves du Roy nightclub, drinking tequila (always with the worm). I tried *not* to keep up, but it was difficult, as he would smack the bottle on the bar counter, kiss me, and pour.

"You are my woman. We drink!" And even though I'd vowed never to drink this evil but lovely drink again, I recall many times when he was called away to "*action*" and I had to get myself home on my motorbike, with no recollection of the weaving journey down the street at that time called the Rue de Corniche to my apartment. I do remember waking up on numerous mornings feeling like I was dying, with that full-blown tequila hangover. Dilys frequently took me for coffee.

But these were the good times spent with insanely exhilarating people, and again, we were ignorant of what was going on behind all that fun. At night, you would hear the odd mortar blow, far in the distance. No one knew that, within less than a year, Najid and every single man, woman, and child from the homes I'd been in and drunk endless teas and coffees with, would all be dead, shot to pieces where they stood.

One day, there was a knock on my door, and I opened it to see my darling Paul Ryan, standing there grinning in his black bell-bottoms,

Celebrating my birthday at Caves du Roy with my boyfriend, Varouche (center, sitting beside me), other members of the band, and their girlfriends, June 3, 1974

silk shirt tucked into a sparkly belt, and those too-great silver-and-white platform boots.

"Hello, luv," he greeted me. "I missed you, so I thought I'd pop over for a visit. I fancied a bit of a holiday."

I started laughing. Only Paul would "pop over" to a relatively obscure Middle Eastern country for a "bit of a holiday." We had a wonderful week hitting the clubs with all my friends, who adored his platform boots, and taking part in Paul's favorite occupation—sunning by the pool at the Saint Georges. You absolutely had to go home with a tan, otherwise how would anyone know you'd been away?

It was starting to feel strange in the city. I knew Paul needed to leave. There was a hum in the air, and I had a sense something was going to pop. I knew I'd feel a lot better if my dearest friend "popped" himself safely back to London. At the airport, I told him I was worried—I had a bad feeling about this town. He got it. He was a super smart guy and an incredibly special man whom I loved dearly and will remember forever. He died ridiculously early of lung cancer when he was only forty-four. We all smoked like troopers back then. It was what you did. And I still miss him with a pain that will never go away.

My new apartment building, where I'd moved just before Paul's visit, was in Raouche, a coastal area of the city about two miles from the Saint Georges hotel, along the Rue de Corniche (now Avenue de Paris). My building offered short-term rentals, so it was quite common to see American families renting for a few weeks, sometimes even months, taking long vacations. The apartment next door to mine was a short-term rental housing an American couple, Herb and Betty May from Kansas. I never knew their last name, but they were a hoot. They owned more cameras and lenses than I had ever seen and were always asking me questions from where to go for dinner to whether the water was safe to drink. I remember looking at them in their Bermuda shorts, Hawaiian shirts, and straw hats and thinking they really should be on a Caribbean cruise.

We also had American Navy ships regularly stopping in the Port of Beirut for a few days to replenish supplies and fuel. The sailors, "ordinary seamen" as they were called, would take advantage of the freedom of where they were and hit the city's nightlife like a charge of white-cottoned renegades. One evening, I was at the Caves du Roy hanging with Varouche and the band. Varouche had broken up with me just before I'd met Najid, but we'd stayed friends—it was all good. That night, I met his new girlfriend, Bianca, a Swedish drop-dead gorgeous girl who was also the sweetest person. And we got along instantly, much to Varouche's relief.

On this particular evening at the Caves, the band had finished up earlier than usual. The sailors were kicking up a racket, drinking like fish and stumbling onto every girl they could see, hands outstretched toward any breasts they could grab. The manager finally decided to end the debacle and shoved them out the door by their collars. Two stragglers came over and plonked themselves down, putting their drinks on our table. Tinty, the drummer, managed to haul them out of their seats and push them to the door. We finished our drinks and the band started to pack up. Suddenly, as I stood up, the room started spinning. Bianca had already left, so I couldn't tell her there was a giant three-foot spider crawling over Varouche's guitar. It started with two and three, then a swarm of long black hairy legs moving slowly up the guitar neck. I slumped back down into my seat, vaguely seeing transparent people moving in front of my chair. The floor undulated and the room turned into a moving jigsaw of more spiders, now with dripping red eyes and long yellow teeth. I was convinced I was dying, or—I had already died and this was the road to wherever the Big Guy was sending me. The floor began to melt, bringing more spiders with longer legs, everywhere. I heard myself screaming, as I'd fallen to the floor and was desperately holding on to a stone pillar in the center of the room. *What the fuck was happening?* The next thing I remember, I was sitting on a chair in the club's kitchen with Varouche, looking like a dark green cockroach, holding my hand.

"Are you okay?"

"I think I'm on my way to hell."

"The sailor dropped acid on you." He looked guilty.

"What sailor? What acid? Where?"

"The one that came to the table. LSD."

"What table? The floor's melting, there are no tables!"

"He dropped a tab in your drink. You're hallucinating." His hand was on my shoulder—it had started growing into a huge, clawed monster paw. Poor guy really didn't know what to do. "We're okay. Are you okay?" was all he could say. I had no idea if I was okay; I sure didn't feel okay. The guys took me home, and for three days, nightmares and yellow-teeth spiders plagued my brain. Finally, I started to feel remotely normal, but hey . . . at least I can say I've done acid.

Chapter 19

Paradise Lost

On April 9, 1973, I was enjoying a beautiful spring evening. I was at home on my night off, drinking tea and listening to David Bowie's "Space Oddity" on the radio. I stepped outside, walking through the glass sliding doors, and did what I did every evening—contemplating life while sitting on the balcony. My apartment was on the corner of the building, overlooking the Mediterranean, and as I gazed out, I heard jet engines in the distance. As they got closer, I saw they were following the shoreline—one, two, then four fighter jets, flying in perfect formation, about two hundred feet off the water.

As they roared past, I dimly saw a blur of blue-and-white Israeli flags painted on the tails. Weird, but I brushed it off. Israel was a neighbor—maybe they were doing evening practice runs, I thought, although deep down I knew something wasn't right and this was no practice run. The feeling grew when I saw a bunch of speedboats, also flying the Israeli flag, speeding full tilt toward the beach. David Bowie stopped telling us about "*Major Tom*," and a voice came on the radio, announcing the airport was closed until further notice, and a curfew was being imposed. The phone rang. It was Tinty from the band, telling me there was a curfew and we couldn't leave our homes. He said troubles had started the night before and there were a bunch of Israeli soldiers in Beirut, arresting Palestinian civilians and PLO leaders from the ghettos and camps.

For most of the past year, the PLO had been firing weapons and grenades at Israel from the Lebanese border (those explosions in the distance I'd thought were mortars). Arafat had finally decided that now was the time, and armed with Russian weapons, he and the boys had been taking aimed pot shots over the fence to Israel, including randomly shooting mortars, attacking and killing Israeli civilians as well as military targets within the country. The killing of innocent people was of little consequence to Arafat; he was on a mission to get his home back and didn't care how the hell that happened, although he'd either forgotten or underestimated his opponent. Israel was one fierce enemy, an enemy that wouldn't back down until the fat man started singing and flying a white flag. Arafat was one scary dude, and he was prepared to go all the way to avenge the wrong done. We never saw it coming—probably because no one was looking, and the bastard was always smiling.

The first thing I did after Tinty's call was to go next door to Herb and Betty May and tell them to be careful and absolutely obey the curfew. They promised they would.

So, here we were—it had finally happened. The soldiers arriving were the Israel Defense Special Forces, here to organize a raid on the Palestinians living in Lebanon. It was named "Operation Wrath of God," said to be partly their retaliation for the 1972 Summer Olympics Munich Massacre, as well as their mission to put a stop to Arafat and his boys lobbing deadly pot shots into their country.

The speedboats I had seen were filled with soldiers launched from missile boats offshore, where Mossad agents waited for them on the beaches with cars rented the previous day. The soldiers were then driven to their targets in the city and later back to the beaches for extraction. During the operation, they surprised three of the highest-level PLO leaders and murdered them in their homes, along with as many other PLO members they could rustle out. They never found Yasser Arafat, however. Along with a talent for smiling, he also had an exceptional talent for hiding.

In the days that followed, the raid escalated. Unbeknownst to the Israelis, the hundreds of Palestinians living in Beirut and working those menial, dead-end service jobs were ready to join their PLO buddies at the take-down party. A mass of them had convened and were ready to fight with their Muslim brothers—but today, Israel had changed the game and stepped up the assault. Along with the beach assaults, convoys of tanks were sent in and out of Beirut daily to hunt down the Palestinian troublemakers, street by street. They took them from their homes, from stores, from their jobs, and eliminated them in the broad light of day. When they were done, the tanks moved out, and it was back to the beaches and into the boats, speeding back to the homeland, where a fresh crew would arrive the next day to step, wash, and repeat.

It's strange—humans are quite adaptable to ignoring what they don't want to see. Now there was no choice. Curfew was a nightmare. Food flew off the market shelves, and people were literally fist fighting for bread and milk. The Israeli clean-up invasion lasted five days, and during that time, their killing spree spared no mercy. A Palestinian woman was strangled in an elevator in her apartment building; her neighbor was shot in the corridor, and many, many more suffered equally spontaneous deaths. It was a week of murderous mayhem. By now I had a permit to be out during curfew—I was an artist, so I was permitted to go to work at the club, as were all the other night workers in the city. Five days later the Israeli commandos abruptly left, and life carefully resumed in between curfew hours.

The city had changed. People were wary and on edge. The Lebanese Muslim community was suddenly awake; they started creeping out of the shadows, weapons in hand. Most people continued their fun-loving routine, but everyone knew that the Muslim community had started to turn on Christians, and the Palestinians had come pouring out of the ghettos like ants, looking to find sympathizers to their cause. It was horrible and so incredibly sad, but in these early days, we were adapting to a new way of life. The airport stayed closed, and we obeyed the daytime's sporadic curfew, which changed frequently. My Arabic was respectable and my French fairly good, which helped, and I could tell the difference between the Christian Arabic and the Muslim Arabic mostly by their distinct dialects. I had a British passport showing I was Christian, and a Turkish passport showing I was Muslim, plus I had—The License. I was covered. I just had to make sure I showed the right passport, at the right time, to the right person.

One morning, about two weeks after the Israeli raid, I took my tea out onto the balcony and was startled by a bizarre sight below. I lived on the second floor and there, sitting fifty yards from the front door, was a combat tank complete with a large cannon mounted on the turret with no flag displayed. In the seat sat a fourteen- to fifteen-year-old soldier holding a machine gun in his lap with about a dozen coils of bullets wrapped around his torso. He was wearing aviator sunglasses and smoking a cigarette, watching the day go by as if he had all the time in the world.

Crap. The Israelis had left—hadn't they? I reasoned that this could be one of two things: the Lebanese had sent a tank to protect the building, knowing it was inhabited and run by a well-populated Palestinian family (who had all disappeared, fleeing with just the clothes on their back), or—and this could be serious—this young soldier could be Israeli, waiting for this family to return and remove them from the earth.

I heard my neighbor's glass door slide open. Herb sauntered out onto his balcony holding a camera and a cup of coffee. Right, I forgot I had Americans living next door. I quickly said, "Herb, go back inside. Don't take any pictures. He could be an Israeli soldier or Lebanese. Either way, it's not happy snappy time."

Herb laughed and said with confident joviality, "Oh, he's fine. He's just a kid. I got two boys back home."

"Herb! Get back inside! Please! And close the doors!" I was hissing out the words as softly as possible, trying not to attract the soldier's attention.

Herb shuffled inside and closed the glass doors. A couple minutes later, something made me go to my front door, and lo and behold, there were Herb and Betty May coming out of their apartment and into the hallway, carrying two cameras, a bottle of whiskey, and one *huge* lens. Are you fucking kidding me?

"Herb? *What are you doing?*"

"We're just going to get a couple shots of the kid for the folks back home," said the stupidest man on the planet.

"He's not a kid, he's a *soldier*."

But stupid has no ears. They were heading down the stairs humming, and I ran to my balcony, my brain riffling through all logical scenarios. Why would the Lebanese put a tank outside? Were they putting tanks outside every building run by Palestinians? Of course not, because since this thing had started, there hadn't been any faction of any visible Lebanese army in the city. Oh, that's right—*there was no Lebanese army*!

It hit me like cold pebbles. Yup, he was an Israeli soldier, waiting for the Palestinian concierge and his family to return. Shit. I looked down as Herb and Betty May came out the front door. My brain was hammering—what could I do?

Nothing, unless I wanted to die.

Herb handed Betty May the camera, now with the *huge* lens attached, and pushed her toward the tank. The boy lifted his head, cigarette dangling.

Herb was waving his passport energetically.

"We're Americans! USA!" He held up the bottle. "Johnny Walker whiskey!"

The boy's head tilted to one side.

Betty May got closer to the tank, holding the camera up.

The boy wrapped his fingers around the trigger. All the while, Herb was laughing, clueless. I watched in silence; yelling was now too dangerous.

"Go on there, baby girl, go on and get your foot up there on that there wheel bit. Let's get us a close-up!" Herb was in charge!

Finger still on the trigger, the boy lifted the gun from his lap and adjusted his sunglasses with the back of his hand. I opened my mouth—then shut it. A few more inches and that gun could point directly at me. I moved back closer to the door. He readied his weapon as Betty May put one pink sandaled foot on the tank, balancing the camera in her hand. I remember her matching pink painted toenails. I stifled a scream as the machine gunfire clattered and two Americans from Kansas dropped like rag dolls, dead to the ground, their bodies riddled with about fifty bullets. The boy put his gun back in his lap. He'd not even taken the cigarette out of his mouth.

Herb and Betty May lay where they died for thirteen days. I kept calling the American consulate, but it was closed, all personnel having been sent back to the States. Finally, a truck came and scraped up the bodies. I think someone had complained about the smell.

That pretty much marked the beginning of the nightmare—instant, bloody, and senseless. It became a civil war that broadly pitted Palestinian and pro-Palestinian Muslim militias against Lebanon's Christian militias, devastating the country in the process. Over the next sixteen years it raged, and an estimated 150,000 people were killed, while thousands more fled the country.

It still feels like yesterday.

After Herb and Betty May were shot, the city and its people elevated the shift, and with the advent of the PLO explosion and the Israeli raid, the Muslim community had begun to rise up and demand to be heard. The Christian government started to slowly fall apart, and the conflict just got ugly. I still went to sing every night, and though the clubs were still full, there was an air of unrest and mounting panic. You had to have eyes in the back of your head, as you never knew when an uprising would start in the streets. Suddenly everyone had a gun or two or three. I think, because I knew everyone and had Muslim friends in the Very Right Places, I stayed safe. Najid assured me I was protected. He and his family stayed up in the mountains, waiting for the call to action.

Never take safety for granted.

An old friend, Ahmed, a disc jockey from Riyadh, Saudi Arabia, had been visiting from London and got stuck in the city because of the airport closure. One evening, we decided we'd had enough of all the troubles and would go have a night on the town at the Casino du Liban, the fanciest nightclub in Beirut, often referred to as "the jewel of Lebanon." That evening, it took us three times as long to drive the fourteen miles because of the dozens of checkpoints along the way, each lit with bonfires blocking

Me and Ahmed at the Casino du Liban, 1973, the night of the ghetto mishap

alternative left or right routes on either side of the street. These fires were six feet high and at least twenty feet long. So if you decided to be a super smarty and just "go around," you'd have to drive through the fire, and of course someone would shoot you on the other side—should you make it through alive.

Eventually, we arrived at the casino and had the most wonderful evening, and at about three a.m., we started the journey back. As we came down the main road leading into the city, there was a fiery checkpoint ahead of us.

"Damn! I know where we are," I said. "Let's just hang a right and cut this corner off." Ahmed made the turn, and we found ourselves driving down a pitch dark, narrow street, with trees intertwined above like a leafy umbrella. The road ended, and our headlights lit up an eighteen-foot-long wooden gate covered in barbed wire. Standing guard in front were two of the wrongest-looking soldiers I had ever seen. "Oh shit! It's a Palestinian compound. Crap! Turn around! We have to get out of here now! Hang a U-ie. Go! Go! Now!"

As we started to turn, we heard the readying of two machine guns, and my heart jumped hearing a loud rapping on the back of the car. We stopped dead, halfway through the turn. One soldier came to each side of the car and motioned for us to lower our windows. We faced two pairs of coal-black eyes, burning into us above the familiar checkered keffiyeh of the PLO militia. We were in very deep shit, and this could easily be the end for both of us—right here, right now. I had to think and think fast; there was no time to be scared. As of this moment, neither soldier had spoken, but they had slid the machine guns in the window, each butt pressed against our heads, Ahmed on the left and me on the right. I can still feel that ice-cold steel circle pressing into my temple. I had to get us out of this; no, I *was* going to get us out! The silence broke as the soldier spoke in Arabic.

"*Hal 'ant Muslim 'am 'ant masihiun?*" He was asking if we were Muslim or Christian. I listened to the soldier's Arabic. It was crude, not very articulate, and tinged with a definite accent.

I sat still and took a breath. My life depended on my answer. I responded in Arabic, telling him "*Ana Muslim*" or "I am Muslim." He leaned in closer.

"Papers and passport."

Again, the clatter of guns being readied. They motioned me to hurry with my papers. I reached into my purse and took out the PLO driving license and my Turkish passport. Ahmed, shaking, *handed* his Saudi passport over, consequently breaking war rule number one. You *never* let your papers/passport out of your hands *anywhere* to *anyone*. I held my passport and opened The License. The soldier's eyes widened like black grapes above his keffiyeh as he peered closely at that infamous signature. He swiftly pulled his gun up and shouted to his buddy to return Ahmed's passport, and standing back, they saluted us three times.

"Allah Akbar! Fatah!" And then they vigorously waved us on our way.

I think Ahmed had peed himself, poor darling, but we were alive. I gave a quiet thanks to my angel, Tony the Mechanic, and yes—I also did silently thank Yasser Arafat.

For the next eight months, I ducked mortars and bullets and scrambled to survive, which had now become everyone's way of life. Streets had to be navigated with care, as you never knew who was waiting down any given alley and with what weapon. One afternoon, Carol and I were in a taxi going to see Susy—my motorcycle had been stolen—and we had to pass through two tanks firing at each other across the street. A third tank behind them had just blown up a house holding Palestinian guerillas. Our driver was crying in terror, yelling for us to lie on the floor.

Anyone could get shot, anytime and anywhere. There were no good guys or bad guys. By now, Lebanon was in the throes of a major civil war. This beautiful city of happy people was falling into ruin. The clubs and restaurants closed down, and some were blown up. Soldiers burned and shot holes in every building they could, inhabited or not, and destroyed the famous Gibran museum, which housed the famous poet Khalil Gibran's paintings and writings. Tony's mechanic shop hung on but was finally burned to the ground with Tony burning inside.

Dilys and most of my girlfriends managed to get out, but some didn't and disappeared, never to be seen again. My friend Carol was whisked out on a private airplane with her boyfriend, Adnan Khashoggi, the famed arms dealer, and I never heard from her again. Susy was so scared that in a constant effort to calm herself from her blinding terror, she overdosed on opium and died. I found a couple of my Dabke boys, Bashir and Hamid, to help me try and get her body out of the apartment, but shells were blasting full force and we had to leave her there. I took three steps away from the building, and in that precise moment, the full and actual horror of what was happening got to me. I just stood there crying—my heart was broken. The boys saw me and ran back, taking both my arms.

"We cannot get her. You must run with us. Hurry!"

And as we ran, the building collapsed to the ground behind us, burying Susy in the rubble.

All my other friends—the other Dabke dancers, my friends in all the bands, teenage kids who wanted to be soldiers, children who wanted to be men—all died. No one was trained to be a soldier. They were just swept up in the high of a totally unregulated war. Our pal Serge stayed solidly ensconced at his beach desk at the Saint Georges—before they destroyed it—handing out serious weapons to anyone who had the cash. Young men who were willing to fight now owned automatic weapons, grenades, and mortars; it was like boy bands were suddenly armed with killing machines. On one of those famous blue, sunny days, Serge was murdered while sitting at his table, and the Saint Georges was burned and bombed so badly that for years it remained a hollow shell of its former grandeur on the Beirut waterfront. Today, the pools and restaurant are open to the public, but the hotel itself—and its legendary bar—remain bare and unfinished.

Najid was shot in his home in Zahlé, along with his entire family and all the other families who lived in the village. Others I knew were shot or caught in mortar attacks, gone forever. Needless to say, I had stayed longer than I should have. I knew I had to get out, but I didn't want to leave—I didn't want to believe my friends were all gone and life there was over.

The airport was still opening sporadically for a day here and there, and one or two flights would get out with all the foreigners. I had a lot of contacts, but it was all about *when* the airport was open and how fast you could get there before the gates closed. Someone who knew someone would be the one who found out, and you got there as fast as you could, hoping it hadn't closed during your journey. Then you had to have cash to get on any plane going anywhere. A month before, I'd withdrawn all my money from my bank, carrying it in various zipper pockets in my bag and on my person. Looting was now prevalent, and the banks ran out of money and finally shut their doors. I was carrying the equivalent of about five hundred dollars, which back then was a lot of money, and for some reason—probably The Big Guy again—I wasn't robbed.

I left Beirut on October 29, 1975, lying on the floor of a taxi stolen by my dear friend Hakim, who drove like a madman as the shells and mortars flew around us. We made it to the airport just as they were about to close the doors. I hugged Hakim goodbye and thanked him for risking his life to get me there. Before I went in, I quickly looked back as the doors were being locked. I can still see him leaning against the bullet-riddled taxi, grinning at me with his hand on his heart.

"Always our friendship first," he mouthed. Swallowing tears, and knowing I would never see him again, I ran and managed to get on a TWA flight to Berlin. As the airplane climbed out of the airport and turned toward the ocean, I couldn't look out the window. I didn't want to see what I could hear and still smell—death and devastation.

The war lasted until 1990, and the horror and destruction tore apart one of the most wonderful, happy places in the world—a true slice of paradise and for three years, the place I called home.

Chapter 20

London and a Broken Heart

I've left out Mother, haven't I? Well, upon her return to Istanbul and finding me gone, she marched right over to Saad, who airily told her I'd gone to Beirut to see my friends.

"I know that! She left a note!" She stood in front of him.

He shrugged. "Good—then you know it's better for Juliette."

"How did she get there?" Her rage fumed. I had committed the inexcusable crime of leaving.

"I gave her a ticket."

I managed to call her occasionally, where she carefully explained her conversation with Saad, whom she described as a selfish, sly Arab, and how could I have just left on his word, blah, blah. Usual Mother speak. Our conversations were always terse, with the usual lament of "what had I *done* to her" and "*how long* was I staying?" In truth, it was nothing short of heaven to be free of the binds that tied me to her, but eventually she buckled and came to visit, begrudgingly admitting it was a fun place with nice weather, which then turned into regular appearances. She used to take the bus from Istanbul to Beirut, a treacherous eighteen-hour journey across Turkey and Syria, but she loved it. She had a ball. There were copious amounts of alcohol on the bus, and she was quite cheery when she arrived at Riyadh Square. She adored Beirut and made quite a few friends, and she loved all *my* friends! I have no idea how her brain worked. Maybe it was being back in the Middle East with what she used to call "her people from back in the day." Who knows?

Eventually, when we returned to England, she became Helen again—bitter, angry, and just plain unhappy in every way. I wish she had talked to me without the accusatory blame. I wish I had understood why she was so miserable and why she did her best to make herself even more miserable by being unpleasant to and resentful of everyone else.

When I did occasionally buck up the courage to ask her a personal question, her response would be cold and direct.

"It's none of your business. It's my life, which has nothing to do with you."

I always knew where I stood.

After my three-hour flight out of war-torn Beirut, the plane landed in Berlin. I managed to call Mother to tell her I was safe. She said she was headed back to Beirut to pick up a watch she'd put in for repair at the jewelry store on Hamra Street. I laughed, not thinking for a second that she was actually serious.

"Mum, Beirut is at war."

"Dear, I *know* war, and that isn't it. Arafat is *not* Hitler. It's my gold watch—I need to pick it up from the jewelry repair shop."

I opened my mouth and then closed it; there was no point.

When I got back to London, I had nowhere to live, so my only choice was Grandmother in Hatch End. The contrast between where I had come from and the cold, silent, brown-paneled gloominess of that house, compounded with the dreary drizzle they called weather, physically hurt. My grandmother fawned over me in a sickening way, probably still carrying a clear memory of the milk incident and was going to make damn sure I didn't get "upset" again.

Days went by as I took walks and tried not to get horribly depressed. One afternoon, I was in my room listening to Cat Stevens when the phone rang. I bolted down the stairs as the kitchen door flew open, but I got there first, beating Grandma to it. It was my mother calling from *Beirut*.

Over the crackle of serious static, she told me she'd taken the bus from Istanbul to get her watch, and her American friend Bill had picked her up in his Mercedes at the bus stop on Riyadh Sol Square.

"Wasn't that kind of him?" she chirped. Through the static, I could hear weird sounds in the background. "He has kindly offered for me to stay at his apartment in town—that's where I'm calling from." She was still chirping.

More weird sounds . . . booming sounds . . . oh shit!

"Mum? What's going on? Am I hearing bombs?"

"Just mortars, dear. They're firing them at the opposite building. Bill's on the terrace with binoculars keeping an eye. We're fine." Her casualness was astounding, but of course there she was in her happy place—crisis mode, being her best, authentic self.

Suddenly I heard an earth-shaking explosion. I screamed into the phone, "Mum? What was that? MUM? Are you still there?"

"Yes, dear. Please don't shout. Some soldier on the opposite roof threw a couple of grenades, you know, one of those men with a tea towel wrapped around his head. I think they hit the third floor. We're all fine here, holding the fort. Did I tell you Bill has a penthouse?"

"I don't know Bill, Mum." What was the point? My mother was going to die today.

"Yes, you do. You met him that afternoon when we had coffee with the Seymours. It's such a shame how awful your memory is. Anyhow, Bill's penthouse is just around the corner from Hamra Street. It's very nice—I have my own room."

I was speechless. My mother was about to be blown up, and she wasn't even fazed. In fact, she sounded like she was having the time of her life.

She was.

I tried to sound rational. I'd been there, and keeping your life intact was a twenty-four-hour challenge.

"You have to get out, now, immediately. Have Bill drive you to the airport, or try and get on the bus back to Turkey. You'll have to go through a bit of Syria, but . . ."

She stopped me with a condescending tone, the one she'd used when I was a child. "Now, dear, be sensible. We can't. The buses have stopped running and the airport's closed. Plus, I have to get my watch."

I was *really* trying to stay calm.

"The repair shop is probably gone," I said as another ear-shattering explosion filled the phone.

"No, Bill drove us past it yesterday and they're just not open today." This was insane, and what the fuck was Bill doing driving a car? And *who* the fuck *was* Bill?

"When do you plan on leaving?" My calmness was running thin.

"After I get my watch. Bill and I managed to get some groceries, I brought English tea, and we have lots of brandy. We're fine." I was just about to tell her again to leave when I heard a loud rapping. "Someone's at the door, dear. Can you hang on?"

This wasn't good. I was sure no one was popping over to visit. I heard sharp men's voices talking in Arabic, I heard my mother ask if they spoke French, and by their response, that was a "no." She came back to the phone. "They're some kind of militia, probably Muslim, Lebanese. They're dressed in black and have lots of guns and grenades on their belts." I sat on the floor. "It's all right, they just want to see our documents. I'll have to call you back." She hung up. I stayed on the floor contemplating how to have a funeral with no body. I suppose you could; people did it all the time with missing war victims.

At least she'll die in a good mood, I thought.

The kitchen door opened. My grandmother stood silhouetted in the gloom of the English evening.

"Who was that?"

"Mum."

"Is she on her way home?"

"I don't know."

She tutted in annoyance and went back to the kitchen, slamming the door.

Two days later, my senseless mother called and launched into a detailed explanation of the "militia visit."

"They were actually quite nice. We showed them our passports—they searched the apartment for guns and of course found nothing. They looked very tired, so we offered them a cup of tea with a couple of brandies, which they gratefully took. All is well, and we're fine. I'll try and call when I'm leaving, but it might be difficult."

No shit.

"And how . . . when do you plan on doing that—leaving?"

"Not sure," she said, living in her element of happiness, as if she were having a lovely vacation and maybe would stay a day or two longer. Only my mother could come face-to-face with probably the most dangerous men in the entire world and escape death with a cup of tea and a couple of brandies. "Have to go! Bye, dear!"

That was that.

I started wondering. If she didn't come back soon, how long should I wait until she was presumed dead?

And that's the way it was. I could do nothing now but face my own dismal life and hope my mother didn't die some ugly death while hundreds of miles away from me. I knew I had to do something other than sit around depressed, but I was painfully sad. I missed my "home." I missed my friends. I missed Beirut. I missed the sunshine and the happiness and Serge and Dilys and . . .

I missed them all and I hated it here in this horrible brown house.

A few days after Mother's call, I was sitting on my small, lumpy twin bed in the sewing room, unable to sleep, miserably pondering. I turned on the radio to The Easybeats pounding out "Friday on My Mind." My old Cat Stevens poster—albeit a bit tattered—hung above the Singer treadmill sewing machine, and I stared at it for ages, listening to the lyrics of The Easybeats. It was time to get moving. I had no money, but my Vespa scooter was still in the garage—miraculously, Granny Dear hadn't sold it! I still had independent transport. I could get a job in London and, okay, so the round-trip journey was seventy-six miles, but who cared? I could do that, easy.

Every day, I bought the newspaper and took the train into town. The Vespa would be saved for when I got a job, which would likely entail odd hours. I thought about trying to go back to Playboy—then un-thought it. I went all over town, searching, finally landing a job at La Valbonne, a trendy disco at 62 Kingly Street, two blocks from Carnaby Street. The club was owned and run by the legendary nightclub impresario Louie Brown, a tall, smooth, slightly slimy man who was stinking rich and drove an E-type Jaguar as well as a Silver Cloud Rolls-Royce. La Valbonne was one of the first real discotheques in London, housing a groovy DJ who sat above the floor in a towered glitter box playing all the latest hits. It was the hippest place to see and be seen. Celebrities flocked there nightly—Princess Anne, Mick Jagger, Freddie Mercury (with an occasional secret lover at his side), Jimi Hendrix, and the ever-crazy Keith Moon were but a few of the regulars.

You entered through red velvet ropes at street level, then climbed a super steep set of stairs to the twenty-two-thousand-square-foot club on the first floor where there were four bars and an abundance of tropical plants to rival the Amazon. Determined to be even more trendy, Louie had had a heart-shaped swimming pool built in the center of the room to encourage "dolly birds" to take a dip and cool off when needed. The decor of the club was in the typical seventies style with red-and-black lacquered tables and stools, deep red flocked wallpaper, faux leather sofas, and the customary mirror ball, all illuminated by pink lighting. Occasionally the Four Tops (or whatever popular band was around) played live on a Saturday night.

There was one super creepy element—Louie had had the entire back wall of the club rebuilt with a purple-tinted two-way mirror that we later found out he would sit behind and watch the action. No one really cared—we were all making money, customers were happy, and we knew Louie was just a harmless pervert.

The club was packed to the gills nightly, and the line would stretch all the way down Kingly Street. Behind the velvet ropes—which were lifted from their brass hooks and swept back to let in the rich and famous—stood at least a hundred guys and gals decked out in the latest fashion trends, waiting to be "chosen" to enter. I had a blast working there and made great money. Occasionally, I would stay in town with either Paul or Barry, Pete and his wife, Chrissie, or my friend Cassidy. At four a.m., that thirty-eight-mile drive to Hatch End was brutal, plus Grandma didn't care if I came home or not.

Cat Stevens, who was always just Steve to us, was around quite a bit. He had just released a rather odd album called *Numbers*, which his record company didn't care for, so he wasn't happy. By then he was a megastar, and over the years since we'd parted and before I went to Turkey, we'd see him from time to time on his UK visits. He was always part of our group but spiritually restless. His brother, David, had given him the Koran, where he seemed to have found a connection. I think we, his old friends, grounded him in a weird way, but as for his peace of mind, we could do nothing for that. He wasn't one to open up and talk about what he was feeling and how unhappy he was, so none of us knew or understood what he was going through or could help him find what he was looking for. He did talk about the Koran and God and the goodness it represented, but I had just come from a world of angry, fighting Muslims who were very far removed from the Koran, and I hadn't seen much of God's work being done lately, so I was tepid in my opinion of his new awareness. He didn't understand *why I* didn't understand. I was Muslim myself, so . . . ? Weren't they my people?

I didn't have the heart to tell him the Muslims I had just come from in Beirut, killing within their own families, were not my people—not in any way, shape, or form. I had witnessed and lived through a violent and senseless Islamic bloodshed, which was something I hoped he'd never have to witness. Even though we were his friends and perhaps a fraying tie to Western reality, I knew he was feeling compelled to move further and further away from this life. He wasn't having a good time being the huge famous pop star the record companies wanted him to be, and I think that troubled him, as he really wasn't sure what he needed to feel fulfilled.

Seeing him was always difficult. I still loved him so much, but he was such a different person from the one he had been. He had a detached coldness that was hard to be around; nevertheless, just the fact that he was there was sometimes enough. I believe, looking back, I loved him for that time he loved me so completely, when I had nothing and no one and I'd lost myself in the refuge of his heart and soul. On his visits, we spent quite a bit of time together, and it was always quite awkward. I used to stay over sometimes and lie there, wide-eye awake, wondering what I was doing. We had hardly anything in common. He didn't laugh much, and I don't think I gave him much peace with all my questions. Sometimes, there would be long periods of silence, then he'd pick up the guitar and this extraordinary talent came to life in some of the sweetest music I have ever heard. I believe we did have a bond. To this day, I know deep in my heart we were connected to each other and always will be, for the rest of our lives.

Chapter 21

The Swiss Adventure

Since the days of working at Playboy, the influx of oil-based, wealthy Arabs moving into London had grown extensively. Every month, dozens more would arrive, settling themselves and their entourages into expensive apartments in and around Mayfair, one of the wealthiest areas in town. And then there were the cars. The Lamborghini Miuras, the Ferrari 365 GTB4s, and the Maserati Spyders, all built to be driven over eighty miles per hour but had been demoted to a pokey thirty-five, relegated solely to driving back and forth from luxury apartments to swanky restaurants and the Playboy Club.

It was a literal invasion. Saudi Arabians were the most prolific arrivals, but the Kuwaitis, who were experiencing their own golden era in an oil-driven period of insane prosperity, were a close second. Their wads of cash, no longer a novelty, were spent like water. Shopping at places like Harrods and being surrounded by every beautiful blonde in town all served to make our new Arabian residents happy. Top-shelf liquor was consumed nightly in vast quantities, and the staff of high-end restaurants in town would fawn over each and every one of them when they showed up as a party of twelve or twenty, doling out tips of over £50 to every employee. Similarly, escort agencies experienced a business boom that was unprecedented. Usually four or five girls were "ordered" for an evening of dinner, dancing, and whatever happened later back in the suite. The agencies, seeing golden apples falling from desert trees, had no qualms about charging anywhere from £1,000 to £3,000 per girl, per evening. Surprisingly, they were all—especially the Saudis—a great group of fun guys. Away from the rigid confines of their Arabian homes and strict, patriarchal rule, they were notorious womanizers, and many a time a hand had to be grabbed and gently removed from an unwanted excursion around your body, but no one got upset and this was largely because no one forced themselves on you. They heard you when you said no. They believed in the Koran, praying five times a day and truly believing that, if they behaved like good Muslims, there were seventy-two virgins waiting for them in heaven. But "good Muslims" in those days were men who believed in God, followed God's word, and did no harm.

I'll never forget coming out of a restaurant one evening with my then boyfriend, Prince Mohammed Mishaal (about ninth in line to the Saudi throne), and seeing a homeless man on the curb asking for money. I knew there were no homeless people in Saudi Arabia, so I was curious as to how Mohammed would react. He saw the guy and, to my surprise, walked over and knelt down beside him. The guy held out his tin cup, and Mohammed dropped in the keys to his brand-new Lamborghini parked fifteen feet down the street. The guy investigated his cup and looked back to Mohammed.

"Wuz that, guv?"

"My car. It is yours. Please?" Mohammed motioned for him to stand. "We must go to the car. The title is in the glove compartment and I have to sign it to you."

There are no words to describe the look on that homeless guy's face. As we walked to the car, I whispered, "Can he even drive?"

Mohammed shrugged. "It doesn't matter. He can sell the car and get an apartment and eat for a few years."

The car had cost Mohammed $19,000—today the same car can be purchased, used, for $1.2 million! We hailed a cab, and as I got in, I looked back to see the homeless man, standing by his new, legendary silver speed ship, holding the keys . . . crying. These were Islamic, rule-abiding, restrained men who'd arrived in a world of unlimited freedom and gave freely of their generosity. In their home countries, they all had a wife or wives and lived a highly regulated life. Women didn't socialize or have any meals with the men, and they all lived in their own separate apartments off the main house. The King of Saudi Arabia at the time, Khalid bin Abdul-Aziz, had thirty wives and had fathered about thirty-five children.

The rule of Islam governing Muslim women was strict and, in its objectification of them, unilaterally favored men. Polygamy was legal, the wives' ventures outside the home were made chaperoned, and all women were appropriately dressed in black hijabs, covering them head to toe. Marriages were arranged by the men, between families suited to one another in rank and status. In this world, sex took place after marriage and for the purpose of begetting heirs—preferably boys, who would carry on the family name. Life for women was proficiently controlled by men. Notwithstanding, the men were expected to also set a high standard of strict behavior adhering to Muslim law. Alcohol, being strictly forbidden, was made punishable by public flogging, fines, or lengthy imprisonment, as was extramarital sex and the possession of pornography. So being confined, when at home, to these rigorous rules, you can imagine what happened when these guys were set free in swinging London. Unsupervised by their families, and with their holy Korans left behind on their nightstands, they went wild with abandon. The Saudis were all well-educated, having been to private schools in England and Europe; hence they spoke perfect English and had wonderful manners. Life at home was never discussed, although they also constantly worried that their fathers might find out they were drinking and carrying on like college kids and send for their return. This often happened.

At this point, I feel it's imperative to tell the following story—it'll give you an idea of how impenetrable the rules of Islam are, even within the family structure, and also how different and divergent both our cultures are. What follows is the gist of what severely fractured the wonderful, close relationship I had with Mohammed—who had already proposed a few times.

Me and Prince Mohammed Mishaal, 1973

Mohammed had a sister, Princess Mishaal, who had been *allowed* to attend school in Lebanon—she had asked, and the family had *generously* given permission. While in school, she fell in love with Khaled, the nephew of the Saudi ambassador to Lebanon, and they began an affair that eventually turned into a serious relationship. Somehow, her family learned that she'd eluded the chaperone and conspired to meet Khaled alone on several occasions, sneaking out of school to break this sacred rule. Now discovered, they were immediately dispatched back to Saudi Arabia, where both were charged with adultery. They quickly planned to escape, and Princess Mishaal faked her own drowning to create a cover-up. Confident she was safe and with Khaled by her side, she disguised herself as a man and they raced to the airport. Unfortunately, the passport examiner at the Jeddah airport recognized her, and subsequently she was returned to her family. Under the Wahhabi law in Saudi Arabia, a person was convicted of adultery (you didn't have to be married) by the testimony of four adult males who had witnessed the act of sexual penetration or by admission of guilt by the two people concerned, stating three times in court, "I have committed adultery."

Princess Mishaal's family urged her not to confess, but instead to merely promise never to see her lover again. On her return to the courtroom, she repeated her confession three times in a row:

"I have committed adultery."

On July 15, 1977, without any trial, both were publicly executed in Jeddah in a carpark near the palace, by the side of the Queen's Building. Nineteen-year-old Princess Mishaal was blindfolded, made to kneel, and forgoing the traditional professional executioner, was executed explicitly by the instructions of her grandfather, Muhammad bin Abdul Aziz al Saud, the king's older brother, by five gunshots to the head. Khaled, after being forced to watch her execution, was beheaded with a sword by one of the princess's male relatives—it took five blows to sever his head. It was a heinous, barbaric, and utterly unfathomable act of murder, creating front page news all over world television and newspapers. I was horrified that this had been done to my boyfriend's sister—surely he would be equally shocked and be on the next plane home. When the news broke, I headed straight to his apartment.

"Mohammed, how? Why? They murdered your sister. You're going home, of course . . . right?"

He shook his head and, very composed, answered, "I have not been called for."

"What do you mean 'called for?' This is . . . was . . . your *sister*!" I couldn't believe it.

His composure didn't waver. "She brought the highest dishonor to our family. Therefore, she received the highest punishment."

I was dumbfounded. I barraged him with questions as to how such a monstrous act could take place, today, in a supposedly civilized country? An Islamic, God-worshipping country? To his *nineteen-year-old sister*, who had apparently committed a crime just by falling in love.

He shrugged.

"It is the law of the Koran. She was fortunate our family showed mercy. She was executed by gunshot."

"Five to the head," I said, now furious.

He put his arm around my shoulder.

"Come, we have reservations at The Ritz. A nice afternoon tea will make you feel better."

There was no further discussion. This man I cared for deeply, and who had proposed *marriage* to me, stood there, utterly unforgiving, but also as if nothing of any significance had transpired. That evening, I looked up this "law," and the Koran's statement is as follows:

"If an unmarried man or woman commits fornication more than once, then they will be punished three times by hundred whips, and if they are proven guilty for the fourth time, then they will be put to death."

Their months in Lebanon had propagated an excess of "four times."

And this was the way it was and had been since the Koran was written some 1,370 years ago. The laws of Islam governed each and every Muslim in some way or another, and no matter that we saw them as a bunch of fun, happy guys—I now understood they were a totally different people with a completely different culture that we would never understand. Their rectitude was based on a distinctive set of values, and their decisions on right and wrong were and always will be alien to us. They killed, even within their own family, all in the name of a god and a righteous honor. In most Arab nations today, nothing has changed, although in some countries, due to persistence by women and support from the West, a small amount of progress has been achieved. In 2017, King Salman ordered that women be allowed access to government services such as education and healthcare, without the need of consent from a husband or guardian. In 2018, King Salman issued a decree allowing women to drive, lifting the world's *only* ban on women drivers, in Saudi Arabia.

I'd been working at La Valbonne for a few months when I met a cool Persian girl named Pashma. We hit it off and started hanging out together, going to lunch, shopping—all the usual girl stuff. She was a student at the London University and lived in her parents' huge, fancy apartment in the very fashionable area of Kensington. The family itself lived in Tehran, also owning a summer home in Lausanne, Switzerland. Every day, Pashma would walk around with at least £300 in her purse, which, back then, could have paid a mortgage on a nice house for at least four months. We had only known each other a few weeks when, one afternoon, she invited me over for tea. I was just about to bite into a scone, and she handed me an envelope.

"My parents have invited me to our summer home in Lausanne next weekend." Her smile beamed. "They have asked if I would like to bring a friend?" The beam filled her face. "Open the envelope." Inside were two first-class plane tickets to Geneva. "Will you come?"

I jumped at the invite and arrangements were made. I got the time off work and told my grandmother I was going away for a few days with a friend. Friday, we were at Heathrow, boarding Swissair, and landing an hour and a half later in Geneva. As the airplane rolled to a stop on the pavement, way off from the terminal, I saw out of my side window a black Mercedes limousine pull up to the side of the aircraft. Maybe we had someone important aboard? The flight attendant came to our seats.

"Please, come with me."

She then escorted us off the plane, into the limo. The Folks must be a big deal. Electric gates opened, and within minutes we were speeding down the highway, en route to Lausanne. I did wonder about customs and why we hadn't shown our passports, but I dismissed the thought—Switzerland was a country that revolved around money, and he who had the most, won. Life was bought and bribed by the wealthy, so I didn't think any more about it.

We arrived in Lausanne at six thirty p.m. and pulled into the Hotel Beau-Rivage, one of Europe's finest hotels. It looked like a French palace, and I wondered only briefly, *Why are we here?* Before I could ask, Pashma said her parents were delayed for a day in Paris, therefore, we would be staying here, at the hotel, for the night. Tomorrow we would go on to their home, a few minutes out of town. We walked through the lobby across floors of pale gold marble shining under crystal chandeliers hanging from the hand-painted ceilings. Cocktails were being served in the lounge, and the soft sound of tinkling glasses, held by elegantly dressed men and women gliding around, reminded me of all those fabulous movies of the forties. We walked up to the mahogany reception desk and were checked in by a young woman dressed in the hotel's blue and gold uniform.

Pashma handed me my key.

"Just unpack what you need for the night, then meet me downstairs in the dining room at seven thirty for dinner." We parted ways at the reception desk, and the concierge tipped his gold-embossed cap as we passed. I stepped into the elevator and took it to the top floor. Down a narrow carpeted corridor, I found room 717. Something felt odd. The lobby looked like the Palais Versailles, yet this room was small, plainly furnished, with a single wooden bed and one tiny window. Maybe the hotel was full and this was all they had?

Isn't the mind an extraordinary machine? It rearranges your doubts and fears, turning them into a perfectly bullshit logical explanation. I unpacked a few things, then wandered to the window. My view was of the front of the hotel and, below the yellow awnings of the rooms below, I could see the Mercedes limo, still parked on the gravel driveway with the chauffeur still sitting at the wheel. Hmm. He had to be in the hotel car waiting for someone.

It started raining.

Then I saw Pashma walk out of the hotel. The driver jumped out and held an umbrella over her head as she climbed in and, with a spray of gravel, the Mercedes sped away down the driveway. My watch said seven fifteen. Maybe she'd gone to get something from a store? Why else leave when she was supposed to meet me in fifteen minutes? I also had another voice in my head, and it was growling.

By eight p.m., I knew something was awfully wrong. I ran to my purse and pulled out my airline ticket—it was a one-way flight to Geneva. God damn it! How could I have been so . . .

The phone rang.

I picked it up and heard a deep voice with an unmistakable accent.

"Good evening, mademoiselle. The sheik will see you in ten minutes. You will be collected from your room."

As my stomach went cold, I knew exactly what had happened and exactly where I was and, worst of all, why I was here. This was A Really Bad Situation. A Really Fucking Bad Situation. I had been lured to the needs of men beyond the realm of Machiavellian immorality. Since they'd invaded

London, the real badasses of our new Arabian residents were the guys from the smaller nations—Abu Dhabi, Dubai, Qatar—who had basically started running a kind of "white girlfriend/slave" trafficking operation, with crude but very efficient methods. They used their wealth to lure young women into a sly and proficient spider's web of no return. There was an almost professional system of recruitment, where a young Persian or Syrian girl was paid large amounts of cash to befriend young women who either lived alone, or at a university, or who just wouldn't be missed. The "friend" would then take her time and get close to the chosen victim. Once "best friend" status had been established, a story was spun and the unsuspecting innocent was lured to a neutral country, usually Switzerland or Belgium, where they would be taken by some sheik or minister or whoever was "shopping" back to their home countries where they would disappear—forever.

During this time in the late seventies, thousands of European girls went missing, never to be found, vanishing into the bowels of vast desert empires, locked away somewhere in the middle of the world. And now here I was, one of them, unwittingly fooled and abducted by a perfectly nice Persian girl who'd taken her time to make me her friend and thus serve her client. I stood by the window as fear became anger, then rage. How could I have been so dumb to not check my ticket? The nonexistent customs? No passport required?

A loud rap at the door made me jump. I opened it to a young boy, no more than fifteen or sixteen, in a white *thaub*—a cotton ankle-length garment with long sleeves—bowing and smiling. He motioned me to follow him along the corridor to a second elevator beside the one I'd come up in. The corridor was narrow and there were no exit stairs in sight. If I'd wanted to run, I'd have to take down the kid—but where would I run to? Shit. My terrified brain wasn't thinking fast enough. Then the elevator arrived and in we went. The doors opened to an opulent living room with about half a dozen traditionally dressed Arab men, all standing around drinking tea. Bowing and walking backward, the boy left the room. An old man who looked about eighty sat in the center in a high-back gilded chair. Frail and thin, his long white beard touched the top of his chest.

I was shown to a chair facing the opposite. Everyone stared at me in silence. Fortunately, there was one important fact, unknown to the present company, that I had to my advantage—I spoke Arabic quite well and understood it even better. The old man squinted his eyes, then let out a roar of Arabian fury.

"You brought me the wrong one! She looks like my daughter!" And with a disgusted wave, he held up his hand to be helped out of the room. I was dismissed. A brief respite of relief hit me—*thank God for my dark hair*, I was thinking, and I stood up just as another voice spoke.

"I'll take her." A very tall man walked out from behind and stood beside me. "My name is Abdul Rahman Darwiche, and I am your master. I will come to you later." And with a nod to the young boy, who had returned, I was escorted back to my room.

When we arrived at my door, I asked the boy in Arabic, "Do you speak English?"

"A little," he replied, his eyes widening in surprise at my knowledge of his language.

"Who is the sheik?" Between his bad English and my hesitant Arabic, he managed to explain that the sheik was the father of Zayed bin Sultan Al Nahyan, the ruler of Abu Dhabi and the United Arab Emirates. Just think, this was the guy who basically owned 32,278 square miles of oil, and Abdul Rahman Darwiche was his financial minister.

"How do you know Arabic?" the boy asked. I put my finger to my lips and put my hand on his shoulder.

"When are we leaving?" I had to plan.

He held up two fingers. "Two days."

"Morning or afternoon?" I was being very trusting, but I had few options. This was a critical situation.

"I think, afternoon. After sleeping."

"*Shukraan*," I told him, which means "thank you." He nodded and ran back to the elevator.

Inside my room, my brain was humming. Two days would pass quickly, but it wasn't tomorrow yet, and that was a good thing. I had to plan to get

Abdul Rahman Darwiche (left) with King Faisal of Saudi Arabia

out of the hotel because once they got me on their private plane, it was all over, and the distant yellow sand would swallow me up.

I was so angry to have been duped so easily. "I am your master"? Really? I knew I had to stop being angry and start getting smart. I went through all the pluses in my head: I knew the culture, I knew all the languages necessary, both with the Arabs and here in the hotel where they spoke French. I knew I would have most of the daytime, as they all slept till noon. I still had my passport and a few English pounds, but I needed a lot more money. Bribes would be necessary, and I needed to buy a plane ticket home. Dumber than dumb on the ticket situation, but hey, what did I know about white slave trafficking and to not take one-way plane rides with strange women?

The phone rang. That voice again.

"I will be at your room this evening at nine o'clock. Be ready for me."

My brain was whizzing at top speed, but before he hung up, I spoke with great authority.

"I need to go shopping. I have no money." It came out as fast as I thought of it. Arabs *live* for shopping—next to Islam, it's almost a religion. Jewelry was their thing, and the more they had, the richer they appeared. It was all about status, especially in the smaller Arab countries, where the need to display this obscene wealth was essential.

"I will send the boy with money. And remember, nine o'clock." Minutes later, the young boy was back at my door, handing me a piece of paper and an envelope. On the paper were instructions that I could sign for anything in the hotel, and inside the envelope was a thousand dollars, which would translate into roughly the same amount in Swiss francs. It wasn't a vast amount—this was Switzerland—but enough for what I needed. The signing thing was going to be the icing.

It was now eight thirty p.m. I had half an hour before Mr. Fucking Master was due. I knew why and what he was coming for and, well, I had other plans, which may have seemed very tough and confident of me, but at that precise moment, I was trying my best not to go into a full-fledged panic attack. I had no idea how to stop what was about to happen. I knew these men thought nothing of forcing themselves on you, that rape was just a means to the desired result. Suddenly, a flash of inspiration came to me! I knew one thing they couldn't and wouldn't tolerate—it was the one thing that revolted them and was definitely against God . . . tantamount to touching the devil. I had a plan! Great! I changed into a dress.

At five minutes to nine, I went into the bathroom and took out my shaving razor, opened it up, and took out just the blade. *Shit, this is going to hurt.* I then tore a small half-inch incision at the top of my leg, inside my thigh, as close to the important parts as I could get; it stung like a mother but did the job nicely. Blood started running down my leg, and for extra effect, I saturated a couple of tissues and . . . waited. The knock was firm and insistent. Holding the dripping Kleenex (yes, it was gross, and I hoped to God I wouldn't bleed to death because of this fucking guy), I opened the door. Abdul Rahman took one step forward, and I held up the tissues, lifted up my dress, and pointed to my crotch, which had an impressive flow of blood running down my leg.

"Sorry," was all I said, standing back to let him in the room.

His face went ashen and, clapping his hand to his mouth in horror and disgust, he let out a sound I'd never heard. It was almost funny. His voice crackled like a burning tree.

"You are unclean! Forbidden! Tomorrow you *must* be clean, otherwise there will *be strict punishment!*"

He turned and ran like a girl down the corridor, and I closed my door and breathed. Tomorrow I would be gone, no strict punishment for me. I was bleeding—a lot—so I cleaned up as best as I could, slapped on a bunch more tissues, tied pantyhose around my thigh, and went downstairs to the lobby. There was no time to waste; it was around nine fifteen p.m., and I knew the sheik and his entourage would be at dinner in the penthouse. I went to find the hotel's jewelry stores, hoping they would still be open. They were—smart Swiss, they knew who shopped at night: young women on "dates." Piaget, Bulgari, and Cartier were all there, side by side in a windowed line along the walkway.

I went into the first one, Piaget. A slender male assistant glided out from behind the counter and guided me to a gold satin chair, which he placed underneath me with the grace of an eel. He slid back around the glittering glass counter and brought up a sparkling glass of champagne.

"Can I help you, mademoiselle?"

Taking the fluted glass, I hoped I wasn't bleeding onto the gold satin seat. I don't remember how much I bought and what it cost, but I do remember it was at least three watches, a few diamond rings, diamond earrings, and a rose stone necklace for my mother. Thousands of dollars. I signed my room number on the dotted line, finished the lovely glass of champagne Mr. Slithery had brought, and sailed out. Back in the lobby, I walked up to the concierge's desk, where I found Monsieur Victor Dupres, our cap-tipping concierge. A dapper gentleman in his early sixties, M. Dupres was proudly dressed in the dark blue and gold uniform of the hotel, wearing a black name badge and his name etched in gold. You knew he'd worked there for years. Standing to attention, he tipped his hat and gave a small bow.

"Mademoiselle," he said, "I apologize, my shift is over, but Monsieur Dancour will assist you." As he turned to leave, I touched his arm and, faintly alarmed, he took a step back. Touching was a gesture unfamiliar to concierges of six-star hotels.

"*Oui?*" he said. I decided to speak his language—to gain rapport. I asked him what time he would return in the morning. "*A six heures et demie.*" Six thirty a.m.

With one eye on the stairs and another on the elevator, watching for the enemy, I asked M. Dupres if it would be possible to get me a plane ticket for the nine a.m. flight to London the next morning? And to order a car to take me to the airport at seven?

There was an uncomfortable pause as M. Dupres gave me a strange look. He absolutely knew who I was, why I was there, and who I was with. I wasn't worried; the Swiss are always neutral, right? White slave traffic? Aiding an escapee? "*Ne signifie rien.*" Did I have enough for his silence? To encourage a positive response, I reached into my bag and pulled out one of the beautifully wrapped Piaget packages that held the earrings, and an envelope with five hundred dollars in cash. I'd noticed a wedding ring on his finger.

"For my ticket and a small gift for your wife—for your trouble. Please keep any extra cash there might be," I said in particularly good French, placing them both on his desk. My ticket to London would have cost about fifty dollars. He opened the package and his eyes shone as he looked inside the box. He nodded, pocketing the cash and the box.

"Ticket and car will be here tomorrow at seven a.m. Come to this desk."

Within five minutes, I was back in my room. As I put my things together, I had a nagging feeling that maybe it had all gone a tad too smoothly. I had to trust the concierge, didn't I? Of course I did—I had no choice—but this was Switzerland. Money talked loud and proud, sometimes coming before morals and loyalty. He who had the most, won.

The next morning, I was downstairs drinking coffee at six fifteen a.m., and everything was packed in my room. Promptly at six forty-five, I picked up my ticket from M. Dupres and saw the car was waiting by the front door. I went upstairs to collect my bags.

As I started walking down the corridor, a chambermaid hurriedly turned off the vacuum and stopped me with a worried expression.

"There is a big Arab man in your room, and he is very angry."

As I ran down the hall, I passed room 710 with a discarded breakfast cart parked outside. Reptilian brain in full command, I grabbed the heavy silver coffeepot and held it behind my back. My door stood open to reveal Abdul Rahman sitting in the small armchair by the bed, his face black with rage. My hidden suitcase lay exposed on the floor, clothes strewn everywhere. A barrage of high-volume obscenities poured out of his mouth, which didn't bother me as much as what he was holding in his hands—my passport twisted in the first stages of being torn in two. Without thinking, I brought the coffeepot around from behind my back and hit him on the side of his head with a strength and force I didn't know I had—it helped he was sitting down and my angle was a dead strike to the temple. He dropped like a stone, tipping sideways off the chair, dropping my passport as he fell.

Blood gushed out of his head like an open faucet, soaking the carpet. I grabbed my yet unbloodied passport, stuffed my clothes back into my bag, and slamming the door behind me, I ran down the corridor with sprinter speed. As I passed the same chambermaid, I said in super-fast French, "There is an Arab in my room, *sleeping*, and he doesn't want to be disturbed for at least four hours." I handed her a Piaget box containing a two-carat diamond ring. She took it, already nodding. I ran down the stairs to the lobby and out to the waiting car, not taking a proper breath until wheels were up and tucked away in the belly of Swissair Flight 22 to London. I did wonder how he'd known. No self-respecting Arab male is up at seven a.m., so probably the concierge had double dipped—ratting on me and keeping all the money. It was Switzerland after all. "*Ne signifie rien.*"

For the next few years, I was paranoid and constantly on the lookout. I asked myself every day, *Had I killed him*? That was a hell of a lot of blood, and if the chambermaid had not gone in for four hours, he could have bled to death, right? Or had he been rescued and survived?

When I got back to London, I went looking for Pashma. She was a predator I had to find before she "befriended" yet another young girl. Her apartment was empty and her phone number disconnected. I honestly believe there is a special place in hell for people like her. I didn't tell anyone what'd happened, not my friends and certainly not my mother, who would eventually throw it back at me sometime, somewhere, usually in front of someone I cared about. Besides, I couldn't tell her; she wasn't here. She was still somewhere in war-torn Beirut, maybe lying dead on a back-street sidewalk with her good friend Bill, teacup and gold watch in hand. Who knew? A small sliver of me *was* worried, not having heard from her since that infamous phone call, but there was nothing I could do. If it was bad, so be it.

Keeping everything tight to my heart was the beginning of my many life secrets, the things I just didn't and don't tell anyone. By now, I knew I was different. I knew that I could survive and succeed at anything thrown my way. I also knew I was very much alone, and that was fine by me—that became who I was and, eventually . . . who I am.

Chapter 22

The Ball and Chain of Mother

Still living with my grandmother, following my Swiss adventure, which is how I choose to remember it, I wandered, not knowing what to do or how to do whatever it was I was supposed to be doing. Then my mother magically returned, unscathed *and* with the damn gold watch. She proudly told us she'd managed to get on the bus back to Istanbul. "Had to duck under the seat every now and again as those wretched mortars flew by," she said with triumph. All the while clearly relishing in telling her dramatic story—finally, she had her own—she then explained how she arrived twenty-six hours later, back to our old apartment on Uftade Sokak. Once there, she called the landlord, closed up the apartment, and gave him back the key.

I didn't bother asking, but I presumed we'd moved back from Turkey.

She came to stay with me and Granny Dear, but three weeks later, she announced we were not living with Granny Dear anymore. She had studied the classifieds for days and eventually found us "accommodations" in a pseudo boardinghouse (we were the only tenants) two towns away, owned by a middle-aged man, Fred something. Fred declared the accommodations were, in fact, one room. We would share the kitchen and *his* bathroom. That fun arrangement lasted two weeks and three days, until he walked in on me taking a bath and offered to "jump in and have a tickle."

It was time to bail out of Freddy Creep Land.

Mother went back to Hatch End, and since I needed to find a job, I was going to live in London.

"Where?" she asked.

"With a friend."

"Who?"

"I don't know yet." Of course, I did.

"What am *I* going to do?"

I moved into an apartment in Islington, North London, with my friend Cassidy. I had some breathing room, managing to live on the few pounds I'd saved from working at La Valbonne—oh, where I no longer worked. Mr. Louie Brown had decided I was to be replaced for no reason. Of course, now I needed to find a place for Mother—the weeping phone calls had to stop.

"Mum, let's find you a flat in town, near the shops you like."

"It would have been considerate of you to have found somewhere for both of us, together, at the same time. Obviously, there's no room where you live now with that rather coarse girl, Cassidy, whom I can't fathom why you seem to like." This comment was swiftly followed by her "go-to" crying as she continued to bemoan her fate. "What have I done to deserve being alone *again*? How could you turn your back on your own mother—after all I've been through?"

Her pain exhausted me.

"You won't be alone," I told her. "I'll visit every day. We'll find you a nice place."

Once again, through a friend of a friend, I accomplished quite the feat of the impossible and moved her into a small, super-cheap studio apartment in Chelsea. Almost every day, I would schlep back and forth from Islington, enduring a journey of over an hour on two particularly unreliable buses. We would go shopping, or sit and drink endless cups of tea in department store tea rooms as she gloried in stories of the war (the German one), Beirut, and near-death encounters she'd had with Bill (who had also managed to get out), at the same time bemoaning the bleak future ahead and how she hated living in one room—alone. Over and over, like an ever-present mantra, she would proclaim, "Everyone and everything I have ever loved is dead." Obviously, my being alive was never included in that deal, so there was no doubt I was never the loved one and only the lifeline.

Mum's studio was in an extremely sought-after apartment block in Chelsea, ten steps from King's Road, the grooviest street in the world. Her building was mainly populated by artists and ultra-cool people who, by some quirk of nature, adored her. Probably because when she was around them, she was adorable. Her neighbor was Amanda, this crazy, gorgeous transvestite who wafted around the building in satin multicolored kaftans with fluffy boas trailing behind her and odd glittery things in her hair. Amanda thought Mother was too marvelous and frequently showed up at her door with a bottle of brandy begging for more of those . . .

"Fabulous World War II stories, darling!"

Amanda was also pals with Andy Warhol who, when in town, would occasionally *pop by* to visit, usually with one or two of his pals, David Bowie, Halston, and others from "The Factory"—his New York City studio. They would often partake in the brandy and war story evenings with Mother. How in the name of God could she not relish those moments with beyond-thrilled-gratitude? Andy Warhol? David Bowie?

One day, I'd come to visit, when Amanda grabbed me in the hallway.

"Darling, Liza [Minnelli] is in town and she's having a little soiree tomorrow evening at her flat for Andy and the gang. We would *love* for Helen to join us and tell those fabulous war stories of her days as a French spy, but she's saying no. Of course we would pick her up. Could you have a chat?"

My mother had been a spy?

I promised I would try, already knowing the answer. I opened her door as she was putting on her coat.

"You're late," she said.

"Mum, I just saw Amanda in the hallway, and she really wants you to come to Liza's soiree thing tomorrow evening." No answer. "That's Liza Minnelli, right? You like her, don't you?"

She started shaking her head. "Tomorrow's too soon for me to be ready."

"They're sending a car, which will probably be a limo. It's Liza Minnelli! You know, the superstar?" I was flabbergasted.

"She isn't Judy [Garland]. I've heard she takes drugs and drinks too much."

"No, she doesn't! She's amazing and talented and—Jesus, mum! It's Liza Minnelli! *And probably* David and Andy and Halston will be there—your friends! And were you really a spy?"

"That's none of your business, and I'm not going."

And that was that. Many no's later, the visits eventually stopped. Amanda stopped asking, and here it was, yet again—Mother had done a damn fine job of alienating all things good and creating the life of solitude she'd predicted. It was hard to see through the haze then—but she was dragging me down with her. For years, I'd felt like I had a rope noose around my neck, and it was getting tighter by the day. I was terrified when she was angry and always "so dreadfully disappointed in me," which was most of the time. Hers was a silent, seething, tight-lipped anger that made me feel ill. I felt helpless and couldn't see any way out. The way I had seen it, as far back as I could remember, was that this was my life and I had to deal with it.

Standing outside her building that day, after trying to appease her and failing, I had an epiphany. It was like something snapped in me. This miserable existence was going to end. I didn't know when, but this wasn't going to be my story. If this was some divine plan, then I was damn well going to change it, and fuck God if he'd put me here as her gatekeeper—I was officially resigning from a job I'd never applied for.

Cassidy and I went out every night. There were so many fun clubs to go to and cool people to meet. We started at The Revolution, then on to The Scotch Club to hang out with Jimi Hendrix, then maybe a visit to The Marquee to catch Manfred Mann or The Animals. Every doorman knew us, and we never paid for anything. Famous people were everywhere—it was still a time where no one was scared of being mobbed by lens-snapping paparazzi or robbed by hooded criminals. Clubs were safe. The streets were safe. Since Cassidy had started dating the actor Telly Savalas, we would usually end our night at the infamous George Raft's Colony Club on Berkeley Square, where we would spend hilarious evenings with Telly and producer Cubby Broccoli, the Bond film guy. I can still hear Telly's nightly greeting as we were escorted to his table.

"Who loves you, baby? Telly does!"

The Colony Club was a London gambling casino and fancy restaurant operated by the American Cosa Nostra mobster Meyer Lansky, of the Philadelphia crime family. George Raft, the American film actor, had been the host and front man, back when the club opened in 1966. Unfortunately, George hadn't been particularly discreet about his close mob ties and in 1967, being labeled as "undesirable," was banned from reentering London. Now it was Pierre who greeted you at the door. "The Host with the Most" Pierre stood at the entry podium, crisply smart in his impeccable tuxedo, flashing a dazzling white smile as he took your coat. No one got past Pierre. If your name wasn't written in his little red book, the smile quickly faded and he would open the door, politely instructing you to leave immediately. After all, this was The Colony Club, and The List was his bible. Sammy Davis was a frequent guest, and it was lovely seeing him again. Wealthy people, politicians, British nobility, famous people, and the ever present, well-dressed mobsters were engraved on The List.

Everyone was happy, funny, and having a ball. Never was any man offensively inappropriate. Yes, as usual, there was a tap on the butt or a giggly suggestive comment, but it was all in good humor. They wined and dined us, treated us like queens, and at the end of the evening, cars were ordered, and we were driven home in style. I brought my mother one evening in the hope that she might actually enjoy herself. She didn't like Telly—he was *another* Greek, and she again reminded me how much my father had hated Greeks. Thank God Telly didn't hear that. She didn't trust Sammy, as he was Black *and* Jewish. The only people she liked were the mobsters. Figured.

I loved every minute, especially since I wasn't "with anyone"—I could just be myself and hang with all these amazing people. In general, dating for me was difficult and stressful. I always messed up, falling madly in love within days, which of course only sent the guys running back to the safety of casual dating. I was a terrible girlfriend. I guess it goes back to my father, or maybe I was too needy, which scared everyone away. If it didn't, eventually they would meet Mother and . . . well . . . unless by some miracle and the stars aligned perfectly, it was yet another awful encounter of suffering. She would either treat them with condescending, one-word responses, causing an uncomfortable shuffling of platform-booted feet and fixated-floor staring, or she would just be silent, teaspoons clinking on saucers as I cringed with embarrassment. She had no idea how to be nice for one hour of visiting with someone *I liked*. Eventually they would all be gone, leaving with a quiet, dishonest mutter of, "I'll call you." I was then usually berated again in regard to my awful choice in friends. I don't blame any of them for leaving; they probably looked at her and thought, "Oh shit—maybe that's Juliette in thirty years—hell, no thanks!"

Here's the thing—I didn't know she was seriously mentally ill. How could I? What did anyone know about the workings of an unbalanced, borderline manic-depressive mind that also exhibited sociopathic narcissism? Nothing. Of course, now it's all so obvious. Her own abusive childhood, orchestrated by a parent who certainly never should have given birth and seriously should have been locked away, didn't exactly set her up for normalcy. But even if we knew something was slightly off, where would she have gone? There was no professional, educated guidance toward diagnosis and the prescription of the correct meds. If you went to the doctor and said you were depressed, you were told to go on a nice holiday. If you were *very* depressed, you were given lithium, primarily used as a psychiatric medication, and if it looked like you were really heading to Doddery Land, you were sent to a mental institution. Mother was alone. No one knew she was crazy—they simply assumed she was moody, had no manners, and was just damn unpleasant.

I have a deep empathy for anyone who has no father, be it the result of death or divorce. The departure or lack of that critical masculine role from such an early age really hurts. It can result in missing a vital part of your person, like a jigsaw puzzle with the center piece missing. Perhaps you start making up for it by *becoming* your father (taking charge of the family's survival) or worse . . . looking for him in every man you *think* you like, hence, the falling in love every five minutes, which creates a steamroller of disasters, sending you down the highway to isolation, or worse—hooking up with violence, or a guy who's weak and wimpy and therefore easy to push around or . . .

There were never any good choices. I could get myself out of almost being shot by the PLO and abducted by a bunch of rich Arabs, but I couldn't handle my mother and the embarrassment and shame I felt when she was rude. I tried to keep boyfriends to a minimum and always a secret, but that involved huge amounts of lying, which was—and still is—not one of my talents.

Then, suddenly, everything changed.

I had on and off dated Paul Ryan (Barry's twin brother) before I went to Beirut, and now that I was home, we met again and went to lunch, picking up exactly where we'd left off. Paul was one of a kind, and I adored him. We talked about Steven and how I had cheated on him with Paul and . . . and . . . Paul waved it away with a simple statement.

"It happens. Steve's funny like that; he doesn't forgive."

After a few weeks, Paul and I were officially dating. There had been mumblings of marriage from him, but it was really just that—light mumblings. Nevertheless, as we were basically together all the time, I knew I had to tell Mother. I was sick to my stomach with nerves—I saw the impending and inevitable scenario lying ahead. Paul had become very special to me, and I was scared to death she would chase him off with her mouth and her madness. Mariam suggested that she could take Mother out to lunch and warm her up.

"No. I mean, you're being sweet, but it wouldn't be pleasant. Really. There is no 'warming.'"

What she didn't know was, my mother hated her too. Mariam was one of the kindest people I have ever known, and she was a princess for heaven's sake! Royalty! But Mother was always brief and to the point—or rather, *her* point.

The lovely Princess Mariam and Paul Ryan, 1978

"She's a princess of Johor, some small, third-world, backward country."

I gave up. I was Napoleon and this was my Waterloo. I just had to suck it up and deal. Nevertheless, Paul, not the least bit bothered, suggested we take her out to dinner. I shook my head.

"It'll be fine," he insisted. "Don't worry—I'm great with mums."

And the dinner day arrived, my nerves getting the best of me for the better part of the day. Then the inescapable evening crept in. Mother was a good drinker, and I figured if we could get a few cocktails in her fast, it could moderate the sting of the inevitable. Paul picked me up and I was a mess, anxiety and panic spurring my adrenaline and vice versa until we got to San Lorenzo's, a super trendy restaurant on Beauchamp Place, in Knightsbridge. After downing two straight-up tequilas, I realized Paul was being brilliant, taking Mother's hand and telling her how wonderful it was to meet her and how lovely she looked this evening. More cocktails were ordered, and she was on her third very dry martini when The Miracle happened. Paul was telling a story of Sinatra and some hilarity that had happened between them, and . . . What was this? Mother was *laughing*? Not a smile-and-nod-tolerating-the-story kind of laugh, no, a full blown, gusty, tears-rolling-down-your-face-gasping-for-air guffaw!

I was speechless. Finally, when she almost fell off her chair, waving at him to stop, I realized, "Oh my God. She LIKES him!" She was also very drunk, but maybe her intuition told her this was one good guy.

Paul Ryan was one of the best humans I have ever known, authentic and brutally honest, while at the same time kind and deeply caring, and oh God was he funny! He could (and did) have you on the floor, holding your sides, weeping with laughter at the simplest observation. His wit was satirical and, along with the ability to laugh at himself, Paul saw "funny" like no one I have ever known. He was also a talented songwriter. He wrote a top-ten hit for his brother, Barry, called "Eloise," and Frank Sinatra recorded a couple of his songs, one of which was "I Will Drink the Wine," which is on Sinatra's 1971 album, *Sinatra & Company*.

It was extraordinary. Here was Paul Ryan, this twenty-something pop singer with long dark hair, dressed in tight white bell-bottom pants with a "V" of sparkling rhinestones in the flare, four-inch gold-and-white platform boots, and a white satin shirt opened way down. This was the guy who was finally batting a hundred, top rating in the Helen Approval Book. All the way home she extolled his virtues. God sure does have a sense of humor.

With life having taken this unforeseen turn, I could now spend most of my time with Paul and our friends, Mariam (who eventually married Paul's twin brother, Barry), Pete and Chrissie Thompson (Pete still hinting the Kray Twins gig was always open), and Clive McClean, always a hilarious part of the family.

Paul brightened my life. He knew how much I loved singing, so he tried to help me by giving me one of his songs to record. I wasn't very good—he knew it and never said a word. We would spend hours sitting in CBS's recording studio with the brand-new, just invented sixteen-track sound board, playing backing tracks of songs he'd written.

I had to get a job—soon. A minor stumbling block was my lack of skills and that I had been fired from most of the day jobs I'd had. I couldn't go back to Playboy because of them discovering I'd been underage when I worked there. I felt the panic starting. I didn't know what to do. Mother kept asking why Paul couldn't help me become famous. As if it were that simple. It was Paul she believed in, when she said that, and not me. I didn't know how to ever get her approval for anything I did.

Chapter 23

Cabaret and the Bailey's Circuit

Surprisingly, my quest for work proved easier than I expected. Through Princess Mariam, I'd made close friends with Oliver Gilbert, an exceptionally talented musician who played the piano and wrote Broadway-style music. He was renting space in Mariam's office to run his one-man company of no one knew what, but we hit it off immediately. He became a champion in my quest for work as a singer, which I'd decided had become my only possibility for employment. Together, we hunted the London nightclubs to see who was hiring girl singers and maybe also needed a piano player. I chose some popular songs and Oliver wrote the charts while we rehearsed in cheap rehearsal studios and got ready to go to work. We played pubs, tiny clubs in dubious neighborhoods, senior homes, more pubs, and pretty much anywhere they'd have us.

By the end of summer, we'd joined the agency of Jimmy Madbone, who booked us on "The Bailey's Circuit," a grueling schedule of one-night stands that had us covering numerous variety theaters and nightclubs in and around the north of England. Each evening's performance predictably consisted of three to four acts appearing in order of status. I was the Girl Singer, usually coming on after the magician and his magical doves, or the ever-ready ventriloquist, both preceding Alice Marvel and her spoon act or

Paddy and his Amazing Poodles. They would do about half an hour, then I would come out and sing for twenty minutes. A short break followed, and then it was time for the top of the bill, a lineup of some of the better-known acts of the day—Ken Dodd, Gerry and the Pacemakers, Freddy and the Dreamers, Billy J. Kramer and the Dakotas, and a bunch of comedians that rotated in popularity. Each one would do their act—usually each performing for an hour or so. You played the one night, then it was back on the road, on to the next gig. This endeavor toward a show-business career was not for the faint of heart. You traveled by car or van, slept in drafty boardinghouses, ate cheap food from cheap cafés, and dealt with the ever-constant hunt for a night laundromat to do your laundry. You were exhausted and run down, and usually cold, but it was a paycheck.

The Bedford Nightclub, built before the war, was a particularly memorable venue. I remember walking into a concrete building, the damp air wafting around me. Being that my star status was just above Alice and her spoons, I did not qualify for a carpeted dressing room or any creature comforts of any note. That night, Ken Dodd was the top of the bill and kindly lent me his two-bar electric heater (reserved only for the star), as my dressing room's window was malfunctioning, letting in freezing cold rain. England doesn't really experience a fall season like one might in other places, unless you enjoy watching brown tree leaves dropping into nasty gray puddles. In any case, one really can't put makeup on with frozen hands, in fingerless gloves. It got to a point where I was so cold, nothing was working. I finally knocked on Ken's door, and he opened it, having just put the final touches on his stage persona. He looked like a cross between Beetlejuice and the Mad Hatter.

My words got stuck—Ken Dodd was a huge star—and all I could say was, "Hello, Mr. Dodd. I'm so sorry to bother you, but do you happen to have a spare heater?"

"I think you need a hot cuppa too!" His voice was high and bouncy.

"Oh yes, please! Thank you!" God, I was sick of this English cold.

Ken Dodd sat me down and gave me a wonderful mug of tea and his own personal heater. He pulled at his spiky hair and grabbed his two "tickle sticks," an intricate concoction he'd designed from two multicolored feather dusters on top of brightly painted glitter sticks. Letting out his famous laugh, he stood in front of the mirror and said, "How would you like to go to work looking like this?"

He was hilarious and kind and gave me a moment of warmth on a miserable night.

My most unforgettable experience was performing at the Empire Theater in Glasgow, Scotland. Our agent had dumbly booked me as the opening act for Billy Connelly—the hugest, most popular and famous Scottish comedian in the country. It was a night of horror. The audience was composed of beer-drinking Scots and . . . more beer-drinking Scots who'd come *specifically* to see their guy. Billy's humor was raucous and blue, and he was adored, so—if there *had* to be a girl singer, it should have been their girl Lulu, a Glasgow native who was always in the top ten of the pop charts. I walked on to the stage to boos and beer bottles flying straight in my direction. The booing soon became a feverish chant, and sandwiches were now accompanying the flying bottles.

I saw my only escape was to climb off the end of the stage and drop down into the bandstand underneath—who had been playing my opening number for five minutes and were still playing it. Covered in egg salad and beer, I slid down almost on top of the conductor and immediately tracked down the stage manager, finding him sitting in the wings, tipped back on a chair, drinking a cup of tea. He started laughing as I stormed up.

"You look a wee bit hammered," he said. That meant battered, defeated—basically done in. And yes, I was!

At that moment, Billy Connelly walked by and stopped. "Is it an egg salad act that you do then?" He chuckled at his own joke and disappeared through velvet curtains, stepping out to a thunderous roar of applause. The stage manager started to walk off, but I grabbed him.

"I could have been badly injured—they were throwing broken beer bottles."

"I saw that. Saturday's always the 'swanky crowd.'" He grinned. "They just wanted Lulu."

My final "road" gig was a three-day stint at Butlins Holiday Camp in Pwllheli, Wales. You did your show four times a day, starting at nine a.m. for the kids who were screaming for ice cream, a one p.m. show for the lunch crowd (the rattle of sandwiches in paper bags and kids screaming obliterated any musicality forthcoming from the stage), and the last show at six p.m. for the seniors, who mainly slept through it. It was raining the entire three days, and Oliver and I were lodged in two tiny concrete bunkers. One lone light bulb poking out of the ceiling, along with a bed and table that were the only furniture. Oh—and it was bitching damp cold. As Oliver and I were driving back to London, an unspoken decision settled upon us, that of Never Again. We were done with the north . . . and Butlins and Bailey's.

At the same time, Mariam had also rented out some of her office space to a questionable character named Johnny Farrout and his record company, Mirror Records. Johnny was in the process of recording a song for Barry Ryan, while at the same time he was booking acts all over Europe. Word got out I was once again on the singing job hunt, and one day Johnny called me saying he had a two-week gig at a nightclub in Liege, Belgium. It paid well, he said, and asked if I would like to take it. I would have to record a backing track tape with all my songs, as the gig was in a disco with a stage but no band, and I would sing along with the tracks.

I agreed to go, and Paul arranged to have the tape made for me and organized all the music. Mother was happy, as Paul had promised he would make sure it was all done properly, and being that he was now her most favorite person in the world, everyone was happy. I could leave without hysteria. Now, being age twenty-six has its advantages—you have few lines on your face, you look good when you cry, and you have health and energy, which equates to being able to stay up all night and still look fabulous the next day. I also thought I was a pretty hip, street-smart person—after all, look what I'd been through, right?

What I didn't realize, as I basked in my few years of hard-earned knowledge and experience, was that . . . I seriously lacked wisdom. Without really thinking, I signed the contract in Johnny's office and, five days later, boarded the plane for Brussels. I hadn't double-checked where I was going, who I was working for, or when I was going to get paid, let alone whether I could trust Johnny Farrout. I packed a bag, this time with the addition of sparkly frocks and a tape of twelve backing tracks, and checked that I had an open-end, round-trip ticket, and then I was off on another adventure.

I arrived in the small town of Liege on a sweltering July afternoon. I took a cab from the airport, which dropped me off at the entrance to a long, narrow alleyway lined with nightclubs and bars. The address was a building in the middle of the alley too narrow for any vehicles, so I walked past a row of small, unkempt gardens to a tall, ornate structure that resembled an old church. Large wooden double doors with brass rings for handles stood open at the end of the cobbled pathway. Coming in from the sunshine, the pitch-dark hallway blinded me, until my eyes adjusted and I saw I was in a corridor leading to a relatively small, black-mirrored room with a bar running along the full length of the wall. The floor was black tile, and there was a DJ stand covered in shiny black satin, perched high, facing down to a ten-foot-round circle of black wood—I presumed this was the dance floor and my stage. The only thing that wasn't black was the disco mirrored ball hanging from the center of the ceiling. As I sniffed at the lingering smell of stale beer, suddenly, a face popped up from behind the bar.

"*Bonjour et bienvenue!*" A small man dressed like he had just arrived from Cirque du Soleil bounded over and threw his arms around me in a huge hug. "*Je suis Charlie!*" Charlie was around fifty years old, thin as a rail, with a little pot belly protruding from his colorful satin shirt with blouson sleeves. He did make a point of telling me, with an insistent flourish, that he was *absolutely not Belgique*, he was *Francais* from Normandy. Charlie was dressed in his "daywear," which consisted of a multicolored shirt unbuttoned to his skinny tanned chest, adorned with gold and red silk tassels—he was a glorious whirl of color tucked into a pair of flowered, pink satin bell-bottoms swirling over a pair of orange and turquoise Turkish slippers. Charlie was quite unique. Woven through his hair was something that looked like a bunch of feathers—I wasn't sure.

"Hello, I'm Juliette," I told him. "The singer."

Charlie clapped his hands in sheer delight. "*Magnifique!*" And just as he was about to launch into an animated conversation, a tall, good-looking man appeared through the front door, dressed in a dark blue Armani suit and tie. He strode up to us and waved Charlie away, sending him scuttling into the darkness. A perfectly manicured hand reached out to shake mine.

"I am Monsieur Armand, the owner. You are Juliette the singer?"

I nodded.

"Welcome to Le Club du Monde." He then went on to ask me if I would like to extend my engagement for two more weeks. I hesitated. "Of course, I will double the original money—here is your new contract to sign." And, out of a beautifully tailored breast pocket appeared a single sheet of paper, which he carefully laid on a table.

"You want me to sign now?" I asked.

He shrugged, producing a gold-plated fountain pen from inside said breast pocket. "Why not?"

Did I have the wisdom to see, maybe, a teeny red flag? Nope, I was poor, and all I heard was "double the money." I signed. Monsieur Armand pocketed the contract, failing to provide me with a copy of my own. Still, I remained oblivious to anything fishy.

"We are open seven days a week. The doors open at nine and we stop at five a.m. You will sing every two hours for thirty minutes here on the stage." He pointed to the circle of black wood in the center. "Luca will play your music." He pointed up to the DJ booth. "It's okay?"

I nodded. Weird. No days off, but . . . double the money. Sure, it was okay.

He picked up my suitcase and motioned for me to follow him. "We will go to your room now."

That's right, "accommodations" were included. We came out of the club and walked down the dark, narrow corridor. Ahead was a winding staircase leading to the upper floors, and as we creaked and groaned our way up, M. Armand explained this was a two-hundred-year-old building that used to be a nunnery. Arriving at the third floor, he opened a glass-fronted door to a large square room; he waved his hand, indicating a well-worn sofa.

"Where you can sit." An ironing board stood in the middle, with a steaming iron propped at the end, and right beside the board was a stand-alone shower on blocks of wood. Through the translucent wraparound curtain, the silhouette of a naked woman could be seen through the steamy water. Four rooms branched off the main room, and a couple had their doors open. M. Armand led me to a room off the small communal kitchen.

"This is yours," he announced, opening a door to a large room with a dresser, closet, and a bed. Two big picture windows covered one wall, and the floor was bare wood boards, probably also two hundred years old by the creaking. "It's okay?" M. Armand looked at me, eyebrows up.

"Yes, it's okay. Thank you." I was holding the door handle, which was loose. I also noticed there was no key in the old-fashioned lock. I asked, "Monsieur Armand, is there a key?"

"Ask Michele, the bartender—he will help you with questions. You start tomorrow night." And then he left.

I didn't know it, but I was never to see Monsieur Armand again.

At about five p.m., I sat on the full-sized bed, which felt decent, and then unpacked and opened a couple windows, letting in the eighty-five-degree air. A couple of the girls who lived in the other rooms came by to say "hi" and introduce themselves. There was Sylvie, a stripper across the street at the Club Bene, and Monique (just out of the shower), a "dancer" at The Crazy Horse across town. They said the other girls on the floor were also "dancers" but away on their day shifts. We chatted, and they explained they rented rooms here since this was the safest place to live in Liege.

"Is it not safe here? In town?"

They lifted their hands and eyes as only the French can do, and Sylvie said, "At night, always you walk with someone."

I asked about Charlie, and they told me he lived downstairs in the room below mine. Apparently, he'd been a fixture at the club for years, working every night, greeting people, and creating the "ambiance" of the evening. Occasionally, Charlie would make the girls his favorite food—couscous. That evening I found a café, had an omelet, and went to bed early, remembering almost as an afterthought that I hadn't asked M. Armand who paid me.

The following night, I went down to the club before nine and met Michele the bartender, an attractive young man about my age. I also met Luca the DJ and gave him my backing tape, explaining how many songs there were and how long it was. All the while, as I was talking, he was slowly staring me up and down, grinning. It didn't go over my head that my words were going in one ear and out the other. He was kind of rock-star attractive, but I also had a feeling someone had once told him he looked like Jim Morrison and he had believed them. He took my tapes.

"Your first set's at ten p.m.," he said, climbing his DJ throne.

I asked Michele where the key to the wonky, keyless lock on my door was, and he looked at the floor.

"I don't think... well... there isn't one. Maybe I'll try to find something?"

Despite my initial encounter with him, where I certainly had my reservations about him, I found him to be another good soul, and he quickly became my friend. Michele was a sharp, hardworking young man studying to be a doctor, and the bartending job was helping him pay for school.

The club was packed every night. I literally had to push bodies away from my precious round black circle to do my show. It was as if no one had even noticed a person was attempting to perform. Luca would announce me, push the button to start the tape, and then descend from his perch to the bar, leaving me to struggle with "I Will Survive." In an exercise of futility, I tried to raise my voice above a hundred others, all talking at the same time. Charlie was my savior in more ways than one. He was nothing short of delightfully hilarious and sweet at the same time. He would stand on the bar and clap his hands loudly in an effort to quiet the crowd. Eventually, he brought a tambourine, which he rattled, totally off tempo, in an attempt to be heard over the noise.

Charlie took me under his wing, and we became great friends. Between my sets, we would sit together and exchange stories. Charlie adored anything Moroccan (hence the endless preparation of couscous) and loved my stories of Istanbul and Beirut. He was working hard to save money to go to Casablanca, where his last boyfriend, Kamal—which meant "perfection"—was waiting for him. Kamal was Moroccan and the love of his life, and Charlie tearfully told me how he had given Kamal all the money he'd saved—close to three thousand dollars—to go to Morocco and buy them a house. Kamal had promised to send Charlie a ticket to come to Casablanca when everything was ready. Needless to say, since Kamal had walked out a year ago, Charlie hadn't heard a word nor received any ticket. He genuinely believed Kamal might be in distress and that, any day now, the call would come and he'd be off to paradise.

"I'm saving more money in case my love is in trouble. He might need me to go and help him." He so wanted to believe. His despair tugged at me, but I didn't have the heart to tell him what I absolutely knew to be true, so I put my arm around his skinny little shoulders and did the best I could.

"Maybe you're right, Charlie, but I'm sure he's fine—just busy. He'll write soon."

And so began a grueling routine that made my Playboy job look like a party. I worked every night until five a.m., then Michele, myself, and sometimes Charlie would go to the coffee bar at the end of the alley to get café au lait and croissants. I would get to bed around seven and sleep till three in the afternoon, when I'd have my one meal of the day consisting of coffee, toast, and one egg. That was all I could afford until I got paid. To pass the rest of the time, I'd go for a walk and sit by the river to contemplate life, then more coffee to quieten the growls in my stomach, then back to my room to change and be back at work at eight thirty p.m. to start the long night again.

Chapter 24

Le Maquereau

Liege is situated in the southeastern part of Belgium. It's a quaint village with beautiful old buildings and gorgeous countryside folding around the River Meuse. In direct contrast, Liege also had the largest concentration in the country of adult nightclubs, drug trafficking, and a flourishing industry of prostitution. French was the main language spoken, but a lot of the "night people" coming in from Brussels for a good time spoke Flemish, the language of the north. Every night, you could count on a reliable flow of unsavory folk skulking in from the big cities to run the dark and unscrupulous activities of the nighttime populace. The dealers pushed the drugs, and the pimps, called "macs" (short for *maquereau*, which means "whoremonger"), walked the streets and ran some very tough "*working girls*" and transvestites, who were quite gorgeous.

The town came alive at around ten p.m., with music pouring full blast out of every disco door until the sun came up. In the twilight of dawn, you often saw people staggering out of bars and falling into a heap outside or wobbling down the street holding the lamp posts for support. Then the town clock struck eight a.m., signaling the appearance of a crazy-efficient clean-up crew, who picked up all the bottles, vomit, and passed-out bodies littering the gutters. By nine a.m., it was as if the night had never happened.

Cute little shops were open for business, coffee shops and restaurants were full, and the locals strolled the streets, going about their day. There was no sign of the wild debauchery, merely hours old, that would commence all over again when darkness descended.

I'd been working hard for over three weeks and had yet to be paid. Michele had finally procured a key for my room, which sort of worked—sometimes. It was fine, as I was only there during the day to sleep, and since there was no one else in the building except me and the girls, all was well. My real and present worry was money. I had none—I mean, maybe I had the equivalent of five bucks in my pocket, but I officially didn't have enough money to eat. I went to Luca, who sent me to the night manager, Louis, who sent me to call Hugo the bookkeeper, who said he would call Monsieur Armand. This charade went on for two days to no avail. Finally, I demanded Monsieur Armand's phone number and called him from the club's office. He was profusely apologetic, saying the club had had unexpected building repairs and to tell Michele to give me 350 Belgian francs (or the equivalent of about a hundred dollars) from the bar's register. He assured me I would get the rest next week—Hugo would send it over.

Something didn't feel right—I had a bad feeling that there might not actually be a "Hugo the bookkeeper," but I ignored it and kept singing, knowing deep down there was probably not going to be any more money without a regular battle with the ever-lovely Monsieur Armand.

Why didn't I just get on a plane home? Why didn't I call Johnny Farrout and get him to deal with this and get me my damn money? Probably because 350 francs would feed me for a while, and "home" was just my apartment and what else? There was nothing to go back to, except for Mother and, maybe, Paul. But what if he felt differently about me? What if he'd met someone else? I had no feeling of having a "home" to return to, a place of safety to regroup and be cared for. I was far away and had to create any care for myself, *by* myself, so I stayed in Liege working, and my strange life went on. Charlie made me couscous when he could, but to make that 350 francs last, I ate my egg and toast meal once a day, drank masses of coffee, and slept as long as I could. Michele would give me cocktail sausages and nuts, but too much of that and I felt ill. I was lucky to be blessed with my youth and my father's tough Turkish genes—it was all that was keeping me healthy through this awfulness. But I should have gone home. I shouldn't have been so stupid and thoughtless.

The weather had gotten hotter. It was summer, and the temperature hovered at about ninety-five degrees all day and well into the night. Naturally, the neglected two-hundred-year-old building didn't have air-conditioning, so Michele had given me the bar's fan to take up to my room, which provided minor relief. I managed to get it pointing straight at me in bed where—if I were completely naked and kept a spray bottle beside me—I could get some sleep.

One morning, climbing the stairs to my room, I was particularly exhausted and wondering for the umpteenth time if I should leave. Luca had approached me earlier in the evening and asked if he could come to my room after he'd closed up for a "visit."

"I've been thinking about you since you arrived," he said with deep "sincerity." And then I thought about it—hell, why not? Maybe an hour of hot, steamy sex would take the dreariness away. The pseudo–Jim Morrison look was cool . . . so why not? I told him I'd leave my door unlocked. The room was stifling, though my cheap kitchen clock said it was 6:10 a.m. I wrestled with the fan until I finally got the damn thing propped up on a chair with a pillow and managed to angle it to point directly at the bed. Ignoring my continuously growling stomach, I collapsed into the rumpled sheets and waited for my hour of steaminess . . . and waited . . . and waited. It wasn't going to happen because Luca wasn't coming—I knew that and, as I felt myself sliding to sleep, I realized—the door was still unlocked.

I thought to myself that I really should get up and lock it, but didn't.

Chapter 25

Revenge

I shot awake with sweat dripping into my eyes and the sound of something being dragged across the floor. Sunlight filled the room and, blearily, I saw the clock—it read 7:55 a.m.—then that dragging sound again. I looked up to see . . .

A man. In my room, weaving toward the bookshelves.

The dragging sound was his feet shuffling across the wood floor. The smell of alcohol hit me, and I was officially awake. *Who the . . . ? What the hell . . . ?*

Either way, this sure wasn't Luca. I couldn't properly hear or understand the words he was muttering under his breath—it was Flemish, that much I knew. He was dressed in a stained button-down shirt, half of which was hanging out of equally stained khaki pants. He stumbled and grabbed the bookshelf, which fell forward, crashing to the floor, all my things tumbling across the floor. A box that I had wrapped in a T-shirt broke open and out fell all my jewelry, including the real stuff I'd got in Switzerland. Why the hell had I brought it, who knew.

My heart sank as he bent down and pocketed the two Piaget watches and the diamond rings. *Oh, shit, shit!* My brain was rolling. *Fine . . . okay, he's a thief. A drunk thief. I can deal with that, I'll just . . .* And then the committee of sanity spoke loud and clear in my head. *You'll just do what? You're butt naked—your clothes are ten feet away on a chair! What are you going to do? Is there a plan? A dramatic take-down of this guy? How and with what? No coffeepot here. Nope, you'll just do nothing right now except be calm and keep thinking.* And then a stupid phrase flashed across my brain. *Ill-gotten means.* The jewelry . . . he'd stolen my ill-gotten wares. I almost smiled—it's funny how the brain works when you're petrified. Turning back to the situation at hand, I refocused on the reality of what was happening in my bedroom. Not a single word had been spoken other than the mutterings of a drunk man fumbling in his pockets with my things. I watched him straighten up and, for the first time, he slowly turned and looked at me.

I felt cold.

He sat on the side of the bed. I pulled the sheet up to my chin.

I felt colder, realizing . . .

He had no intention of leaving.

He stared at me and pulled a large switchblade out of his pocket, the long blade snapping open. He moved forward on the bed and laid the blade flat against the front of my throat. In very rough French, he said, "*Je te râpé ou je te tue.*"

I rape you or I kill you.

My brain had slowed to a snail's pace. I remembered the PLO in Beirut, I remembered Abdul Rahman in Switzerland. *I could do this, right? I could get myself out of this—with my jewelry! Yes, I could . . . I think.* Okay, but thinking needed to be done quickly and carefully, although in the immediate moment, my choices were slim. I was naked, trapped in the bed. I had no weapon, and this stinky, weaving shithead had a big knife blade right up against my throat. The whole deal didn't look good, but I was absolutely *not* going to die in this crummy place, by the hand of this piece of garbage, so . . . I vaguely remembered reading that rapists wanted their prey to be scared; it was apparently more of a turn-on or something. Maybe if I presented a strong, calm attitude, he'd lose interest?

I was wrong. Though I stayed calm, he went to work, with the blade against my neck and, relentlessly, in all the vulnerable places, he raped me over and over and over and over . . .

He wasn't a normal guy—in the sense that he wasn't built normally. He had a tiny, deformed penis that didn't work, so he used the handle of the switchblade to perform his iniquitous deeds in and out of my body. The hours ticked by. I hurt, especially my face from holding my jaw closed in a vise grip, first to deal with the pain and then in case the bastard thought of kissing me.

I was angry—a silent, motionless, seething rage.

Who the hell was this fucking guy in my room? Raping me! Then the committee piped up. *You left the door open. You didn't lock it—now you must think. Be smart. Pay attention. Remember everything. Feel everything. See everything. Bolt that in and shut him out.*

I heard the muted sound of voices coming from Charlie's room below and wondered if I should scream. No, too risky—this guy might get nutty and do something evil with that knife. I stayed silent. My surroundings were eerily quiet except the muffled sounds of mutilation. Four and a half hours later he stopped, rolled off me, snapped the blade closed, and put the knife back in his pocket. He stood up. He was done. He pulled up his pants and left, quietly closing the door behind him. I was lying facedown on the floor, blood smears all around me. Was I hurt? Yes, I was hurt. Was it bad? I really wanted to lock the door behind him, but I knew I had to get up, get out, and get help.

I dragged myself up and tried to walk a couple of feet to grab my robe off the chair—that was not happening; I fell right back down. "Shit!" I had pain in places that were mildly scary. I didn't look, but I knew I was bleeding from my lower extremities. "Get up! Move." Somehow, I got to my feet and struggled to the door. The kitchen was empty, and everyone was sleeping. I held the walls and made my way to the stairs. Taking a deep breath, I somehow hobbled down to Charlie's door. I knocked just as my knees gave out, dropping me back to the floor. Charlie opened the door and started screaming, seeing this blood-smeared naked woman on the ground.

"Oh! *Mon Dieu!*" Then he saw it was me and screamed louder.

"Charlie, I need help," I said, reaching up to him. He was crying as he helped me inside and onto the sofa. I felt bad; blood was seeping all over his Moroccan treasure—Kamal's legacy. Charlie didn't seem to care as he bounded into action, getting a bowl of hot water, towels, and a first aid kit.

"My darling Juliette, what has happened to you?"

"I've been raped and robbed."

He gasped in horror and clamped both hands to his mouth.

"Mon Dieu! Who? Was it that awful creature Luca? You know I don't trust him." He ran to the dresser and poured a huge glass of brandy. "Drink."

I sipped the brandy gratefully—I was feeling very woozy.

"No. It wasn't Luca. Charlie, I have a lot of pain. Please—I'm sorry to ask, but—can you see . . . if he did something bad?" Charlie nodded and carefully rolled me over. I never thought how he must have felt staring at my naked butt, but I was in pain and my butt needed to be seen. He carefully examined me all over.

"Not too bad under the blood. Okay—we can fix it. Did you know him?"

I shook my head. "He was drunk and dressed like a . . . dirty drunk."

Charlie nodded. "A mac . . . he was a mac. A pimp looking for money for drugs."

"I think I need a doctor, and I have to go to the police." I was worried that I could be in bad shape.

"You can't go to the doctor! They will report you." He bustled around getting antiseptic, hot water, and a bottle of something that smelled like iodine.

"Why can the doctor report me—for what?" I was incredulous. He shrugged (as only the French can).

"You are an *artiste*, nothing better than a whore on the streets—no one will listen to you." He very gently bathed my hurt parts. Whatever smelled like iodine was doing the trick. I was starting to feel a bit better.

"You'll take a couple days off, drink brandy, eat some couscous and savois! Just a bad memory." He tried to smile. Bandaged and fixed, he gave me one of his prized Moroccan robes and took me back to my room. He put the bookshelf back in its place and pulled the sheets off the bed. "I will bring you new ones."

"Charlie, did you hear that fall?" I pointed to the bookshelf. He looked sheepish and guilty.

"*Oui*, I am so sorry, I thought perhaps . . . you were . . . having some fun . . . *avec* someone . . . *jolie*. I am so sorry." The irony was . . . well, it just was.

"How would you know? I didn't scream."

He patted my head. "How are you feeling?"

"Better. Sore, but I'll be fine," I said resolutely. "But tell me again why can't I go to the police? Didn't this mac guy just commit a federal crime? Isn't rape a crime here?"

"No, not crime, very small misbehave, and you must *not* go to the police." Charlie was almost panicking. "They will think you are a *prostituee* and this was your mac and you had a fight and . . . all no good. The doctor, if you go, he will have to call the police. It is the law. They will arrest you and perhaps they take you to the *Palais de Justice* and it is all bad. Stay here. I will look after you. Remember, I am downstairs."

He hugged me and left.

I sat on the chair and thought about what had happened. A man had walked into my room and attacked me. For four long hours, he'd done awful things to my body. He'd hurt me, stolen my stuff, then walked out, and now I was being told not to do anything? No police? No doctor? I wondered how many times this happened. Nightly, weekly? And how many times per night—per week? So what if you were a prostitute or a stripper or an *artiste*? Obviously, you had no rights here. You could be raped, robbed, or whatever else, and you were supposed to do nothing? What if I'd cleaned out the cash register downstairs? You bet they'd have hauled my butt straight to jail.

It got me thinking about the future. Strange, but something was talking to me deep down, and I instinctively knew that if I didn't finish this, I would be affected for the rest of my life. I would carry this nightmare with me and it would mess me up—my view of men would take on a whole different meaning. I would make decisions from a mind based in fear of "what had been done to me and what could be done again." It would become my story, and young as I was, I knew I had to do this right and end it right. That pimp was out there walking the streets, free as a bird, selling my jewelry with no concern of what he'd done. I was nothing but a small part of his depraved day, a dim memory soon to be erased by the evening's ubiquitous offerings of degeneracy. I had to make a plan to find him and get him arrested, preferably while he still had my jewelry, but how? This was a guy from the streets, a slimeball who could be anywhere, even back in Brussels for all I knew.

I lay down on the bed and closed my eyes, but they immediately shot open. I was too amped up. I got dressed and went back down to Charlie's apartment, but he wasn't there. I walked down to the club and heard Edith Piaf. Charlie was standing at the bar, making coffee, singing along with "La Vie en Rose." Michele was pulling bottles out of a packing case across the room, and Luca was fixing the turntable. I walked up to him, saying nothing, and his eyes stayed down as he continued his very absorbing task.

Charlie ran over. "*Chérie*, you should be—"

I cut him off and, standing as close to the DJ stand as I could, I spoke clearly and loudly.

"A filthy pimp walked into my room at 7:55 a.m. and raped me. For four endless hours."

Luca didn't raise his head, but I continued. "I'm going to catch the son-of-a-bitch and put him in prison."

Charlie had stopped speaking and just stood there, his mouth dropped open. Michele, holding a bottle of scotch, looked up at me, but Luca kept working, head down. "And I'm going to need help finding him."

Charlie fluttered, "Oh, no! He is a bad man. You can't find him. Macs. They're all out there in the streets."

"Do you think he's local?"

"Who knows, maybe he comes from Brussels a few times a week. They come and go, like cockroaches. What will you do if you find him? No one will believe you." He was visibly shaken at what he perceived was my insane declaration.

"Yes, they will. I'm going to have him arrested." I was totally mission-oriented. "Can I do that?" There was silence. Charlie just shook his head and moved away from me. "Can I do that?" I think I was shouting. "Hey! Luca? Can I do that?" I *was* shouting, and Luca turned away.

"Yes, you can," Michele said in a strong, clear voice. "First, we must find him, then we bring the *Police Fédérale*. You say first, he robbed you—that is a real crime—*then* you say he attacked and raped you. They will come and arrest him, but you *must* be sure. Otherwise, it is bad for you." He came and stood beside me. I looked back at Luca, still eyes down working on his turntable. Charlie was back at the bar, polishing shot glasses.

"You said 'we'?" I asked Michele.

"Yes, I will help you."

"Thank you, Michele."

"Do you have a plan?" he asked.

"No." I hadn't gotten that far.

"Okay. We'll just go looking." He sounded confident.

"It's a small town, right?"

Michele nodded.

"Even if he comes from Brussels—he'll come back, right?"

"Yes, this is a town for macs. He has much business here," Michele said.

"Okay, good plan." No, it wasn't, but it was all we had.

Every night (morning really) after work, Michele and I would tread the streets. We'd go to every bar, strip joint, and nightclub in town. We went down dark alleys and into every sleazy basement haunt of the macs and drug dealers. Someone Up There must have been looking out for us because nothing bad happened. It should have, because we were going where two young respectable people had no business going, and how we never got jumped or hurt is a mystery, although I do believe my total and complete commitment to my mission alerted the attention of the Big Guy Up There and, for a second, he stopped doing whatever divine things he was doing and figured he'd help these two crazy kids down here by at least protecting us from death by night people. This was our ritual for over two weeks, and there was no backing down. I kept thanking Michele and telling him he really needn't do this every night, as we had already covered endless miles, trekking the underworld of Liege. He wouldn't hear of quitting. He would take my hand and not let go.

"We will find him, maybe tonight."

I was so grateful. I couldn't have done this alone, and he was a friend who had generously decided to help me. I often remember what a treasure he was, and I so hope he has a wonderful life somewhere, as a doctor, with someone who loves him very much.

One morning, at about seven thirty a.m., Michele and I were sitting drinking coffee in our usual café at the bottom of the alley, which was in the typical style of local cafés, with a long countertop where everyone sat side by side in a line on swivel stools. Suddenly, I felt fingers brush the back of my neck as someone passed behind me. I turned just in time to see HIM! The guy! Calmly walking out the door!

I grabbed Michele and spluttered out a whisper.

"There he is! That's him!" Michele immediately got up and quickly followed him outside, returning moments later.

"Next door, left, in Le Pussycat, in the back, sitting at the counter."

I had no idea what to do next. Police? Michele guided me up and out. We slowly walked next door. I followed in behind Michele and peeked over his shoulder. Peering into the darkened room, there HE was! Sitting at the bar, drinking a beer, smiling, and chatting with the guy next to him. My heart was literally banging in my chest. I felt a piece of paper being pressed into my hand as Michele handed me the phone number for the Special Federal Police. He looked deep into my eyes and asked, "Are you completely sure?"

I nodded.

"Then . . . okay, call now." He handed me a bunch of coins. I walked to the pay phone on the wall and dialed. A woman's voice answered, announcing the Federal Police Department, and in my best French, I said, "I am in the Pussycat Bar on [whatever street it was], and there is a man here who robbed, attacked, and raped me two weeks ago. I would like you to come and arrest him—now, please." She asked for my name and said they were on their way. I hung up the phone. I looked at Michele. "That was easy," I said.

He nodded.

I felt triumphant. "We got the bastard."

"*If* you are correct in your identification."

He was seriously concerned I might have made a mistake. I wasn't worried—I was confident in my identification. It felt like five minutes, then two open military jeeps with sirens screaming, flashing blue, red, and white lights, roared to a screeching halt outside the dim windows. Everyone in the bar stopped talking and looked up in alarm—these were the scary cops. Four heavily armed soldiers in full combat gear, wearing red berets, stormed in calling out for no one to move. Glasses and bottles went down on the counters.

"*Qui a fait le rapport?*" There was silence, everyone looking at everyone. Michele went up to them and spoke a few words, pointing at me. Two of the police came over and stood on either side of me as the third soldier turned to me.

"*Qui est l'homme que vous as rapporté?*"

I pointed to where the guy was sitting. They headed toward him, and he turned with an "*Oh shit*" look on his face and, in a split second, a soldier pulled him off his bar stool. I could see the fear on his face as they dragged him out the door, and I made sure we made eye contact. I wanted him to see me.

The two police who were now holding my arms escorted me out to join them in the second jeep.

Why was I . . . ?

And as we tire-burned down the street, sirens blaring, I turned to see Michele on the curb, watching us leave with a very worried look on his face. Neither one of us had known I would be going too, or had he? Maybe it had been the reason for his intense questioning as to the certainty of my identification.

We arrived at the Palais de Justice in a matter of minutes. I was escorted inside and put in a room with a single chair, a table, and a glass of water.

I saw them take the guy away down the corridor. I sat in the chilly gray room, feeling scared. *Had I been arrested too? Oh shit. Had Charlie been right? Were they going to charge me with being . . . something? Someone . . . illegal?* About an hour later the door opened and a young man entered, introducing himself as the judge's clerk. He took me to another room where an older man, dressed in a dark gray suit and tie, sat behind a large mahogany desk. The clerk introduced him as *le Juge en Chef.* The chief justice: the man who made decisions. He started by asking me to tell my story of what happened the morning of the fifteenth.

I did the best I could, but we were speaking French and I was trying to sound respectable and truthful, but at the same time I was scrambling for the right words in a foreign language that I was not a hundred percent fluent in. Eventually, I got the story out, and there was silence as the chief wrote notes on a pad. He then thanked me, and I was escorted back to the chilly gray room. Two more hours went by, and the same clerk returned, walking me back to the same office. The same chief justice greeted me, asking me to sit down and repeat my story of what happened the morning in question. I complied. He thanked me and I was taken back to the gray room. This time, a fresh glass of water sat on the table.

This scenario repeated itself six more times—each time the clerk returned, I was taken back to the same chief justice to tell my same story. Occasionally, he would ask a question. What was the man wearing? Did he speak French? Finally, on the seventh time back to the office, there was another man in the room wearing a white coat, standing by the door on the opposite side. The chief justice introduced him as Docteur Dubois, then leaned over his desk and looked me straight in the eye, prompting a pause that would have made Pinter proud. I could smell the garlic sausage he'd eaten for lunch. He then asked me, was there *anything else* I could remember about the man? Something particular? Something *only I could know* from being in that situation with him?

Having been in the building for nearly sixteen hours, without sleep or food, I was exhausted. They'd brought me water and coffee and allowed escorted bathroom breaks, but my head felt like mush. The problem was,

I knew they didn't have enough. If I'd been examined, I had no visible wounds; the mild abrasions had all but disappeared and, let's be honest, if there were any remaining marks, I could have easily gotten them from rough consensual sex—it was my word against his. Suddenly, a thought popped into my head. It was almost silly, but I had nothing to lose. Well, except that I did—I could lose here and that creep would walk and I could potentially go to jail for a wrongful accusation—but what the hell, I turned to the chief and spoke.

"He has a deformed penis."

Frowning, the doctor moved closer. The judge cocked his head, puzzled.

I waved my hands around. "It's tiny and sort of broken. Also, he has the skin of a wet fish." I pulled at my skin for "skin." Thankfully, I remembered the word *poisson* for "fish," but I was dead in the water for "deformed penis." Bewildered faces—I asked for a piece of paper and drew my best version of a tiny, crooked penis in a hairless genital area. The two men looked at the paper and I pulled at my skin again. "*Poisson*."

They looked at each other, then at me, and finally the chief justice handed the piece of paper to the doctor, who left the room. I thought we were done again, and it was back to my gray box. I stood up, but the chief quickly told me to sit. Fifteen minutes passed in complete silence. I watched the chief writing carefully in a large leatherbound book. I could see his handwriting was tiny. The door bounced open and the doctor returned—smiling; he looked weird. His words tumbled out quickly, but I understood all of them, he was almost excited. He said it was incredible! I had described his penis and skin exactly. Yes! It was exceedingly small and broken and yes! His skin was like a wet poisson.

The two men exchanged a few words, and the chief wrote something down, closed the book, and I was taken back to the room. Another hour passed, and then it was back to the chief, who shook my hand and thanked me for my time and for telling the truth. He also thanked me for staying awake, not a particular feat of brilliance—a single metal chair on a concrete floor facilitated wakefulness quite efficiently. He said they would be holding the man here in prison to await trial. I would be escorted back to the club, and they would let me know when the trial was going to be held. I would be required to testify within two months.

I had to tell him I wouldn't be here, as my engagement at the club ended in two weeks. Not a problem—I should go downstairs to the office and collect a voucher for a train ticket from London to Liege and another for a three-day stay at the hotel they used for witnesses. They would let me know the date of the trial by letter. He finally pushed a card across the table of the person who would liaise my arrival and attendance at the trial. Another shaking of the hand and thirty minutes later, voucher in hand, I was walking through the tall iron gates back to the club.

That was it. They had believed me, and we were done . . . for now. He was in prison and would stay there until judgment day. I was amazed and, I have to say, immensely proud of myself. I had been truthful and, for now, some of the nighttime girls of Liege would be safe from this predator. He might have been just one guy, but he was one son-of-a-bitch who would never harm another girl ever again—*if* I won the trial, which of course I would. I'd made it a primary "must."

I returned to the club and told Michele the story of my seventeen-hour sojourn at the Palais de Justice. He was amazed and relieved that I wasn't the one behind bars. We agreed he would accompany me to the trial. Charlie was *beyond* amazed at what I had done and said I was his hero and the bravest person he had ever known. He'd told everyone why I wasn't singing last night—I was being a vigilante for the *artistes* of Liege! And now the stinky bastard sat in a cold, stone jail.

There is no better feeling than justice.

Two weeks later I was back in England. The club hadn't paid me any more money, but Michele had given me some cash from the bar register. I'd managed to talk to Monsieur Armand, who promised to send me the rest of my salary as soon as the "*repairs*" were completed on the club.

Liars are funny people. They always think you believe them.

Chapter 26

La Vigilante

When I got back home to London, my first visit was to Mr. Johnny Too-Fucking-Far-Out, to tell him about the Le Club du Monde rip-off employment gig.

He looked surprised.

"I had no idea. Why didn't you call me?"

Ah, there's the rub. I hadn't called anyone.

"Just please don't book me anywhere else, ever again," I said in my best snooty voice. He feigned more surprise, but I knew he was aware the whole deal was suspect from the beginning. I never told anyone of my "incident in Liege." Not Paul and Barry, not my best friend Mariam, no one, especially not my mother. Just like "the Swiss adventure," this was my secret to keep and withhold as I saw fit.

I went back to my apartment with Cassidy, and life went on. When the letter arrived from the Liege Justice Court, informing me the trial date had been set for September 12 at nine a.m., I had to think up something to tell both Cassidy and Mother as to why I was going to be away for four or five days. I honestly don't remember what I came up with, but whatever lie it was, it must have been good enough, since neither one asked any questions.

On September 11, Michele picked me up from the Liege station and drove me to the small hotel the court had chosen for my stay. He said he would meet me outside the justice courtroom the following morning at eight forty-five a.m. I had already learned—and firsthand—that the legal system in Belgium was quite different from ours, and I also understood by now that crimes like rape and petty theft (neither considered major nor considered a federal offense) were heard by the Court of First Instance, and decisions made by this court could be appealed. There was no jury, only a panel of three judges. Not having made bail, the guy had been confined in jail until this court date. I knew I'd better be on my game—I had to win this thing.

The trial began with a lot of back and forth between lawyers and prosecutors. They interrogated the guy, who was being tried for robbery and soliciting prostitution—the rape was included as secondary crime. I sat at the prosecuting table on the right side of the courtroom, and he sat across the room at the defense table, flanked by two lawyers. Behind him in the front row sat his entire family, consisting of a sobbing wife, four kids, and a grandmother. I sat alone, with no papers and no lawyer—just me with Michele in the row behind. They questioned me, again in French, and I repeated my story accurately, just as I had done for the chief the previous month. The morning wore on. Finally, they asked me to repeat how I had positively identified him. In my best French, I replied, "*Il a un pénis déformé et la peau d'un poisson mouillé.*"

A burble of sound rolled around the courtroom. His wife buried her head in shaking hands.

At one p.m., we took a lunch break. I asked Michele how he thought it was going, since I was trying to understand this complicated procedure in legal French. He said he wasn't sure—the guy was denying everything, and his defense was saying my evidence was weak. The afternoon went on and I was questioned again. The guy had a couple of witnesses, then his wife took the stand, and I felt sorry for her. Obviously, she didn't know what a horrible scumbag her husband was, but my precise identification of his body parts had made for an unquestionable conclusion, and now she knew that he'd committed a go-to-jail crime. Finally, the day was over. I was told to come back the following morning, which started promptly at nine a.m. and progressed much like the day before. The guy's lawyer pleaded his case, and then I gave my story one last recount—my French was starting to wane—and then it was over. We were told to go outside and wait. Michele said this was strange, as the verdict usually took a few days and they sent the prisoner back and everyone else home. An hour or so later, we were summoned back inside the courtroom. One of the judges stood up and read from a piece of paper, starting with a summation of the case, and then a proclamation of the verdict.

"*Coupable des deux chefs!*" Guilty on all counts!

And for some inexplicable reason, the judges sentenced him to fifteen years in prison—without appeal! Apparently, they'd put the rape and attack above the lighter crime of robbery—all highly unusual, but Michele did say that the guy (we never did remember his name) had been arrested many times before for various nefarious activities, and Michele thought the court had basically thrown the book at him once and for all.

Of course, I didn't get my jewelry back, but nevertheless, I was thrilled and relieved. Michele hugged me and said I had done something great for all artists in town. We went for a celebratory dinner. When he picked me up early next morning, Michele was holding up the front page of the newspaper. The bold headline stood out declaring me as "*La Vigilante!*" My picture was just below, with the report of how my attacker had been sent away for fifteen years, which apparently was remarkable, considering the charges. It felt good to have this over, but it also felt good to have finished the story. Had I done nothing, I knew it would have haunted me for many years. I knew I *had* to have him caught, and even more, I knew I *had* to have him put away. Now I would never be one of those women who carries a lifelong burden of shame, guilt, and pain and all the other shit that goes along with having been raped. To this day, I am grateful for whatever genes I have that made me brave.

I didn't bring the newspaper when I left. Instead, I left it lying on the table in my room, being deathly afraid of who would see it at home. Yeah,

I may have had a ton of courage and strength when it came to catching a bad man who did very bad things to me, but I couldn't seem to have that same fortitude of conviction when it came to dealing with my mother and the story she would tell everyone, each time embellishing it ever so slightly. I imagined she would have framed and hung the newspaper clipping somewhere prominent for all to see what an amazing daughter she had and how I got it all from my father and his father, my grandfather.

Comparing me to Dad was just fine by me, but constantly equating me with my grandfather was not okay. Gramps was a Russian Cossack and cavalry leader within the Ottoman army who had marched with his soldiers into Armenia in 1915 to enforce the extermination of one and a half million Armenians, mostly citizens within the Ottoman Empire. It was an act of unfathomable carnage that my mother constantly and pridefully held up as an integral part of my heritage. I never contradicted her or asked her to stop reveling in that part of rotten history that lived deep within my bloodline. I just sat there cringing as she held up Grandad's photograph with him in full Russian uniform, complete with fur hat and a saber across his lap, recounting the atrocious story to anyone who'd listen.

I did once pull up my courage bootstraps and asked her, "Mum, wasn't that pretty much what Hitler tried to do? Annihilate an entire race of people?"

Her response was almost flippant. "Armenians were really *bad* people, and they just had to go."

I was horrified. Those words *actually* came out of her mouth, and I sat back and said nothing to contest them. I couldn't see my fear—no, terror—of this one sad, bitter woman who affected every aspect of my life. I had neither the fearlessness nor the courage to dispute the frequently heinous statements of *her* truth. I saw my mother as someone to put up with, someone who was a dark cloud over my being that might go away—but only if I went away—far away. Or she died. None of which seemed likely to occur in any near future, or at least not one that I could envision. For the time being, it was a matter of doing the best I could with what I had.

Chapter 27

How Not to Become Famous

Oliver had gotten me an audition for Le Boulogne, a nightclub in the West End of London, just off Piccadilly on Wardour Street. Owned by Mr. Hamed, a Turkish gentleman, it was a pseudo-French burlesque dinner/show spot that had been there for more than eighty years, catering primarily to tourists and out-of-town businessmen. Mr. Hamed had known my father and remembered me as a child, all of which helped get me hired as the lead girl singer performing with a group of sequined showgirls and one male singer, Tony Money, who truly believed he was London's answer to a bald Frank Sinatra. Our show was a compilation of fancy dance numbers and popular songs, and my co-girls were a wonderful bunch of hardworking Londoners. We all got along famously.

Since the pay wasn't great, I got two other singing gigs; one involved subbing with the band at the famous Café de Paris on Regent Street, and the second was at the well-known Chaplin's on Swallow Street. Little did I know that at Chaplin's I would be working for the notorious Oscar Owide, once dubbed "Britain's biggest pimp." With his pencil moustache, slicked-back hair, and old-fashioned BBC announcer drawl, Oscar Owide may have seemed the perfect 1950s gentleman, but in reality, he presided over a tacky, self-proclaimed sex empire. For more than thirty years, he ran Chaplin's and other "hostess bars," where girls tricked gullible customers into paying vast sums of cash for bottles of watered-down champagne and, if the customer could afford to keep paying the bar bills until three a.m., he could take a girl home for sex at a minimum of £500 a night.

I was one of the lucky ones—Mr. Oscar had hired me solely as a singer and was nothing short of charming and polite toward me for my entire run. Tucked halfway down Swallow Street, Chaplin's was in the epicenter of the hippest nightlife scene in London. You walked through a black door and down a long flight of stairs lit by fake candles, into a small clubroom that seated about seventy-five people. The décor was primarily blue and gold velvet, with satin drapes enclosing "private seating." All the girls, including myself, were instructed to call him "Mr. Oscar," which was supposed to convey a kind of reverence and respectability, although "Mr. Oscar" merited neither. One of the many scandalous stories that came out, much later, was that a visiting prince used to send a servant known as "the doctor" to bring girls to his suite at the swanky Dorchester Hotel. I remember one young lady in particular who was paid £8,000 for her services, though of course Mr. Oscar took his customary 70 percent cut. It was quite astounding how he managed to run his Soho Empire of prostitution and racketeering for nearly thirty years, miraculously getting away with it. It wasn't until 2004 that he was caught for some unrelated charge and had to pay a steep fine but no jail time.

Back in the summer of 1976, the place was packed every night—with a primarily male "audience"—and I did my show to a half-listening crowd of guys, some still in their office suits, their sole desire to drink and get laid. I adored all the girls who worked there, and we laughed all the time. Mr. Oscar treated me well and paid me every Saturday night, in cash. Between the three clubs, I worked four shows a night, six days a week, with Oliver working with me at the Boulogne as the piano player and band leader. I was beyond exhausted but making some decent, much-needed money, and that was a good thing. I haven't talked much about Oliver; it's a difficult topic. He was my dearest and closest friend and possibly one of the most extraordinary musicians I have ever known. A pianist and songwriter, he would sit down at the piano and genius would flow.

Oliver's story ends under very painful circumstances—we'll talk about that later.

Mother was about to be evicted from her studio rental in Chelsea. She had missed paying rent too often, and since she'd ostracized herself from all her friends, including the tenants of the building who'd often reached out to her, no one came to her rescue. I was also getting tired of Cassidy's numerous boyfriends—skinny, pasty-faced young men who regularly stayed over and who I would regularly run into, either stumbling out of her bedroom butt naked, or making morning tea in the kitchen, dressed only in Cassidy's flowered robe.

"'Ullo, I'm Mike . . . Bill . . . John . . . Nigel . . ." whoever was the latest guy would say, and there were many. Once I found one in the bathtub, buried up to his neck in the bubbles of my quite expensive bubble bath.

"'Ullo, I'm Roger. Wanna jump in?"

It was time to live in a house with no roommates—well, probably Mother would have to be included, but at least I knew I wouldn't be finding strange men in the bathtub. Farouk, a dear friend and wealthy Kuwaiti businessman I'd known in Beirut, kindly gave me the money for a deposit on a house on Orchard Avenue in Finchley, a residential neighborhood in North London—about fifteen miles from the West End. It was a four-bedroom Victorian house with a big garden that cost £23,000 (about $40,000). Today that house is worth £2.2 million (close to $2.4 million). Our mortgage payments were around £50 per month, so if we both kept working, we could manage. Mother still had a secretarial job in the city, a forty-five-minute subway ride each way, and she would get home just as I was leaving for work. Oliver would pick me up at five p.m. and we would drive into town to commence the endless parking search on Wardour Street. It felt good buying something rather than paying rent, and I rarely saw my mother and didn't have to put up with her endless waiting for me to come home anymore. When I used to go out (back in the day), she would wait up; I can still see the glow under her bedroom door from the solitary bedside lamp, clicking on when I reached the top of the staircase. I will forevermore hear that high-pitched voice calling out, "Juliette? Where have you been and with who? I've been waiting."

I always had to open her door. She'd be propped up in bed in her thick pajamas, white faced, seething in tension and anger.

"Sorry. I was at The Revolution and then the Scotch."

"With whom?"

Why was I sorry? I had the indisputable excuse for coming in at four a.m.—I was working to keep a roof over our heads.

"I'm sorry, I didn't notice the time."

"Who were you with?" She was almost shouting.

"Jimi Hendrix, Jeff Beck—Cassidy and I were having great fun." There was a "scoffing" tone in my voice, but for once I was being truthful. Jimi was one of my favorite people, and a good friend.

"Oh, that's nice. Now I have a daughter who spends her time with drug-taking hippies," she spat out with absolute conviction.

"No, mum, they're not hippies. They're my friends."

"Why are you associating with drug addicts? Are you taking drugs? Will this ever end? These *people*! Cat Stevens, Jimi Hendrix, and those awful rock bands? How can you make me worry like this? When will it end? You're an awful daughter! You bring me nothing but pain, gallivanting all night with the dregs of humanity." And here was the kicker. The one to the gut. "Your father would be ashamed of you." This line was then followed by copious weeping and sobbing and fist pounding into the bed. I used to stand there feeling nothing, waiting for it to stop, and it did, in an immediate recovery where her head would whip around almost 180 degrees and a voice resembling the devil would growl, "Don't you understand? I've been through a war and lost everyone I have ever loved."

I was numb, only wanting to get out of that room. Long ago, I'd stopped asking why I was continually included in all the lost, dead people, but in truth, I honestly didn't care.

My night life was a grueling schedule. I would start at the Boulogne with the eight p.m. show, then, armed with music charts, sparkly frock, and glittery shoes, would sprint down Piccadilly to Swallow Street for the nine thirty show at Chaplin's. At ten thirty, I sprinted back to the Boulogne, dragging on my red sequined costume and feathered headdress for the eleven p.m. show. The night would end with either the Café de Paris one a.m. show or Chaplin's late show. This juggle fest would go on six nights a week and would earn me about £400 a month, or about $650. I decided to audition for a popular television show called *New Faces*—the first talent show and one that spawned *Britain's Got Talent* and all the other talent shows that popped up in later years. I was chosen and went on television one month later, singing a Stevie Wonder song.

Stevie Wonder? What was I thinking? I was terrible and got crucified by the judges. Mickey Most, the famous record producer and a definite forerunner to Simon Cowell, said I was the worst thing he had ever seen . . . and *who* had let me onto the show? They should be fired! I remember leaving in tears and embarrassment. The next night, when I got back to work at the Boulogne, a heavy silence blanketed the dressing room. *Everyone* had seen it. The girls had propped up the TV in the dressing room, and the entire staff had gathered around, holding their respective glasses of bubbly, ready to be wowed as they witnessed my rocket to stardom. That night, I went back to work, and the girls were all sitting at the long makeup counter, intently looking straight ahead in the mirror as they applied their false eyelashes with pointed care. Occasionally, one of them would turn and shoot me a quick smile, then it would disappear. It was the kind of smile you use for visiting a terminally ill person in the hospital. It's funny how we deal with other people's misery, often not knowing what the right thing to do or say is.

Finally, Sally, our lead dancer, came over and put her arm around me, and her deep cockney accent was comforting.

"We bloody hate Mickey Most anyway, right? He's a conceited prick with long hair and a fucking ginormous ego. What does he fucking know about anything, right, love? Fuck him." And with that she slapped down a shot glass of vodka. "This'll make you feel better, and we gotta 'ole bottle in the back!"

I was grateful for the kindness, but what was I doing? I wish I could go back in time and stop moving for one second, long enough to realize I was just running down a blind road leading to nowhere-land. I knew I wasn't a very good singer and *New Faces* should have been my wake-up call, but I loved being on stage, and something deep down felt right about it. For some crazy reason, I'd somehow put it in my mind that I was going to be the next Liza Minnelli. Why? Perhaps because Mother had pounded it into me that I was just as good as her and no way should I *ever* stop trying, that I was a born entertainer and that's where I belonged.

No, it wasn't.

There was no way in hell I had anything close to Liza's singing talent—maybe it was because someone once said I looked like her mother that I doggedly pursued this course. I used to think if Liza was suddenly stricken with some awful condition that stopped her singing, or she quit the business or . . . died? I would be ready! What a terrible thing to even *think* about someone. I thought that if I became famous, I could give Mother a chunk of money and leave. She would be happy because I was famous, and I would be happy because I had enough money to go far, far away and never come back.

And maybe if I was famous like Steve—he would take me back.

Messed up? Sure, but I had no identity of my own. There was no "me." I was always trying to be someone else—because someone else always looked better. Better life, better friends, better parents, better everything. I'd convinced myself that becoming famous would solve all the problems.

I had no concept of what I looked like. I always thought I was fat and not quite pretty enough. I used to stare at magazine photos of Twiggy and Jean Shrimpton and long to be them. I starved myself on outrageous, crazy, dangerous diets in an effort to be rail thin. When I look at my old photos now, it almost makes me cry. I was beautiful and at a perfectly normal weight. If you had asked me to tell you something about myself, I would have quickly grappled for something witty and cool, nothing of any substance, just something that sounded impressive. If someone gave me a compliment, I would knock it down with an axe. It took me over twenty-five years to be able to say "*thank you*" when someone said something nice to me.

Some of my issues ran much deeper than my insecurity over my appearance, but in those days, no one discussed their feelings, serious problems, or anything private like emotions. No one ever asked me about Beirut and what it was like spending months in a war zone. Having a mother such as mine had already alienated me from reality. I did make friends easily, always making sure they were shielded for as long as possible from Mother, who didn't help by being who she was and hating everyone interesting or different that came into my life. In short, I had become an unwilling permanent caregiver to someone who didn't care about me and most likely never had. I was her charge—her duty to my father who had, ironically, always instructed her to "look after our precious child." But her words always resounded clearly in my head.

"Everyone I have ever loved is dead."

Chapter 28

Words of Wisdom in Scotland

In the seventies, we would all sit around for hours into the early dawn, having deep intellectual conversations about the meaning of life. We all put flowers in our hair, quickly realizing we'd better stick to fake ones, as real flowers wilted and died. We smoked cigarettes day and night. Marijuana and hashish crept in, and suddenly everyone was lighting up. Drinking was still the main drug of choice, and thankfully I wasn't much of a drinker. There was some cocaine and heroin floating around in the dark, but those drugs were not yet in the mainstream. I tried marijuana once, but putting my mouth around those nasty little wrapped, soggy butts of weed made me sick to my stomach. Our language was changing. You were "groovy, man" or "far out," and everyone needed to just "stay loose, man."

We found great joy in discovering bands and music, which then became the backdrop and narrative of our youth—Chicago; Blood, Sweat & Tears; the Eagles; Earth, Wind & Fire; and of course The Beatles. I knew the lyrics to every song on *Sgt. Pepper*; we all did.

I stayed close to Mariam, Paul and Barry, and Steve, when he was around. Pete and Chrissie Thompson and my darling Clive McLean, photographer extraordinaire, were also constant companions. We did everything together and laughed all the time. Clive went on to be the number one porn photographer of all time, working for *Hustler* magazine for nearly thirty years. He often said to us, "You gotta be bloody good to shoot nudes." He was right—he made naked women look so beautiful. Clive saw the funny in everything, and that's what made him special. He loved animals and he was kind, and that's all I needed to call him my friend. Clive died of lung cancer at sixty, as did Pete Thompson and a lot of our gang. We just smoked too damn much! Who knew it was killing us?

Oliver had pulled off a miracle. He'd gotten me the opening slot for Des O'Connor in Edinburgh, Scotland. It was a Saturday night booking at a prestigious nightclub, and this was a huge deal. Perhaps one of the biggest British stars of that time, Des O'Conner was a singer/comedian who currently had his own number one hit television variety show on the BBC. He was also a dear friend from back in the Playboy days, where we had dated off and on when he was in town. He was hilarious with that delicious Irish humor that is always so unique and endearing. The year previous, he'd been very kind and put me in a skit on his TV show, which almost closed the show down since I wasn't in Equity, the actors' union, but Des managed to talk us all out of trouble.

He knew how much I wanted to be a successful singer, so when the booking agent for the Edinburgh club asked him if I could be his opening act, Des was very complimentary and agreed immediately. He knew it could launch me into a lucrative career at bigger and better clubs across the country. It would also pretty much ensure I could now get a decent agent and poor Oliver wouldn't have to keep scrounging around for jobs. I didn't give a moment's thought to the fact that Des had never heard me sing and (thankfully) never seen *New Faces*. Mother was thrilled because Des O'Connor was one of her favorites, so for a brief time happiness and optimism filled the house. Mother was convinced this was the break to launch me to stardom. The London Palladium was next, and Liza could just step aside.

I managed to get the time off from all my clubs, and Oliver and I chose the songs, sticking mainly to show tunes and pop songs of the day—Stevie Wonder was expunged from the list. We rehearsed and rehearsed and rehearsed . . . and then rehearsed some more. I got myself two new sparkly dresses with matching shoes, and finally the day came for us to leave for the long drive to Scotland. Mother stood in the chilly sunshine and waved us off from the front garden, dabbing her eyes with a handkerchief. It was a ridiculously sentimental departure.

Edinburgh was a six-hour drive, and money was horribly tight. The only place we could afford to stay was about ten miles outside town. I honestly don't think there are words, in any language, to describe the bitter, mind-numbing cold that greeted us as we stepped out of the car at the Brass Bell Boarding House, owned by a hardy woman named Miss Scottie (I think it was a nickname) who showed us to our rooms. The temperature was a damp forty degrees outside and only a degree or two higher inside. Most of the windows in the house were thrown open and when, between chattering teeth, we suggested they be closed, Miss Scottie declared with gusto, "A wee bit of fresh air is good for the soul!"

Oliver slept in all his clothes plus an overcoat, and I did the same. My "soul" was beyond caring what was good for me. I was in a place where the cold had deprived you of the ability to speak a fully formed sentence. The next day we hurried out, declining Miss Scottie's cold cooked breakfast, and ran to the nearest café, which thankfully had a modicum of heat coming from an old iron stove propped up in the corner, and then it was on to the club for band call. I kept on my winter coat and gloves, as I didn't have a scrap of trust that any place in this damn country was heated—and I was right. The club's main room was beyond frigid.

The band was an assembly of solid, first-rate musicians who threw my music up on the stand and read the "dots," playing perfectly. As my musical director, Oliver took over at the piano, and I saw the rest of the band nod in approval. I went through my numbers one at a time and, halfway through "Don't Cry Out Loud," the band suddenly stopped playing. Oliver stood and followed the club manager's beckoning finger into a windowed office; the band muttered something about a smoke break, lit up cigarettes, and left. I figured I might as well go back to my dressing room to try and warm up beside yet another ancient metal stove spluttering out a few gassy fumes of heat. It was noticeably quiet. I sat and waited, listening to the rhythmic sound of a small kitchen clock ticking on the dressing table. The door finally opened, and Oliver stood there holding all the song charts in his arms. His face was white, and he was biting his lip . . . hard. My stomach dropped.

"What?" I asked, not really wanting the answer.

"You're . . . we're . . . not"—it was difficult for him to talk—"going on. You're not going on."

I just stared at him. My mouth instantly dried up. He came over and sat down, still holding the charts close to his chest. The words came out hot and fast. "They are replacing you with another singer. They said you . . . you sounded . . . were flat . . . not good . . . not good enough to open for Des." And tears started rolling down his face.

I sat there, stuck in time. It was one of "those" moments when everything stops and you have these odd fantasies about rewinding the last six minutes.

"I'm so sorry," Oliver said with his head down. I could see big, wet tears dropping onto his perfectly pressed blue suit pants.

"Am I flat? I am, aren't I?"

He nodded.

"Is Des here yet?"

He shook his head.

"Pete just arrived." Pete Marshal was Des O'Connor's personal assistant who had been with him for a hundred years. A solid, loyal man, Pete looked after Des and got him where he was supposed to be, and occasionally, with the utmost discretion, where he wasn't supposed to be. Des was on his second marriage, but he just loved women. He was a lovable Irish rogue, and the odd philandering here and there was beyond his control. We had a brief affair back in the *Playboy* days, and he'd come over to my apartment on various afternoons, always in disguise because someone might "see" him. His dress-ups were awful—crooked wigs, oversized coats . . . just ridiculous. We both knew this thing was going to end, and it did, in hilarity. Des asked me if I would wait eight years until his children left school, then we could be together. I think I laughed so hard, it made him laugh too. We stayed good friends because, well, he was that kind of guy. Here, on this rotten day in Scotland, I knew I could talk to him. I went back down to the club floor, where the manager saw me and scurried into his office, closing the glass-paneled door behind him. I saw Peter and walked straight over.

"Did you hear?"

"Yes, love. I'm so sorry." He put his arm around me.

"Can I see him?"

He nodded.

"He's still back at the hotel. I'm running band call . . . hang on, let me give him a ring and the car can run you over."

The hotel was a short distance from the club, and in less than twenty minutes, I was knocking on room 129. Des opened the door in his traditional before-the-show satin robe. I walked into his arms and we sat on the sofa.

"Pete just rang," he said gently.

"They've replaced me."

"I know." He looked at me intently. "What do you think?"

"They said I was singing . . . flat."

"Were you?"

"I don't know." I could hear a clock ticking. Scotland was all about ticking clocks—everywhere you went there was some form of grandfather clock ticking, and I hate that sound to this day. We sat in silence for a few minutes, and I was trying so hard not to cry. "I was nervous," I said. "Maybe? That's what it was, bad nerves?"

Des stood up and crossed the room. There was a flowery china tea service set up on the table, and I became fixated on the huge cabbage roses painted on the cups and saucers. He poured me a cup and brought it back to the sofa, sat, and took both my hands.

"Here's what could happen. Right now." His voice was calm. "I could pick up that phone and make a call to the club. I could tell the manager you *are* opening for me. I *am* the star of the show—I am Des O'Connor and I can do that, right now. They'll cancel the replacement, and you'll go on tonight as my opening act. Pete says the place holds eight hundred and we're sold out." He stood up. "Do you want me to make that call, Juliette?"

I sat in silence as my mind rolled around like the inner workings of the ticking clock. Somewhere in between the wheels, common sense voices spoke. I looked up at Des's sweet, kind face.

"No, they're right and . . . it wouldn't be right."

"I am very proud of you." He put his arm around me and spoke with great intention. "Listen to me, you *are* special. You have something—you just haven't found out what it is yet. It's always going to be hard for you because you're different. People like you don't have it easy. They have to work ten times harder than anyone else and put up with much more rejection and difficulties, but—there are a few shining lights in this world, and *you are one of them.* Don't ever stop looking and trying. You *will* find it one day, I promise."

I nodded. This had come from a man who spent most of his time telling silly jokes, singing schmaltzy songs, and laughing when women threw panties on the stage. Rarely was he this serious. In truth, it didn't really sink in that day because I was feeling so shitty and I thought he was being kind, and I didn't realize I would remember these words and this moment for the rest of my life.

We didn't say much more that afternoon in Scotland. Des went on to do the show with the new opening act, and Oliver and I left the next morning. On the drive back to London, we didn't talk about what happened. I don't remember what I told my mother.

I do remember it wasn't the truth.

Chapter 29

The Judy Garland Story—Italian Style

Saturday night was always my favorite night in London. Everyone was out and about, dressed in their best glitter and tuxedos, having a good time. You could be on the streets at two a.m. in a skimpy party frock and you were safe as you could ever be. You stayed out of the bad areas of town, which were mostly on the south side, across the river, and locked your doors at night. You gave up your seat on the bus for old ladies and helped blind people to cross the street. There was an order and rite of passage we all followed, and it worked. We had no idea how profoundly safe we were.

One Saturday night, Oliver and I arrived at the Boulogne to see a line that stretched down the block. Happy Mr. Hamed stood in the doorway beaming, then sternly tapped his watch when he saw Oliver and I running down Wardour Street after having battled the nightly parking nightmare. Fifteen minutes in the dressing room, a quick banter with the girls, and I was ready for our first number. Holding my feathers steady, I left the dressing room to sneak a quick peek at the audience. Immediately, I saw a large table of six noisy Americans, who honestly looked like they had just stepped out of *The Godfather*. There was even a dead ringer for Jimmy Caan in the bunch. I heard them call him, "Tony Three Fingers." (Yes, really.) Dressed in dark suits with white or black ties, all sporting Frank

Sinatra fedora hats, they were Central Casting's classic mob dream. A magnum of Dom Perignon sat on the table, nestled in an icy silver bucket. The guys were merrily clinking glasses.

"To fucking life! Yeah! Bring on the girls!"

I went back into the dressing room, where Sally was putting on her feathers.

"Sally, I think those guys out there think they're at a strip club." She stuck her head out the door and laughed.

"Nah, they're just a bunch of bloody yanks—'armless."

Our show went well that night, though the yanks threw pound notes onto the stage, greatly offending Sally, who threw them back. "Tony Three Fingers" waved a £50 note in the air, indicating he would like to place it between anyone's breasts. That was the final straw for our Sally, who, with the ease of Fred Astaire, took her silver-tipped cane (we were in the middle of "Singing in the Rain") and, with a forehand to make a tennis champion proud, whacked the bill straight out of the offending hand, missing his fingers by a hair. The whole table roared with laughter, blowing kisses to us.

"My kinda broad!" came out of one of the guys who had a fedora hat pulled down over most of his face.

After our closing number, I grabbed my bag and ran through Piccadilly to do my set at Chaplin's, only to find the show was canceled. Half the staff had come down with a terrible flu and there was basically no one to serve, sit on laps, or play in the band. Holding my music wrapped in my sparkly frock, I stood in the hallway outside the dressing rooms. Mr. Oscar wasn't happy, not because everyone was extremely ill, but because this had been looking like a sold-out night. Now all his customers were leaving, and all his girls were gone.

"Why couldn't everyone get ill on a fuckin' Sunday?" Mr. Oscar was pissed. When I came back to the Boulogne early for our eleven p.m. show, the Americans were still there ready and waiting. They tried throwing money again, and this time Sally scooped up the notes and stuffed them into their champagne glasses. They thought that was the funniest thing, and more roaring laughter ensued. The show ended, and as I didn't have a third gig that night, I got dressed and came back out to the room to wait for Oliver to pack up. The Americans were still there, and Tony called me over.

"Hey sweetheart! We got champagne! Join us!"

I gave them my best British withering look. I do not respond to *sweetheart*, and frankly, I hate champagne, but there was something very entertaining about them, so I casually strolled over and sat down. They all introduced themselves as Joey this and Frankie that and Marty something. A slick, dark-haired man dressed in a pinstriped suit stood up and held out a deeply tanned, diamond-ringed hand.

"Andy D'Amato, and kid—you were fucking fantastic! Right, guys? What a fucking voice! Did anyone ever tell you, you look exactly like Judy Garland? Huh? Am I fucking wrong, boys?" He looked around as all the guys nodded vigorously in agreement. "You could be her double. Hey, Frankie! She could do the movie, huh? Whaddya think?"

Oliver walked up carrying his well-worn leather music case. He was blinking in slight shock at all the language flying our way.

"Maestro! Sit!" Tony swept out a chair for Oliver, who gingerly perched on the edge. Oliver was a British gentleman, and this was not his kind of crowd. We sat with them for about an hour. Oliver chuckled eventually, feeling almost cool, maybe for the first time in his very conservative life, bless him. They asked me all about my life and again told me how fantastic I was and how I *was* Judy and that they were in financing movies and casinos in Vegas and lived in LA and New York City and had just finished the final financing for the Garland picture and . . .

I could see Oliver's eyebrows raise in cynical doubt, but they were hilarious and quite convincing. I was young and ignorant, and they were American and glamorous and so much more exciting than English people, so who cared? They said they were staying at The Ritz Hotel, and Andy invited me and *my mother* to lunch the next day.

"Why is he inviting your mother?" Oliver whispered in heightened suspicious mode. I shrugged.

"Don't go; they worry me."

"You know, you're awfully boring sometimes and absolutely no fun whatsoever! Why don't you just keep living with your mother and playing the piano."

Yes, sometimes I had a mean streak.

Lunch at The Ritz was amazing. Knowing exactly who they were, Mother was in her element. The Boys adored her, and she reveled in their company. At one point in between courses, she leaned in and whispered in my ear with great conviction, "You know, the Mafia all love their mothers." Frankie kept kissing her hand, telling her she was a Parisian babe, wine flowed, and over the peach flambé, she tipsily whispered in my ear, "See? I told you. I think they're wonderful—they love mothers."

I whispered back, "And they kill people."

"Only when they deserve it." She looked very "part of the group" as she lifted her glass for more wine. Why the hell did she marry a Turk? She would have made an excellent "Cosa Nostra" wife. At the end of the meal, Andy D'Amato pushed an envelope to *my mother* across the table, and she opened it to find two tickets to Miami. Andy then proceeded to say he'd been on the phone all morning, and it was a done deal. Mother and I would be going with him to Miami for a few days' vacation, then Andy and I would be going on to Las Vegas to meet the producer of the Judy Garland picture. He pulled a contract out of his briefcase with the name and logo of the production company printed across the top—a totally authentic, legitimate document in my name to star in *The Judy Garland Story*. I wish I still had the darn thing—it was a work of art. Not quite as brilliant as the PLO driving license, which I also wish I still had, but definitely a respectable runner-up.

Andy then said I should give my notice to the Boulogne tomorrow because we were leaving the following weekend. "Tell everyone you'll be gone for a while," he said, "but that you'll come back fucking famous, kid!"

I hesitated. Mother didn't.

"It's the opportunity of a lifetime."

"Listen to your mother, kid. You're gonna be a star!" He said that—he really did.

And so, it came to pass, the following Saturday afternoon, my mother and I were on board National Airlines—"I'm Lisa, fly me," for those who remember—to Miami. Oliver was not happy, as I had literally quit and was abandoning him. Thankfully, the Boulogne kept him on, so I didn't feel too bad. He was always way too cautious . . . Anyway, I thought he could escort me to my premiere.

Chapter 30

Las Vegas and Rachmaninoff

We arrived in Miami and were met by a chauffeured limo, which took us to the Eden Roc Hotel. Mother and I each had our own room in a three-bedroom suite with televisions everywhere, including the bathroom. Hopping straight into vacation mode, we spent the next four days sunning by the pool, going to fancy dinners, and shopping—Andy said to sign for everything. We met the manager of the hotel, along with a host of other wealthy businessmen and hotel owners, who all treated us like royalty.

"This is the gal who's gonna play Judy Garland in a new major motion picture, and this is her Parisian French mom who was a spy in the war." Oh, yes—lunch at The Ritz had loosened Mother's secretive mouth to her new Italian pals.

On the fourth day, Andy disappeared. He called from the airport, leaving a message on our room phone, saying he had a "thing" and wouldn't be back until tomorrow. We should go ahead, reminding us to sign for everything and have a ball! That afternoon, a slightly distressed hotel manager stopped me in the lobby, looking for Mr. D'Amato. Did I know where he was?

"No. I'm sorry, I don't."

Looking even more distressed, he asked, "How long is he expected to be gone?"

"He said he'll be back tomorrow."

His agitation increased. "And how long will you be staying with us?"

"I'm not sure."

Even more distressed, he shook his head and hurried away. A small flag started to flutter, but it was still a mere shade of pink, and I didn't know enough to worry. Andy finally showed back up the next day and said it was time to head to "Vegas, baby!" The next morning, Mother had a thousand crisp hundred-dollar bills tucked in her purse and was happily seated in first class on National Airlines, headed back to London. Soon after, Andy and I were boarding a flight to Vegas. We had not checked out of the Eden Roc, just picked up our suitcases and walked out, straight into a Lincoln limousine. I suppose it never crossed my mind that something was wrong, or more to the point, that something wasn't right. After the past evenings of socializing with Miami executives and upper crust hotel management, Andy disappears, then reappears, and within hours, we're leaving town like speeding bullets.

I just couldn't shake the face of the distraught Eden Roc manager.

We arrived in Las Vegas late in the evening. I remember flying in the darkening skies and then suddenly, out of nowhere appeared this rolling line of brilliant lights, a glittering magic carpet leading over the horizon to infinity. It was September 1976, and the Mob still ran the show. Howard Hughes, who'd owned seventeen hotels, had died the previous year, and Elvis would die in August the following year, just after performing his last concert at the Hilton. The strip was a miniscule size of what it is today; the main action was downtown on Fremont Street, housing the Golden Nugget, Binion's Horseshoe, and a host of other casinos. The southern end of the strip was still a sparse, dusty road peppered with a few big hotels. The Flamingo sat across from Caesars Palace, and there was the Sands, which housed Sinatra's famous Rat Pack Show, and of course the MGM Grand, Circus Circus, the Dunes Hotel, and the Hilton. As far as I'm concerned, this was always and always will be the real Vegas.

Another black stretch Lincoln limousine picked us up from McCarran airport—then just a small, dusty desert airfield—and drove us to the

Me and Mother having dinner at the fancy Eden Roc Hotel

Dunes Hotel at the southernmost end of the strip. Together with the Sands and the Desert Inn, the Dunes was known as one of the "Three Kings of Las Vegas." Built for $3.5 million, the equivalent of $33 million today, the hotel opened in 1955 during the casino building boom. Sitting on a thirty-five-hectare site at the southern end of the Strip, diagonally across the road from the Flamingo, the Dunes boasted two hundred rooms and a twenty-eight-meter pool, the largest in the country. The hotel was dominated by a ten-meter-tall fiberglass statue of a Middle Eastern sultan and was owned by three somewhat shady partners, one of which was Joe Sullivan, who was later reputed to be a "front man" for cash investments that actually came from mobster Ray Patriarca, head of a Rhode Island crime family. Sullivan kept his interest hidden, expecting to reap under-the-table profits from the casino. The Dunes had achieved its present lofty status due to many years of Mob rule.

Opening the darkened glass doors of the Dunes, we entered through a blast of cold air-conditioning into an enormous room of sound and neon flashing lights, each one declaring various guarantees of instant wealth. "Your win of ten thousand dollars is moments away!" Someone had just thrown a 7 or 11 at the craps table, and a deafeningly loud roar almost drowned out the dinging of slot machines. The air was filled with cigarette smoke, creating a pale blue haze, which was trapped in the windowless, clockless room. What time was it? Daylight or darkness? No one knew nor cared—that in of itself was a welcome mystery to the plethora of strangers huddled together in their various cocoons of money and play.

Andy and I checked into two suites. He handed me my key and hurried off back to the elevator, throwing over his shoulder, "Meet me in an hour on the top floor, in the executive offices."

My exceptionally spacious room overlooked the deserted Strip. Other than a few cars and limos passing by below, all the action was contained within the casino walls. I will always remember that first day looking out the window, breathing in hot, sandy air through the glass. The desert had a smell that was unlike anything I had ever experienced. I felt as if I'd come home, which was definitely peculiar, as Vegas is and was the most un-home-like place on earth, but somehow I felt I knew this country and this would be where I would eventually know and understand myself.

An hour later, I was seated on a red velvet sofa outside a windowed office, watching Andy and a very elegant man deep in conversation. The door opened, and Andy introduced me.

"Juliette, this is Arte Riddle, general manager of the Dunes."

In its early years, the Dunes staggered from one misfortune to another, but by the early sixties, it was on the rise thanks to the savvy mind of its new general manager, Major Arteburn Riddle. A beautifully manicured hand reached forward as a deep, silky voice said, "Major Arteburn Riddle at your service. If you need anything, anytime, please don't hesitate to come and see me."

"Thank you," I said, shaking his hand.

The next few days were just plain strange. First, the limo driver disappeared, and Andy had me driving the Lincoln. He said I should get used to driving on the other side of the street, although I would have preferred a small Volkswagen Beetle instead of a thirty-foot monster equipped with seating for eight. Driving that thing was no easy feat in and around the two-lane Strip and narrow side streets, but eventually I got the hang of it.

We spent a lot of time at the Dunes, and I noticed Andy seemed to have full run of the casino. He could walk in and out of the "cage" and take cash whenever he wanted. He spent many hours in the executive offices, and we ate every night at the *Dome of the Sea*, the five-star restaurant at the top of the hotel. It was all very fab, but I just wished I didn't have this continual nagging flutter sitting at the bottom of my stomach. On the fifth afternoon, Andy led me through the neon world and swooped us through the glass doors. The heat billowed up from the ground and swallowed you, hitting your body like a blowtorch blasting through a hair dryer stuck on high. As we walked to the car, picking our way across the stickiness of the smelting tarmac, I asked when we were going to meet said producer of said Judy Garland film.

Andy kicked the Lincoln into life, announcing, "Now, baby! We're off to meet the wizard!" He roared with laughter at his own joke, cranked the air, and we drove two hours out into the desert—where it was even hotter—to a metal warehouse that looked like a government bunker. There we met Marco, the producer of the picture, inside a large room of about two thousand–odd square feet, where the only contents visible were an ornate Victorian desk with matching chair and a ten-foot projection screen with a camera sitting atop a tripod to the side. Marco launched into a long, meandering dissertation about the role and the script—which he didn't have because it wasn't completed.

I asked where we would be filming.

"Oh, that would be at Rachmaninoff's great-granddaughter's house, right here in Vegas," Marco quipped. Now, even I, with my total lack of movie making wisdom, knew that was weird.

"What does Rachmaninoff's great-granddaughter have to do with Judy Garland?" I had to ask. Not even trying to answer, Marco assured me I would love her and we were lucky to have her on board. This rambling went on and on until we left, with promises from Pete the assistant producer that shooting would begin in a couple of weeks and would last at least six months. I never saw a contract, let alone signed one. That same afternoon, we drove out to Rachmaninoff's great-granddaughter's house and had tea by the pool.

"This is Rachmaninoff's great-granddaughter. You guys are gonna love each other!"

A long, thin-fingered hand reached for mine.

"Enchanted."

I shook hands with a tall, grand lady in her fifties, wearing a long, flowing kaftan with heavy gold and silver necklaces draped around her neck. We talked about Italian painters and London, though her Russian accent (was it, though?) was almost impossible to understand. Thin fingers kept stroking my face, telling me I was lovely.

The next day Andy told me "they" (who?) had gotten me an apartment. I couldn't stay at the Dunes for six months, and so I would be moving today. Back at the hotel, I packed, and we drove a few blocks down the Strip, squeezed the Lincoln down a side street, and stopped in front of a row of townhouses. Andy handed me keys to number 22, and we walked into a nicely furnished two-bedroom house, which apparently belonged to one of the other producers, who rented it out to movie people.

"Andy, this looks very . . . lived in."

"Homey, right?" Sure, if you can call a place covered with family pictures and personal knick-knacks and other people's stuff in drawers and a fully stocked kitchen "homey"—yup, that it was. "Marco wants his stars to feel comfortable. They do all this"—he said, pausing and waving an arm around the room—"to make you feel like you never left home. The set guys are great with this shit." He then handed me the keys to the Lincoln. "Drive it until we get you a car." And wrapping a beefy arm around me, he chuckled. "We'll get you a Caddy—you gotta move in fucking style, right? A Cadillac Seville. You're gonna be a fucking movie star, kid, and we can't have you driving around in a fucking Ford!" He then tried to kiss me.

I quickly stepped back, ready for . . . whatever was coming next.

He looked at me seriously. "You know I'm in love with you, right? Let's get fucking married! Whaddya think?"

"I think . . . that sounds . . ."

"Like a great fucking idea! We'll do it at the Dunes! Bring Mom back!" He pulled me in for a serious kiss, angling our feet toward the bedroom. I turned it into a kind of fumble-hug, squeezing myself out of his arms, and he laughed. "You're beautiful, kid! See you tomorrow!" He opened the front door and ran down the steps. I watched him cross the street and jump into a dark blue Mercedes idling by the curb. As it sped down the street, I thought, *Odd. I didn't remember seeing that car when we got here . . . obviously it'd just arrived . . . he didn't say he was . . . it's fine . . . he's going back to the Dunes. For work.*

And the flag turned red.

Chapter 31

The Scam

Good criminals have a well-executed plan, down to the last detail of timing and finesse. *Great* criminals do all that but with inestimable style. The expensive suit, the confidence behind every word, is guaranteed to inspire absolute trust. The abundance of cash is always neatly folded in a gold money clip or rolled inside a rubber band. For every question asked, there is a complete and logical answer, to which you find yourself saying, "Of course. That makes perfect sense."

The blue Mercedes disappeared around a corner, and the pit of my stomach bounced into life. I suddenly knew he was gone this time. Really gone. It took four days to really sink in—which in Mob time is relatively long—during which I spent most of my waking hours trying to figure out what to do if he *was* really gone. Here I was again with no money and no ticket home.

He'd be back, right? Sure, definitely, he wouldn't leave me stranded?

Daily, I drove back and forth from the Dunes to the Desert Inn, where we'd also spent a lot of time, as well as the Tropicana. I would see the shows, visit with the various managers and cabaret room directors, all asking me where Andy was and when he was coming back.

"Great fucking guy!" They loved him.

All flags were flying red, and I knew—in my gut—it was just a matter of time before this house of cards would come crashing down like broken rock crystals. I loved the casinos here, which seemed so much more vibrant and exciting than the ones in London. I was fascinated by the rows of little old ladies clutching their buckets of nickels and quarters, mesmerized by the potentially "hot" machine in front of them, their eyes shooting laser beams on *their machine*. They all had their favorites, and don't you dare be caught in *their* seat! You would literally be yanked out by an eighty-five-year-old slot warrior!

I had made friends with a lot of the casino staff in the various hotels I'd frequented with Andy. People were extremely impressed that I had been a Playboy Bunny and I could deal three games—roulette, blackjack (twenty-one), and craps. The Tropicana offered me a job, which I promised I'd think about. I'd learned, way back in Beirut, when you're in a new place, make friends—lots of friends—and make them in the absolute right places. I can attest to forty years of gratitude to the eternal kindness of strangers all over the world, especially Las Vegas in the fall of 1977.

By the evening of the third day of his departure, a lot of people were asking me where Andy was, and now the "asking" no longer had "great fucking guy" attached to it. Here was the awful truth—Andy D'Amato had officially disappeared. A few days later, at seven forty-five a.m. on a Sunday morning, the apartment's front door opened, and in walked a man carrying two suitcases, followed by a woman with two small children. She walked into the bedroom, saw me, and screamed. The man came running in behind her, holding up a suitcase in attack mode. I sat up in their bed, barely able to breathe.

"Who the hell are you?" the man shouted, holding the suitcase high. I think he was scared more than anything. I would have been scared shitless finding some strange naked female in my home, in my bed! I found out very quickly that day that the place I was staying in was not an apartment owned by a producer for "movie folk." It was the home of Bill and Francine Mayer and their two children. They had been on vacation, and somehow Andy had known—even though the Mayers had never heard of him. Keys had been made or procured somehow, and here I was, living in a broken-into home of complete strangers. I started sobbing, croakily explaining my preposterous story, which must have sounded so ridiculous. Francine was kind, sat me down, and told me to tell them everything. To a pair of widened eyes, I started at the beginning, in London with Mother, then Miami, Judy Garland, Rachmaninoff . . . right up to this moment.

I think there must be some kind of spiritual energy that comes out of a person when they're telling the truth. These lovely people did not call the police, and instead they asked me if there was anything they could do to help. I said I was fine and so deeply sorry. They were kind and sweet and told me I should never trust an Italian in this town and then asked me why I was driving an eight-seat limousine.

"I have absolutely no idea. It was what he gave to me . . . to drive."

They then helped me pack my stuff, and I left. I really think it helped, my being British, as I must have said "sorry" at least twenty times.

Not knowing quite what to do or where to go, I went to the Dunes and parked the Lincoln in the car park. Before I got out, I looked in the glove compartment and took out the registration, which was in the name of the Summa Corporation, which I remembered was the name of Howard Hughes's company when he owned the Desert Inn. The limo belonged to a recently dead Howard Hughes. Great. I went up to the executive offices and, as I walked into the reception area, a terribly angry Major Arteburn Riddle blasted out of his office, yelling at me.

"Where the fuck is he?" I didn't know what to say. Riddle's face went purple as his voice rose to a crescendo. "WHERE'S D'AMATO, THE MOTHER FUCKING SON-OF-A-BITCH? HE'S GOT TWO MILLION OF MY HOTEL'S MOTHER-FUCKING MONEY!"

That would have translated into about eighteen million today, so he was understandably flustered.

"Oh . . . sir . . . I think he . . . left, sir." My mouth had become sandpaper.

"LEFT?"

"Yes, he left town."

"To fucking where?" His face was almost black. "With my two fucking mil? Did he fucking leave with my two million dollars?"

"I don't know, sir. He left four days ago . . . in a blue Mercedes."

That was all I had, and damn it if I didn't start crying again. This was bad, and I felt so stupid and scared that . . . well . . . these people didn't ask many questions before you "went for a drive." I had no idea if Major Riddle thought I was a part of whatever was going on. And even if I wasn't "going for a drive," I still had no idea how I was going to get home. I had a useless one-way ticket from Miami and no good common sense. And no money. This was no Pashma on an Arab girlfriend hunt—this was really scary shit. I had been fooled by an extremely smart criminal, and now I was in a potentially big mess in a town where that was certainly not an optimal situation. Suddenly, I felt an arm go around my shoulders and the overwhelming smell of Aramis cologne fill my nostrils. Arte Riddle led me into his office and put me in a silver leather armchair. They didn't kill you in offices, did they?

"You didn't know, did you?" His voice was gentle.

"No, sir. All I knew was I was going to play Judy Garland in a movie."

Arte shook his head in disgust. He believed me. Maybe it was that aura thing again, but by now I'd gotten to know quite a few members of the Vegas Italian Contingency, and I could have sworn that these guys could smell the truth. It was many more years before I discovered the full story of the "sting" Andy had been a part of—it would become a prolific scandal in Vegas and many other cities growing in wealth and prosperity.

Basically, an "Andy" guy, posing as a high-end building contractor's agent, would spend months courting and becoming close friends with prospective clients such as large hotel and casino owners, and GMs in five-star hotels, all over the country. He would begin by renting a high-end apartment in the respective town and throwing lavish parties, procuring beautiful "girlfriends" when needed, giving expensive gifts, and doing the occasional legit deal, where he would purposely bend the profit in favor of the client. This showed his worth and established trust, and he eventually became "their guy"; they would then move him into a suite in their hotels. Never in a hurry, though—he would come and go, doing "business" in

London, Paris, and various glamorous cities, returning to Vegas (or Miami, or wherever else) to close the final big money deal, which was either an extensive renovation, a brand-new piped-in oxygen system, or a new addition to their hotel—for which he would then take a hefty deposit to start the contractors. Then he would swiftly and totally vanish, carrying however many millions he had procured, usually in the form of a check that was miraculously cashed in less than twelve hours. A few years would pass, where the obligatory erasing of the old identity and procurement of a new one would take place, all the while making sure a financial low profile was kept. Then a new "*Andy*" would emerge, with a different name and identity, and start all over again.

Everyone knew the scam existed, but the key was—could you see the "sting" coming and . . . could you catch the culprit before your millions vanished into the hands of these very suave villains? The problem was that hotels and casinos were all getting facelifts in those days, so it wasn't unusual to have a building contractor's agent arrange everything and take hefty deposits. Andy D'Amato had easily scammed his name onto the agent list, allowing him to embezzle the Dunes out of two million in less than a week. God knows how much he'd taken out of the Eden Roc, which had most likely kicked off this round of swindling.

I had just been an "extra" in this con movie. His ruse had been the whole Judy Garland fiasco, along with the inclusion of my mother to ice the cake. God knows who the Rachmaninoff great-granddaughter chick was, and of course Marco and Pete the producers—characters on the chessboard of tricks and riddles.

I knew none of this as I sat shaking in Arte Riddle's office that afternoon. He asked me to tell him what I knew, and I told him the location of both the warehouse and the great-granddaughter gal. I later found out the warehouse had been a porno movie studio, and the Rachmaninoff gal's house was bare-floor empty. I did mention the limo belonged to the Desert Inn, and Arte said they too were looking for Andy.

Arte truly was the epitome of kindness. His arm went around my shoulder.

"It's a fucking shame. You're a beautiful girl, and that fucking moron thief took advantage of a beautiful girl's innocence." He squeezed me closer. "Bringing you here to Vegas, promising that you were going to be a movie star—it's just fucking wrong." His arm dropped as he went over to his desk and reached into a drawer. The arm went back around my shoulders. "You are a guest of the Dunes," he said, pressing a room key and two crisp hundred-dollar bills into my hand. "The front desk will take care of your first-class ticket back to London and your transport to the airport. Until then, sign for everything." His arm dropped and he held out his hand. "I'll take the keys to the Lincoln." I thankfully handed them over. He smiled and patted my hand. "You have a friend in Arte Riddle and the Dunes Hotel. You're welcome anytime." He meant every word.

Three days later, I was back in London where things felt different. It was weird . . . I missed Vegas, even though it'd gotten hairy. I'd called my mother from the Dunes, telling her I was coming home, supplying the necessary Cliffs Notes of the Vegas story, which seemed to appease her enough to keep her from asking too many questions. Yet again, I had disappointed her. When I walked into our cold house and dropped my bags in the ever-freezing hallway, Mother was standing in the doorway of the kitchen, drying a plate.

"Well, what happened?"

"Nothing. The movie got canceled." I really didn't want to do this.

"Why?"

"I don't know, maybe money."

She turned and walked back into the kitchen, calling over her shoulder. "Well, I hope you've learned your lesson. I'm making tea."

What lesson?

Oliver had recovered and wasn't mad at me anymore, but I think he was in trouble with the police. He said he'd been let go from the Boulogne because another act had brought in their own pianist, but Sally told me he'd been caught stealing the band money.

"I might go and live in America with my cousin Sylvia," he said casually.

"Who? What cousin?" You think you know a person, and then it turns out you don't.

"You don't know her—she's wonderful."

Barry and Mariam had gotten divorced, which was sad and painful, and her mother, who lived in the Grosvenor House hotel, was dying. I would sit with Mariam for hours in her big townhouse, helping her cope with both losses. Steve was making a new album in Los Angeles, and as usual—and once again—I didn't have a job. I knew I should start the hunt again, but my heart wasn't in it. Mother was her usual depressed, disappointed self, worrying about being poor—actually no one was particularly interested in what I'd been doing, and that was fine; I wasn't interested in telling anyone.

And then I had a resounding thought—it was time to leave.

Six weeks later, I was on a plane to Los Angeles with Arte's two hundred dollars in my pocket, a single suitcase, no driving license, and the name and address of Oliver's other British cousin, Michael. Oliver had arranged for me to stay with him and his son, Ashley, until I got settled doing . . . something. I'd figure it out. Plus, Oliver promised he'd be out there soon to see Sylvia. I told mother I was going to have a look at California, a holiday of sorts.

I only knew one thing. I was gone. Really gone.

Chapter 32

Los Angeles

Michael and Ashley lived on La Jolla Avenue, two blocks east of La Cienega and one block south of Olympic, in a pretty house with a cool little backyard full of flowers. After the gloom and gray of England, the abundant sunny days of California were nothing short of dreamy. Michael was beyond kind, and his son was a sweetheart. They'd both met me at the airport with flowers and the warmest welcome.

Ashley was seventeen, still in school, and Michael was in his midforties, working as the manager of the furniture department at Bonwit Teller. He took immense pride in his job, carefully dressing each day as if he were meeting with nobility. He wore two shirts daily, each perfectly laundered and starched, one that he left wearing in the morning and one that he would change into after lunch. I don't think I have ever known such a clean, crisp man. He always had a tan, and it was real. Sunday was his sunning day in the garden, and he would lay on a cushioned chaise, sipping his gin and tonic.

"Getting golden, darling!" He was hilarious with a great sense of humor, and we would laugh about how great it was not to be in England. We'd have endless conversations about the gloom and doom and rotten weather we'd left behind. I would often ask him about his life, but he scoffed my questions away. "Oh, darling, I'm just an old bore. Nothing interesting to know!"

He advised me to take my time figuring out if I wanted to stay in the US and let me know I was welcome in their home for as long as I liked. But he said that if I decided to stay, I'd have to figure out how to become legal. Michael explained that he had a green card and Ashley had been born in New York, so that made them both legitimate residents. At the very least, I would need a Social Security card to open a bank account and get any kind of job. Bank accounts could wait; my princely sum of two hundred dollars wasn't going to last long. Maybe I could get a job singing somewhere without a work permit? Michael thought it was a great idea, and knowing full well I didn't have a driving license, he didn't seem to care and kindly let me use Ashley's car while he was in school. Every day I drove around this insane town trying not to get stuck, constantly getting lost on the endless freeways and avoiding LA's finest on their motorcycles.

I ended up hanging out a lot at Tower Records on Sunset Boulevard, chatting with all the musicians, and that's where I heard they were auditioning acts at Budd Friedman's Improv Club. Studying the latest Van Halen album was a guy I had talked to a few times. I couldn't remember his name and wasn't always keen on talking with people I didn't know well, but I bravely walked over.

"Hello," I said.

"Hey, what's up?" he said, his eyes staying on the album cover.

"Does the Improv hire singers?" I chirped.

He looked at me kinda funny. "Don't know. Go down and ask—Budd's cool."

The Improv on Melrose and Mitzi Shore's Comedy Store on Sunset Boulevard were the places to be seen and discovered. Great! I just had to get the gig, then be there long enough to be seen, liked, and "discovered." With a renewed sense of purpose and optimism, I asked Ashley to drive me to Melrose Avenue. We pulled up outside the club.

"I'll wait for you."

"Okay. Thanks."

I walked into the Improv, coming face-to-face with Budd Friedman. With his famous monocle dangling by his lapel, he was a no-nonsense, down-to-earth guy who loved comedians and performers and made a point of helping them get a break. Budd could be fierce—they called him "The Benign Dictator"—but he created magic in that tiny place, and people came out of it transformed. Budd looked me up and down when I entered.

"Mr. Friedman?" I asked.

"Budd," he corrected. "What do you do?"

"I sing."

"Can you play?"

"Play?"

"Piano, guitar . . . ?"

"Oh, no, I just sing. Do you have singers here?"

"We do." He smiled.

"Do you have an accompanist?" I asked. He kept smiling.

"You're British."

"Yes, I am." Was that something?

He walked away, indicating for me to follow. Holding my sheet music closely, I trailed after him down the hallway to a large room crammed chair to chair with checkered cloth–covered tables. The walls were decorated with giant murals, and the elevated stage was big enough to hold the baby grand piano that sat off to the side. I later found out the bricks on the back wall were made of plastic. The scene was completed with a lone microphone standing sentry center stage.

"Go ahead, jump up and sing." Budd waved me to the stage and called out to a guy in the back of the room. "Jimmy, got a minute to play for this young lady?"

Budd switched on the microphone, and it beeped into life as Jimmy ambled over to the piano. I'd brought my music and handed it to Jimmy. He peered at it for a minute, then played the intro to "Queen Bee" by Barbra Streisand. Budd stood in the doorway, watching as I finished the song and stepped off the stage. Jimmy wordlessly went back to whatever he was doing, and I walked over to Budd.

"You can have the seven p.m. slot. Two songs, Fridays and Saturdays." He started walking back to the front door. I followed.

"Mr. Friedman?"

"Budd."

"Budd. For how long?"

"As long as you don't empty the room."

"How much do I get paid?"

At this, Budd stopped dead, turned, and stared at me, laughing. "You're funny. Do you do comedy?"

"No, I don't think so." What did that mean? He took my arm and pulled up a couple of stools to the bar.

"Sit."

I sat, and for the next fifteen minutes, Budd educated me on working the clubs in town. You auditioned, be it as a singer or comedian, for the privilege of being able to perform onstage in front of the public, for free.

"Oh, okay."

He must have seen the disappointment in my face. "Hey, try and put some funny in your act. Bette Midler tries out her new material here sometimes—she's funny and a hell of a singer. Johnny's scouts are here regularly." He stood up and patted my hand. "See you Friday. Don't be late, otherwise you'll lose your slot." I figured "Johnny" must be Johnny Carson.

"How'd it go?" Ashley asked as he started the car.

"I'm not sure. I sang my song and Budd gave me a slot, and I'll sing two songs on Fridays and Saturdays for no money, hopefully catching the eye of Johnny Carson's scout and get three minutes on *The Tonight Show*, even though it looks like he only gives slots to new comedians."

Ashley's face brightened. "Hey, maybe you'll be the first unknown singer to get a slot."

"It'll never happen. I'm not funny . . . I mean, I'm not a comedian."

"You never know." He spoke with confidence. "*The Tonight Show* is where everyone starts, you make *me* laugh, and this is LA—anything can happen. Living the dream, baby!"

My current dream had been to get out of England—I'd done that, and now I'd pretty much run out of dreams. Singing had been one . . . but . . . should I try and do comedy instead? Would that be a better way to go? Was I funny? I'd have to talk and write a funny act, write jokes—I hated jokes—and make people laugh, a lot . . . and . . . all of which was . . . mind-blowingly terrifying and out of the question. I was living such a rattled life—nothing about it seemed funny. I didn't see, then, that I could have stopped and asked myself one question: What did I really want?

Singing was something I knew I could scramble along with, but did I enjoy it? When I stood onstage, I always felt anxious and scared—not so much of being onstage; it was the singing part that made me nervous. When the song was over, I'd vamp-chat as long as I could until the music started and I had to sing again. That's when nausea and panic reared their ugly heads and I inevitably forgot lyrics or blew a flat note and fell into the dragon's mouth. *I thought* I was smart and knew exactly what I *had* wanted. Remember? Liza Minnelli, retired from her career, living in some lovely beach house far away so I could take over? Ridiculous.

Now, the great Budd Friedman had given me a slot at his improv show, so I couldn't be that bad. Hey, Rod Stewart sounded like a cheese grater and he'd done pretty well, right? Wasn't there room for the odd and different? Living in my mind was like living in an orchestra pit with everyone tuning their instruments at the same time. I did know I didn't want to go back to London ever again, and I believed to my core that this was now my home. I knew with absolute conviction that I was going to be fine and good things would come to me when they were ready to.

Michael drove me to the club the following Friday, and we arrived early.

"I'll wait in the car," he told me.

"Don't be silly. I might be here late, and it's only a fifteen-minute walk home."

Michael paled in horror. "Oh, darling. *No one* walks in LA! My God. Call me and I'll come and pick you up." He shook his head as if recovering from the shock. "Promise? I'll be up late."

I promised.

Budd greeted me from his desk at the front and said to go sit over with the guys at the bar to wait for my set. I pulled up a stool beside a young man with an impressive mop of black curly hair.

"Hi," I said.

He smiled. "Hi, who are you?"

"Juliette. I have the seven o'clock slot."

"I'm Jay." He thrust out his hand, and Jay Leno and I started chatting. The other guy eventually wandered over, and Jay introduced me. "Dave, this is Juliette."

David Letterman nodded, looking uncomfortable as he always would around people. "Dave's got the eleven p.m. slot."

The third guy at the other end of the bar waved.

"Richard. Good luck." He sounded tired.

At that moment, the front door flew open and a human tornado blew in—a five-foot-seven-inch-tall cyclone wearing a pair of baggy colorful pants, a brilliant Hawaiian shirt, and a very French beret. There was a blur of red and orange as he hurtled over to the bar and landed on a stool.

"YES!" He saw me, and a smile from beyond enveloped his face as he did two perfect pirouettes. "Ohhhh!" he crooned as he extended one finger like E.T. and touched my nose. He then squealed in delight and leapt a couple of feet into the air. "Pretty!" he squeaked and went into a thirty-second pantomime of sounds and actions that, together, created an insane reverberation of hilarity. He baby-gurgled, making sense of my nose, and drawled like a southern blues player looking for his hat, then sat himself on the bar, crossing his legs and transforming into an interior designer busy with redecorating the room. Finally, he jumped down, threw his arms around me, and gave me the best hug I have ever had. "Very pretty! Like flower!"

And that's how the incomparable Robin Williams came into my life. Here was genius you could see, touch, and feel. These were pre–*Mork & Mindy* days, and Robin was just another starving comedian working the nail-scraping crawl up the ladder of stand-up. He had the ten p.m. slot at the Improv, but he'd popped by before his set at The Comedy Store to visit. He plonked himself back onto a stool and we chatted, which was no easy feat. Keeping up with Robin was a workout in and of itself, but he was so kind and genuine that you willingly rode the wave of madness and brilliance pouring out of his mind. He took you from laughing until your body hurt to suddenly sad, then breathtakingly poignant, and back to hilarity all in the space of a couple of minutes. He was like no other.

It was now seven p.m. The main room was still empty. The stage was lit with spotlights trained on the brick wall. The microphone stood alone, center stage. Suddenly, I was terrified. This was not the Boulogne or Chaplin's—there was no Oliver and not even Mr. Oscar, who was evil but at least familiar. My hands started shaking—*shit*! Then at seven fifteen, Budd came over.

"Slow start tonight; better luck tomorrow. You're welcome to stay and watch." My relief was intense—no people meant no going on. I thanked Budd—and baby Jesus—and stayed to watch the show. That Friday night, and on many more nights to come, I watched history unfold as Jay Leno, David Letterman, Robin Williams, Larry David, Robert Klein, and Elayne Boosler—to name a few—stood on that tiny brick-backed stage and created brilliance. For the next twelve months, I became part of those who sat at the bar and waited for their set and, depending on the room count, I would either go on or not, but I would always sit and watch the acts well past the wee hours. I was present as each one rose a few notches in their careers—or didn't—and, justifiably, I developed a reverence for stand-up comedians. No one in the business works harder or suffers the slings and arrows of merciless rejection more than the funny guys.

I tried desperately to understand the darkness some would go through. I had no idea what depression was, but seeing the deep sadness in Robin, in those few moments when he was just—Robin—I learned more than I knew *how* to know. I saw Jay Leno finally get his spot on *The Tonight Show* and watched excitedly as Johnny asked him to sit down! Rock star! You were on your way with the king's blessing. Robin became Mork from Ork and rocketed to unbelievable fame in a matter of weeks, stunning the country with his extraordinary talent. I saw Andy Kaufman, Richard Pryor, George Carlin, and Billy Crystal turn that tiny room into a cavern of roaring laughter as their careers rose up and over. I also remember the ones who didn't make it, including some who took their lives in the pain of rejection. Needless to say, I was not "discovered." I didn't do funny, so there was no spot with Johnny, though I did learn how to work a room and, by the generosity of my fellow bar stool compatriots, I learned how to read a crowd. I learned what these guys' dreams meant to them and marveled at their resilience and stamina. I will always be eternally grateful to Budd Friedman for giving me the chance to be there at the Improv and bear witness to that historic time.

Oh—and Michael eventually broke down and let me walk home.

Chapter 33

The Kindness of Strangers

LA is a show business town and always has been since 1911 when the first movie studio opened. Of course, there's a civilian world there as well, but it's inconsequential when compared to what's always referred to as "The Business." It's a town that operates on who you know and how well you know them, which amounts to whether they will take your call or not. The last one's massive. If they do, you may have a shot at a career. Then there's the A- and B-list parties. For an aspiring actor, writer, songwriter, director, or scriptwriter, it's about being on the list for the right party. The A List was for the big guns, the heavy hitters, the super famous, and sometimes the ones desperately wanting to *stay* famous. The B list, more of the younger up-and-comers or reluctant returnees from fame gone by, a divided nation of those who would eventually get lucky and score an agent or job, or those who could no longer endure the pain and quit . . . after one last party, of course.

It was a brutal system, and the parties were critical for achieving success. Back in those days, they were pretty much the only way—other than if you were already working on a movie or TV show—to meet *anyone* who could maybe introduce you to *someone* who could introduce you to *another someone* who could *maybe* get you an agent and/or an audition for that movie or pilot TV show that *maybe* would get picked up for a series. Then there were the *other someones* who could get your script read, or your song heard, or introduce you to a guy who knew another agent or *anyone* higher up the food chain who might get you work. It was an unrelenting, constant nightmare of stress. The waiting alone in your apartment for The Phone Call was an endless mental highway of exhaustion. Those who made it were the ones who had the stamina and terminator-level strength to battle through the pain and misery of refusal at every corner. If you had talent—that was a bonus that could keep you working. But first you had to get the job—any job. Even if you didn't have talent but you were "interesting," that might help . . . but only if you met the right producer or agent who "liked" you. The system was just plain miserable.

It was a couple of years later, but I will never forget one afternoon, sitting on the living room floor of a modest Beverly Hills home with my friend, a prominent singer-songwriter, watching as she made maniacal, frantic phone calls to everyone she knew trying to find out IF she was going to be invited to a certain movie star's A-list party that following Saturday. She'd recently been dumped by a famous actor, and her career was teetering on the aging laurels of a two-year-old Academy Award nomination. She started crying as her poor addled brain tried to make sense of why she hadn't received The Call, and it was looking precariously close to her not being invited—which was terrifying and unacceptable! Especially since that fucking bitch L***** was going *with* the movie star who'd just dumped her! It was extraordinary, watching this sweet lady crumble in panic as she tried to claw back her fading career.

Transport had now become a "must," and through a friend of Ashley's, I managed to acquire an ancient, ugly, paint-chipped Chevy station wagon. The friend wanted to get rid of it and just gave it to me.

Beware of people giving you very old, very free cars.

I carefully drove it around, managing not to get stopped, in which case I would have had to show the officer a license that didn't exist, ignoring the coughing and spluttering and all sorts of sounds and smells that indicated bad things were coming. Michael's mechanic looked at it and basically told me that the vehicle was a solid piece of crap heading toward the last days of its life. Nevertheless, I was going to give it those last days and deal with the consequences whenever they arrived. One day, I was driving to Warner Bros. Studio to audition for Jerry Bruckheimer and Don Simpson, whom I'd met while visiting Dick Donner. Dick and I were pals now, and he was being particularly kind, telling me it was a hard business and if there was anything else I could possibly do—do it—but go ahead and give movies a try, because Jerry and Don were good guys and, hey, you never know!

"You could get lucky, kid, and make it!" Such sound advice.

On my way to the audition, I got as far as the 101 (Ventura Freeway), and the car died with a loud clunk and a gush of black smoke—an all-too-familiar scenario. I pulled off on the side of the road and watched the cars whizzing by, not having the slightest clue what to do. Ah . . . life before cell phones! A kind person stopped, pulled a shiny Nissan onto the shoulder in front of me, and called AAA, which arrived, called time of automobile death, gave me a lift home, and took my ancient Chevy station wagon to its grave, accompanied by my one-time opportunity at the big time, as I never got another audition.

My two-hundred-dollar stash had crept its way down to fifty dollars, and I had to do something that didn't require a work permit. I also absolutely had to get a car, this time one that wasn't going to blow up. I wasn't particularly worried. I had to make a little magic happen, although I had to make it happen fast. Then . . . out from the universe, magic appeared in the form of Jack-Who-Lived-Next-Door. One evening, I was standing in the front yard smoking a cigarette, when a young hippie guy with blond dreads and a tie-dye shirt came barreling over from the direction of the flower bed. I had seen him coming and going and we'd said "hey" in passing but never talked.

"Hi." He put out his hand and we shook. "How's it going? I'm Jack." We sat on Michael's garden bench and talked for almost an hour. He lived next door with his parents, explaining he was a comedian but "coolin' it" between gigs right now, and I have no idea why, but I ended up telling this scrappy-looking kid all my problems. He listened intently, then stopped me when I got to the Social Security card part. "Oh, I can help you there! Easy-peasy!"

He ran into his house and came back with pen and paper. He took my name and birthday, and a week later we were back on Michael's garden bench with Jack handing me a brand-new Social Security card. I was dumbfounded.

"What is this?" I asked him.

"What does it look like?" he quipped back.

"Is it real?"

"Yup."

"Really? Like legal real?"

"Yup. Really, legal real. My sister works at Social Security and processed your paperwork. You applied and got accepted."

"But . . . I didn't have any paperwork and . . . she doesn't know me."

"I know you and she's cool. Besides, your application was accepted."

I looked at the official and very legitimate Social Security card in my hand and realized this was one of those moments when a tiny window opens and you understand there just may be some kind of Divine Being living in a Divine Universe that every now and again looks down and does shit for you.

"Also . . ." Jack handed me a phone number. "Call Jimmy and he'll set you up for a job where I work. You can ride in with me. I earn good money."

"Doing what?"

"Selling stuff over the phone, all totally above board." He beamed and did an awfully bad impersonation of Steve Martin. "I'm a legal kinda guy!"

With flashbacks to my PLO driving license, I pocketed the precious Social Security card. That afternoon, I called Jimmy and got hired over the phone. He ran what was called a "boiler room," where anyone from anywhere could come and work. You sat in a large basement with about twenty-five other people, all sitting in tiny cubicles facing the wall. The job involved cold-calling businesses in every state to try and sell them, in this case, photocopy paper. The businesses had no idea who you were and really didn't want to talk to you, so you ended up making fifty odd calls a day hoping that one or two might hit. Printed on a laminated card and hanging on the wall in front of each tiny desk was our "pitch," and we had to follow every word religiously.

Jimmy's operation wasn't particularly scrupulous, and he hired just about anyone, from illegals to ex-convicts to hookers to homeless people. If you could sell, he made money, and you made 25 percent commission for everything you sold. Jimmy would sit in the center of the room at a huge, ornate wooden table, processing the orders, the music coming from his cassette player seemingly only playing Johnny Cash on an endless revolving track. Jack and I sat at either end of the room, and I think I can honestly say it was the most dreadful, depressing thing I have ever done. I was ostensibly one of the early telemarketers. It was a humiliating and degrading experience I would never wish on anyone.

Primarily, we called the East Coast, so our workday started at five a.m. and ended at eleven a.m. People shouted at me, cursed me, told me I was a scam—how dare I inconvenience them—and, still cursing, would slam their phones down. Even though I did manage to sell, getting up at four a.m. physically hurt. I was miserable and, most of all, suspicious. There was a noticeable lack of inventory, with no boxes of photocopy paper waiting to be shipped and no deliveries ever made or received. I asked Jack, who shrugged and vaguely said Jimmy probably had some shipping warehouse somewhere. No, I was pretty sure he *didn't*—and that we were selling nothing to innocent people and taking their money.

One Friday, about four weeks in, I took a smoke break and thought about it. Yesterday I had sold a bunch of photocopy paper and made two hundred bucks. Jimmy gave you your money in cash at the end of each morning. Here was my dilemma: Should I be righteous and walk away from an obvious criminal operation? Or should I just make enough money to buy a car? To paraphrase Charles Dickens, "These were desperate times, when desperate games were played for desperate stakes."

I made a decision.

I would stay long enough to make three thousand dollars. That would be enough to purchase a car in decent shape, and God would understand, because this was one of those odd moments of immorality that was necessary in the name of survival. It took another three months of wretchedness until the day finally came and Jimmy handed me $700, which brought my grand total of earnings to $3,500.

I left, never to return. Jack drove me to a used-car dealership in Pasadena, where I bought the prettiest car on the lot for $2,500. It was a shiny bronze Cadillac Coupe de Ville, at least twenty feet long, with a white leather interior and a white roof. The salesman told me it had belonged to a pimp in Hollywood who'd just got busted and was doing twenty years, but the pimp had cared for the car like a baby. I too loved that car as much as anyone can love a machine. It retained a faint smell of patchouli for as long as I owned it, and I loved that too—it reminded me of Jimi Hendrix. That car was everything England was not. I thanked Jack, telling him that he'd gone over and above for me, a total stranger. He said it was nothing he wouldn't do for a friend. I then drove back to Michael's in my beyond-fabulous car and parked it behind his Volvo. I saw the curtains part and Michael's horrified eyes peek through the crack of the window. Twenty seconds later, he barreled out and stopped dead when he saw me in the driver's seat.

"Darling! What on earth is that?"

"Isn't it fabulous?"

"I thought you were a gangster!"

"I bought it from a pimp." I felt very hip and cool. "He's in jail."

"It'll eat gas," Michael said as he shook his head at my madness.

"I don't care. It's gorgeous and so un-British!"

"You'd better get a driving license." He must have noticed me grinning. "Which you can't do without a Social Security card." I continued smiling. "And don't forget insurance, because . . . why are you *smiling*?"

"We don't have that problem anymore," I said. "I have a number."

"We don't? How did you . . . ? Oh well, doesn't matter—that's great." He was confused, poor darling.

"You'll probably have to take the test in Ashley's car because you *certainly* can't use . . . that."

"Okay, thanks Michael." I was in a particularly good mood.

Michael looked at me, shook his head again, and went back inside.

A few weeks later, I was on my way out, though I still hadn't gotten a driving license or dealt with insurance—I figured I'd get around to all of it soon—when I saw Jack pulling out of his driveway in his beat-up VW van. Through the hiccupping of black fumes, he waved and shouted, "Good luck! Going to do a gig in Omaha!" And Jack was gone. He'd basically blown into my life and saved it. Now our short-lived friendship was over, and I never saw him again.

Chapter 34

Yusuf Islam

Having transport made a huge difference, but even though I was studying the test book without an actual driving license, it was quite nerve-wracking being constantly on the lookout for those men on motorcycles. There was something ominous about the LA bike cops. Maybe it was the gold-rimmed Ray-Ban sunglasses, along with the almost Germanic top boots—or the guns strapped to their sides in plain view, I'm not sure, but after the British bobbies with their singular truncheons, these guys were some scary dudes.

My car seemed to eat a tremendous amount of oil, along with copious gallons of gas, and now and again made odd coughing sounds. I didn't exactly care—I had glamorous wheels, a few bucks, and somewhere to live . . . oh, and Mother wasn't here. I dutifully made the occasional phone call home, ensuring her incoming fame was just around the corner, and with the appropriate amount of positivity and excitement, I described the Improv as a glitzy, trendy nightclub full of famous people who thought I was great. Mother was suitably impressed. Finally, I took the driving test in Ashley's car and passed.

Then I decided to make The Call to Steven.

He had told me he was going to be in town for a few months, either making or finishing an album—I couldn't remember. I found the number he'd given me—the office of his manager, Barry Krost—and stared at it for a while. I hated making phone calls, due largely to that irrational fear of calling at the wrong time and maybe upsetting the recipient of my call, causing him to begin to avoid me and avoid taking my call forevermore. In this case, I was about to call a big-time manager and ask a secretary to give Cat Stevens a message "from a friend." How many times did *that* happen in a day? Steve had become enormously famous, and even though we'd hung out at home in London, why on earth would he want to see me here, alone and thereby out of context, with none of our friends around? He'd probably given me the number to be polite, right? I really shouldn't call. Damn it! This neurosis was all my mother's fault—she always used to thrust the phone into my hand for me to make the call, to either the bank manager or a debt collector or someone in authority who was coming to get us for the plethora of unpaid bills.

"You call. You're good at this. Make them go away."

I always did, and I hated it.

I went into the kitchen and picked up the phone. My mouth went paper dry while dialing the number, and I hung up. After taking a deep breath, I gave it another try, and a nice secretary answered.

"Oh, hello," my words rattled out. "My name is Juliette and . . . umm . . . I'm a friend . . . a good friend of Steven . . . Cat Stevens, and he said to call this number and you would tell him . . . I'm here in LA."

"That's great. What's your number?"

I dictated the numbers of my home phone in a trembling voice.

"Great, I'll give him the message."

"Oh, right. Thank you."

"You're very welcome! Have a nice day!" she said with super perkiness.

To my shock and surprise, Steve called that evening sounding happy and saying how brave I was coming to LA all by myself and would I like to go to dinner tomorrow evening? My heart stopped. Yes, I would love to. I gave him Michael's address, and he said he would pick me up at seven. I hung up the phone and started crying. The love of my life was taking me out to dinner. I knew he wasn't a casual person who went on casual dates, so . . . did that mean . . . we were? I told myself I wouldn't think about it until after I had seen him. There was simply no point in speculating on such a gross unknown and thoroughly torturing myself in the process.

The next evening the doorbell rang promptly at seven p.m. I'd told Michael I was going to dinner with a "friend," so when he opened the door and saw Steve, he literally gasped and staggered. I came out of the kitchen, and Michael was holding the door handle with a vise grip to stop his knees buckling.

"Darling!" His voice sounded at least an octave higher. "You never told me who your friend was!"

Steve shook his hand. "Hello, I'm Steve."

"Yes! Yes! I know!" Michael was beyond jubilant. "I have every record you've ever made and more! Please, come in. Sit, can I get you a drink? We have everything!"

"No, thanks." Steve politely took a step back; I think Michael was overwhelming him. I stepped forward before it toppled into "awkward." A few moments of small talk and we left, with Michael waving goodbye from the doorway.

"Come to dinner! I'm a marvelous cook! You'll meet my son, Ashley—we're 'Father and Son'!" He was so happy he'd just thought that up.

I can't remember where we went that evening, but I do remember how strange it felt being with him again. I realized how much I still loved him, but ten years was a long time and much had changed—*I* had changed. I can still hear his voice as we were sitting in Mr. Chow's restaurant, eating our Chinese noodle bowl.

"I've embraced Islam. I am now Muslim. I have surrendered to God," he said with great seriousness. *What? You've done what?* my brain whispered.

"Ah. Okay, I understand," I said with not an ounce of conviction but definitely a few pounds of shock. He explained David, his brother, had given him the Koran to read, and it spoke to him as nothing else ever had.

"I'm learning to speak Arabic. I want to read the Qur'an without a translation," he said, looking deep into my eyes. Was I supposed to say

Me and Cat Stevens, reunited in 1978

something meaningful? "I have changed my name. I am now Yusuf Islam, and please . . . from now on . . . call me *only* by my chosen Muslim name." He waited for my reply. I moved a piece of chicken around my plate. Jesus this was weird. He looked hopeful. I could only hope this was one of those odd phases he sometimes went through.

My response was wobbly.

"Okay, so . . . that might be a bit difficult . . . awkward. I mean, this is so fast. I've known you ten—"

"But you are Muslim." I will say I was impressed he'd remembered I was Muslim, but I didn't have the heart to tell him it was only on paper. I almost brought up Mohammed's sister but ultimately decided that would be a bad idea. He continued in a soft voice, "Maybe this, you and me, maybe it was meant to be." I lit a cigarette and drank a gulp of wine. He moved the wine glass and plucked the cigarette out of my fingers. "I would ask that you give up drinking and smoking immediately." Seriously? This was happening?

"Okay." I nodded.

"I will teach you Arabic." I nodded.

"A Muslim is someone who serves God and is a servant to him," he added.

My brain was rattled. What did "meant to be" mean? Meant to be what? And what did this "serve God" business mean? He said he was going to be coming and going to and from LA on a regular basis and we would now be together—it was more of a proclamation than anything else, and of course, all I could see was that here was the love of my life sitting before me and we were back together again and "meant to be" could mean . . . what? Did this mean he thought we could be something *permanent?* But this God thing was a troubling caveat. I wanted to ask him if he loved me, but I was too scared to hear the answer.

Chapter 35

Goodbye to the Stars in My Soul

B eing back with Steven—I just could not call him Yusuf—was both fabulous and awful. He would travel back and forth from LA, to London and other places, sometimes with weeks in between. He did finally come to dinner at the house, and dear Michael had every piece of Wedgwood bone china and Waterford crystal he owned carefully set at each place setting. He'd spent all day preparing an elaborate dinner of shrimp cocktail followed by roast pork, mashed potatoes, and green peas from his garden. There were also copious amounts of red and white wine—cocktails were to be served first.

Watching him put the pork in the oven, I was in a horrible dilemma. There was the wine thing, then I had a really bad feeling about the pork situation. Pork and Muslims *do not* go together. As Michael was peeling potatoes, singing the lyrics to "Morning Has Broken," I knew I should have said something, but I didn't, and what followed was nothing short of excruciating. Steven politely refused the shrimp, pork, and of course the wine. He picked at a small amount of mashed potatoes and peas on Michael's Wedgwood bone china dinner plate, and we all ate in the dreadful silence of the embarrassed. I felt so bad. Could I have prevented this? Of course, but overcome with the whole thing, I hadn't said anything, thinking and, well, hoping maybe Steve hadn't quite gotten to the food thing yet. Dinner was over quickly, and conversation over coffee was . . . stilted. We left to go back to the hotel—this time, there was no Michael waving from the porch.

Then there were the wonderful days where Steve and I would go for walks and to A&M and Island Records, both, at the time, the largest independent record labels in history. In the US, many of Island's record releases were issued on A&M, hence we visited both studios. We would also have wonderful dinners, but talking to him now was different and almost difficult. He had discovered his final calling in life and was passionately obsessed with his purpose in Islam and learning the Koran. He said this was going to be his last album and he was thinking about leaving the business, which included getting rid of everything connected with his musical past. Knowing I had taught myself to play guitar in London, he gave me his precious Ovation.

I was still too young to have an adult understanding of what was happening. I loved him so much and I was trying so hard to *like* his new way of life, which was completely foreign to me. I was also trying so hard to believe I could be a part of it. The smoking thing came up again. He said I needed to stop immediately, so every time I drove to L'Ermitage, the hotel he stayed when in LA, I would chain-smoke cigarettes during the twenty-minute journey. I always stayed the night, so I got in as many as I could, driving slowly to the hotel.

Everything would be lovely until it was prayer time. Muslims pray five times a day.

I tried to be supportive and understanding, but it was hard—I didn't get it and, honestly, I didn't really want to get it. At dawn, the low drone of his voice would wake me up with a jolt. In the evenings, I would sit on the bed, watching and listening, feeling more awkward than I can ever describe. Our intimate moments were just . . . uncomfortable. Yes, we did make love, but there was that detachment, that coldness. I had this distinct feeling his higher calling was occupying his entire being and had propelled him into this strict world of emotional dedication to one thing—God. It was not my world, but . . . would I jump in and be a part of it? For love?

It was a miserable decision. Steve was my world, and I knew in order to be a part of that world, I would have to wholly embrace this new calling. My father had been Muslim, but I never saw him praying five times a day or devotedly following the practices of Islam. Dad drank wine and his beloved gin and tonics every evening and usually partook in a brandy to end a meal. He knew how much to drink and never did I see him overindulge. I realized Steven's Islam was a brand-new way of life *I knew* would be impossible for me to accept. Yet, I said nothing, thinking, hoping that again, maybe it was just a passing curiosity and he'd be back soon.

One day, I arrived at the hotel and he announced he would be going to New York City in a couple of days to meet with some producers. He asked if I'd like to come along. I had never been to New York, so of course I wanted to go. Two days later, we were on a plane heading east, and for practically the entire flight, he was teaching me how to read the Koran in Arabic. I was impressed with how much he had already learned, but I had to concentrate on not letting my mind wander. Trying to comprehend a language that, to me, looked to be written in a bunch of random squiggles—not to mention, you read backward—was hopeless. He was very patient and showed me how to write my name in Arabic. He kept looking at me with an "isn't this great?" kind of look. I smiled and nodded as energetically as I could.

We got to New York, and the car took us to The Carlyle Hotel on Madison Avenue, where Steven always stayed when he was in the city. The hotel had an old-world elegance from the thirties. In the elevator, he leaned in and whispered, "Did you know this hotel has a scandalous history?"

Wait. Did I just hear what I heard? Steve had gossip? I was elated. Maybe he was back! He went on to tell me that, when John F. Kennedy was president, this hotel had become known as "The New York White House," and for the last ten years of his life, Kennedy owned an apartment on the thirty-fourth floor. A few days prior to his inauguration in January 1961, he stayed at the apartment, entertaining a widely publicized visit from Marilyn Monroe, who was sneaked in through the service entrance on East Seventy-Seventh Street.

"Cool stuff!" I said. He laughed. I laughed back—yay.

The following day, he didn't have any meetings, so we took a long walk around Central Park. He held my hand and told me how happy he was and how his life was now complete. I didn't know what to feel or think or whether I should say anything. In the distance, we heard a guitar playing, and the strains of "Peace Train" filled the air. Then rounding the corner, Steve put his hand on my arm.

"Look." He pointed to a young man sitting on the ground against a tree, playing the guitar, his back toward us as we walked over. Steve went around and stood in front of him, smiling. "Sounds pretty good." The man's face drained of color and his mouth literally dropped open; he was speechless. Steven knelt and took the guitar from him, gently stating, "You haven't quite got this right." And he played that familiar riff we all know—the riff that makes that song "Peace Train." He then gave the guitar back to the man, who was yet to say a word or move from his position, and touched his shoulder. "Allah be with you," he said, and we walked away.

The next day was packed with meetings, so Steve suggested I see the city and do some shopping—he gave me fifty dollars and left. Now, I was the sort of person who would get lost, hopelessly and irrevocably, even with a map—which I didn't have. To this day, I have a directional curse that has never left me. My brain can't seem to figure out how I went where I did or how to get back from there, maybe because I never digested the process while going in the first place. I didn't know New York, and I especially didn't know it was a grid, with numbered streets across and avenues up and down, making it easy for even the most directionally challenged person.

I decided the safest thing to do was to walk Madison Avenue in a straight line, up and down. Oh, that's another thing. You would never say "Avenue" or "Street" but just say the name itself, as in Madison, Park, Fifth, and so on. Get this wrong and you scream newbie! Madison Avenue is just over six miles long, and I got as far as Thirty-Fourth Street before I turned around, remembering I still had fifty bucks in my pocket. At Sixty-Fifth, I suddenly stopped dead beside the most beautiful store I had ever seen. In the window, perched on a silver shoe stand, hung a pair of fire engine red stilettos with three-inch silver heels. Now, I'm not a big shoe person, but these were a work of art, and in those days—thanks largely to the Playboy Club—I was *comfortable* walking all day in high heels. They were priced at $49.50. I walked into the store and stood in the middle of a very glittery room. A pretty, lively young lady arrived in front of me.

"Can I help you?"

I pointed to the red shoes. "May I try them on?"

"Of course!" She bounced away, returning moments later holding a beautiful gold and silver box. She parted the frosted tissue paper and reverently handed the shoes to me. I put them on and my heart fluttered. Not with joy at these wonders on my feet but at hearing a quiet voice in my head. The quiet voice of reason.

"Not a good idea. Don't do it. Listen to the flutter," it said.

I took the shoes off and handed them to the pretty, lively girl. "I'm so sorry—they're not quite right. Thank you anyway."

"No problem. Thanks for coming in! Have a nice day!" And off she bounced.

Back at the hotel, I sat on the bed, realizing as much as it may have pained me, I'd done the right thing. Although I could have bought them and hidden them, I'm not that kind of person. But then again, if I'd bought them, could I honestly see myself holding them up like a proud parent? "Aren't they gorgeous?" Nope. Something way deep down inside—that feeling no one should ever ignore—was saying I'd done the right thing. The respectful thing.

I turned on the TV—*Godfather II* had just started, then about ten minutes later Steve came back. He looked happy.

"We have dinner reservations at seven."

The evening was lovely, we chatted about everything, and I really tried to listen. To understand him. To feel his joy for myself and join in with his enthusiasm, but I should have known I was heading down a slippery slope of cowardly deception. I should have told him I couldn't be this person, that this was *his* faith and could never be mine. The truth is, I was waiting for him to change back—to become Steve again. Love really is blind, and I was being disastrously optimistic in the face of the impossible.

Steve's business in LA came to an end and he went home to London. He had walked away from everything—his manager, his record company, and everything representing his incredibly successful career. He had given up the life he had known for the past twenty years and the music he had created that had become the tapestry of so many people's lives—for God. I don't know if anyone understood the courage that must have taken.

We would frequently talk on the phone and, one day, the call came asking me to come to London. Here it was. This was real. I mumbled and stumbled with words that were nothing but weak and spineless.

"I can't . . . no. I can't."

"Why?" Shock reverberated through his voice. "I'm buying a house in Hampstead."

"I can't walk behind you . . . covered in one of those black . . . covering things."

"It's called a hijab." His voice had become icy cold. "And why are you saying that?"

"Right. Yes, that. I can't do it."

"I never asked you to walk behind me. I never told you what to wear."

I didn't argue. There was no point. I sat on the edge of my bed listening to the silence echoing through the phone. I was confused. I wanted to hear the traditional, "I love you. Will you marry me?" But, despite my convenient confusion, I knew this had been coming, and . . . I knew I could have been kinder and more understanding. I shouldn't have been so inwardly contemptuous of an ancient tradition he wanted so much to embrace because—finally, he'd found the peace he'd craved for so many years. I also knew how much he wanted children, and I should have told him—a long time ago—that I didn't and never would want children. I should have explained that I'd looked after enough people in my life, and the thought of having more people to look after was . . . well . . . abhorrent. I should have respected the joy he felt at having finally found himself and been compassionate about that joy, but I couldn't see myself living as a traditional Muslim woman.

"I can't come." I felt sick. I also felt his disappointment at my refusal, but this was my fault—I'd been a coward—wishing, waiting, and hoping for an illusion that would never happen. He had every right to feel disappointed. I'd been dishonest. I'd never made it clear I couldn't be what he needed. I had said nothing, waiting and hoping for the Steven I knew to say, "I love you—will you marry me?" I had indicated all the while that I was ready and willing, all the while pretending to be someone I wasn't. Naturally, he'd assumed I would be eager to come and be with him. I would have been, if he was the way he used to be, which I see now was a cowardly excuse. Of course he wasn't going to be "the way he used to be"; that was just selfish on my part. But, on the other hand, I'd had my fill of the Arab world—I'd seen the darkest side possible and wanted no part of it. Our conversation ended with a chill.

"Then, this is goodbye," he said, and hung up.

The phone calls stopped, and he was gone. My dream of being with him for the rest of my life was over, and by my own hand—ten years of waiting had ended.

When I think back on that day, I remember it so vividly. I wish I could have been aware of how profound a lesson had been presented. Here was the man who was the love of my life, saying all the things I'd imagined him saying but asking me to be something I *couldn't ever imagine*. I was too young to understand that if you *intensely* focus your mind to manifest something, it *will* happen—you *will* get what you want, but it might not be on the terms you expected.

Chapter 36

Hugh Hefner and the Playboy Mansion

Knowing I wasn't going to be a married woman, I had to get another job, a real one that wasn't based on disreputable deeds. I was still doing my two songs at the Improv on weekends, but money had pretty much run out. Ashley suggested I try and find a job waitressing—there was a restaurant nearby on La Cienega and Melrose called the Melting Pot, and he'd heard they were hiring. Great! Armed with my newly minted Social Security card and recently acquired driving license, off I went to the Melting Pot. It was one of those cool LA bistro-type places, super trendy with pop music playing all the time.

I walked in and found the manager, Greg, told him my background with Playboy, and was hired on the spot. I would start with breakfast and lunch shifts to see how it went. If I was good, I'd graduate to dinners. I started work the next day, and by the end of my shift, I'd served Steve Martin breakfast, Stevie Wonder lunch, and made nearly twenty bucks in tips. I'd passed the audition! Greg was satisfied with my ability, and aside from the almost impossible task of trying to park my twenty-foot pimp-mobile every day, I was happy and relieved.

Early one evening, I was clearing out the side pockets of my suitcase and found the phone number for Playboy Mansion West.

"Call Hef when you get to town," Victor Lownes had said when I paid a visit to Playboy before I'd left London. He'd thrust a piece of paper into my hand. "I'll let him know you're coming."

That had been months ago and, as I have already mentioned, I would rather chew raw glass than make a phone call to the unknown. I had to work myself up to making the call. *It's not the bank manager*, I told myself. *Mother's not shoving the phone at you, and I highly doubt Mr. Hefner has been sitting by the phone waiting for your call. Just do it.*

In agony, I picked up the phone and dialed the number, which was immediately answered by Mary, Hefner's secretary. She was super kind and welcomed me to LA, saying she would talk to Hef and call me back. Two days later, I got the call inviting me to the Friday and Sunday night parties the following weekend. Mary gave me driving instructions and how to announce myself at the gate.

"See you Friday at six!" she chimed. She was very sparkly.

My heart thumped as anxiety hit hard. Yes, this would be a good way to get to know more people, but the thought of going to Hugh Hefner's house by myself, knowing no one, was nothing short of torturous. I looked at the driving directions, which might as well have been directions to a street in Shanghai.

In sharp contrast, Michael was hopping with excitement.

"Darling! Cat Stevens *and* Hugh Hefner? You're never moving out! I want all the details and gossip!" He was laughing as he threw me the massive fifteen-pound LA street map book. "It's a bitch to read, but you're going to need it."

Friday evening, I set off feeling nauseous. These were the days before GPS, so navigating LA was a challenge at the best of times, especially for a Brit on the "wrong" side of the road, shaking with nerves in a huge gold Cadillac that had suddenly started belching long fumes of black smoke. I got to Westwood, parked, consulted the book, and sort of figured out the maze that would lead me to the mansion. I set off, winding around the rolling green lawns of Holmby Hills, passing tall, ivy-covered brick walls shrouding the mega homes of the rich and famous. The roads were narrow and dark, as tall trees blocked out most of the sunlight, and just as I was sure I was hopelessly lost, I do believe God or baby Jesus took pity and delivered me to the Playboy Mansion. It literally came upon me as I bent the Cadillac around a tight, narrow curve, and there it was! A fifteen-foot wall parted to reveal a narrow gated driveway. The numbers on the curb matched my scrawl on the map book. I made the tight right turn, nearly hitting the massive iron gates that stood before me, blocking my passage. It was a very Sunset Boulevard moment.

I'd heard about this place—the mansion where the famous and potentially infamous would be among the guests, plus lots of beautiful girls. I put the car into reverse and started backing. I had no business being here, but—I put my foot on the brake—what if this turned out to be a golden opportunity? To what? I had no idea. Fuck it—no fear, and I was going in. I pulled up, stopping abruptly beside a pole that held up a black box with a keypad inside of it. I looked at my instructions from Mary, which told me to push the button. I leaned out the window and pushed.

"Name?" crackled the box. I responded hesitantly, speaking very loudly and slowly. (Why do we do that?) A long minute went by, then the gates opened inward, just like the entrance to heaven might open. I'm not sure I was breathing. A sharp right curve, then the steep driveway continued up and around a few hundred yards, ending in front of a beautiful Victorian mansion set among manicured gardens. A nattily dressed valet bounded up to my car and opened the door.

"Welcome to the Playboy Mansion," he told me.

I thanked him and stepped out as my car was whisked away, coughing black fog down the continuation of the driveway. I saw other people getting out of shiny cars that had nothing but fresh air coming out of their exhaust pipes, heading to the open front door, chatting together with the ease of familiarity. I was wracked with nerves, my stomach tight as a rubber band. What was the "routine" of the evening? Did you just walk in to "hang" and mingle? Did you get your own drink? Did you have to meet

Hef and wish him a good evening first? I felt paralyzed. Everyone seemed to know each other, and I was ready to get back in the car, when I realized... of course the car had disappeared to an unknown parking location. I was stuck. I felt sick to my rubber-band stomach. *Do not throw up!* I told myself. I had started shaking ever so slightly. *Shit!* I thought... and then, *Fuck it!* What would be, would be. I took a gulp of air and walked in.

The hallway was a big, open room with vaulted ceilings and wood-paneled walls. To the right, the dining room door stood open, revealing a large mahogany table and four smaller tables, set for dinner. Next to the dining room was an ante room leading to the kitchen. Left of the hallway were two *Gone with the Wind*–type staircases flanking a short corridor between them and leading back to the living room. Straight across the hallway, you stepped outside to the patio bar facing the gardens. In the distance, you could faintly hear the sounds of exotic birds and... monkeys?

The bartender was another pretty young man, and he politely asked me what I was drinking. I took a double shot of tequila to calm me down. The place was filling up. I saw Robert Culp talking to Bill Cosby; the director Richard Brooks was grumbling to Michael Cimino about the fucked-up state of the industry. Mac Davis was laughing with someone who looked famous, Bruce Jenner was socializing in very short white tennis shorts, and James Caan and Tony Curtis were sitting side by side at the bottom of the staircase, both staring at their drinks. More people kept walking in and greeting each other. I think I was smiling, but my face felt like it had frozen, immobile with paralyzing fear. Eventually everyone had arrived, mingling like they were in their own living room. I walked into the hallway, clutching my glass. My heart thumped, and I was in the process of figuring out how to leave, maybe feigning some awful illness that had just taken ahold of me, when Mel Tormé gave me a big smile as he passed and Robin Williams walked in. It wasn't his customary rocket-launch entrance—instead he stood quietly in the doorway looking as uncomfortable as I felt. Amid the hubbub of mingling—no one had noticed him yet—I literally ran to him.

"Yes! Friend!" he said with exuberant relief, grabbing my arm and steering me back to the bar. Over two strong cocktails—I was now feeling much happier with a friend and four drinks swirling around my head—Robin confessed he was scared shitless. This was the Bunny House of Infamy, housing Hugh Hefner and everything erotically erotic. Robin knew no one, but *everyone* knew him; Mork was here! One by one, people came up to revere and adore him, which was handy as they inadvertently greeted me too. All I had to do was smile and nod. It was a good slide in and, thanks to Robin, eventually I was chatting somewhat comfortably to people. About half an hour later, Hef came down the long stairs from rooms unknown dressed in red satin pajamas, with the familiar pipe positioned in the corner of his mouth and a beautiful blonde by his side. The evening had begun.

Hef greeted everyone and chatted with supreme ease to all his friends. All the while, I wondered, *Should I go and introduce myself?*

I was saved from making the decision by another pretty male waiter announcing dinner was served. We all went into the dining room, where an elaborate buffet was set out with more pretty men serving. I saw a four-seat, empty round table by the window and sat down. I figured I'd wait until people arrived at the buffet before I would get in line, although I had no appetite whatsoever. Robin had been guided to another table and was seated with a group of famous and almost-famous guys—he waved to me reassuringly.

The three empty chairs around me were quickly filled. Dick and Annie Stewart were the first. Dick had hosted his own TV show back in the late sixties and was one of Hef's closest friends, and Annie had starred as the 1967 Playboy Centerfold. They were mansion fixtures. A minute later, Robert Culp joined us. I am painfully shy around strangers, but thankfully, all three of them made me feel welcome, and I instantly fell into easy conversation. Annie, knowing I was "new," explained the way of the mansion. It was run on an exacting schedule of activities, with Sunday being a regular evening of dinner and socializing, and Friday being first-run movie night. Hef, like the nearby Spellings, was on the "Bel-Air circuit," an "inside" name for a loop of homes that had access to movies as they hit the theaters. Hef was a devotee of all things film, and he used to say, "My life comes from the movies."

The garden of the Playboy Mansion

Every Friday, after dinner, Hef would come into the dining room to do his rounds of the tables, politely conversing with everyone. The corner round table was his last visit, and it was immediately obvious my table mates were some of his closest friends. Dick introduced me, and Hef was charming.

"Welcome to the Playboy Mansion," he said. He then turned to the room to give his familiar sing-song announcement. "Iiiitttt's movie time!"

Everyone stood up, and we all walked back between the *Gone with the Wind* staircases and into the living room, which was set up with about twenty plush armchairs that faced a full-sized movie screen. That first evening, Dick and Annie invited me to sit with them on the coveted velvet cushions, spread on the floor in front of Hef and the current girlfriend's chair. Those cushions, reserved only for The Chosen, became my place on movie night for the next three years, as well as the round dining table by the window.

I will be forever grateful to Dick and Annie for including me as part of the family. They had no idea I wasn't used to thoughtfulness and people being aware of my painful shyness—they'd just given their friendship without question. Since I'd come to LA, I'd been shown more unconditional kindness from total strangers than I ever could have imagined. From where he sat on his chair behind the cushions, occasionally Hef directed a few words in my direction; once I even made him laugh. He never spoke to me much. We would all be at dinner and he would lean on the back of someone's chair, discussing some important *60 Minutes* topic that would be coming on Sunday and never say a word in my direction. It felt strange. Probably because I was new, and he didn't know me, and . . . it would take time. My permanent cushion neighbor was Harry Reems, most known for the famous 1972 porn movie by the name of *Deep Throat*, and his 1974 conviction by the FBI for federal charges of conspiracy to distribute obscenity across state lines. Harry was a sweetheart, but his dream to star in a TV sitcom would never happen—he was forever "unclean" and thereby unemployable. Hef understood the unmitigated unfairness of it all and welcomed Harry into his home. He didn't care what show business thought; Harry Reems was his friend and was always welcome.

I was invited up the following weekend and all the weekends after, and life fell into a routine of ease and regularity. I worked at the Melting Pot, finally opened a bank account, and started to save some money. The Cadillac temporarily stopped belching black stuff and was running sort of okay. The beautiful blonde that first night on Hef's arm was Sondra Theodore, a sweet, innocent gal from Bakersfield, California, who had fallen in love with the world's biggest playboy. Sondra absolutely loved Hef in the purest way. She was energetic, upbeat, and constantly fun. We became best friends, so much so that, in a matter of weeks, I had moved out of Michael's and in with Sondra. Michael was very disappointed—with me went all the colorful mansion stories and potential movie star revelations.

Sondra and I shared a cute two-bedroom, two-bath apartment in Westwood for the princely sum of six hundred dollars a month. I had no furniture or apartment stuff, so Sondra, in her infinite kindness, arranged for everything I needed to be sent from the mansion. The day after we moved in, Sondra organized a queen-sized bed, sheets, blankets, towels, a chair, and a large dresser for my room—all sent from the mansion. I was overwhelmed. My beloved, belching Cadillac barely fit in the driveway, its butt sticking out about a foot over the sidewalk, but no one seemed to care, probably because no one ever walked on sidewalks in LA. To illustrate this point, I only need to relay the story of when I was taking a walk down Sunset Boulevard—I was the only person on the street—and a police car

Me and Sondra, best friends

stopped beside me. Two cops got out and stood on either side of me front and back. For a moment I flashed back to the Bulgarian checkpoint.

"Why are you walking?" one of them demanded. "Where are you going? Meeting someone?" It was actually scary. I looked around and realized I was totally alone on this very long street. The cops took a step forward. This time I flashed to the Palestinian ghetto in Beirut.

Are you Muslim or are you Christian?

Common sense screamed in my head. *For God's sake, this is America! They don't just* shoot *people for walking alone. Right?* So, in my best and most clipped British accent, I said, "Actually, I do so desperately want to see the Troubadour club where James Taylor and Carole King played—it is *so* famous." And then I flashed my best smile.

They stared at me and then at each other for a minute, and then the one in front said, "Don't walk alone here anymore." And off they went, one of them muttering "crazy British tourist" under his breath.

Yup. Got it. You don't go for sightseeing strolls down Sunset Boulevard or any empty streets.

Chapter 37

By Invitation Only

Sondra instinctively knew how shy I was and helped me get to know everyone, and thus fitting in became easier and easier. Daily, we went up to the mansion and hung out by the pool or in the house, mingling with the constant group of people coming and going. Hef's generosity appeared extraordinary, as many of his friends had 24/7 access—always men, although Barbi Benton did come up one day. They were guys he'd known a long time and were his closest pals and confidants . . . and then there was Dr. Mark Saginor, affectionately nicknamed "Dr. Feel-Good" and called that by all who knew and depended on him.

Dr. Mark, as he was known to his loyal customers, was Hef's longtime personal physician and friend. He was in and out of the mansion every day and most evenings, prescribing drugs to visitors and Playmates, as well as to Hef, on a precise and regular schedule. He was on call virtually every night to attend to the mansion's guests and of course to the man himself, who was up all night doing whatever with a bevy of beautiful whoever, until dawn. There was also a multitude of young women, most of whom were sweet, innocent, and terribly naive, drifting in and out at random. It was not unusual, on any given day, to see five or six girls sunning themselves by the pool or floating in the grotto's Jacuzzi, secluded in a rock cave behind another bar at the end of the garden. Everyone was welcome during the day to use the Jacuzzi, as well as take a shower and change clothes, while at night it was "by invitation only." When you were downstairs in the house or out by the pool, or at any of the parties Hef threw on a regular basis, you behaved like a lady or gentleman, with polite dignity. There were no naked girls running around, no blatant fornicating whilst tucked away in a corner or by the pool, and no one coerced anyone upstairs, expecting "something friendly." At least not from my observation.

For three years, I was at the mansion pretty much every day and saw nothing but an elegant house run with dignity and decorum. This was Hef's home, and like anyone else's home that one would visit, it was to be treated with respect. Now, what went on at night, after everyone left, upstairs or in the grotto, was only your business if you were included.

And I never was.

The daytime traffic consisted of a constant stream of "regulars" who could be seen sitting around the table in the kitchen's ante room, ordering their meals and liquor, which appeared within minutes on silver trays carried by young, pretty male butlers.

With Hef sleeping most of the day, his visitors would have run of the place. Everyone used the house phone, which resembled a pay phone and hung on the wall inside a small mahogany booth in the hallway. People using the phone could call anywhere they wanted at any time, nationally or internationally. The house was treated as if it were an all-inclusive resort, which doubled as an office for some. Most of the time, it was the same crew hanging out—Bill Cosby, Robert Culp (not quite as frequent as the others), Shel Silverstein, Jim Brown, Jimmy Caan (who had his own room upstairs in parts unknown), Patrick Curtis (recently divorced from Raquel Welch and very much a lost soul), and Peter Lawford, who would regale us with hilarious stories involving Marilyn Monroe, JFK, and Elvis as he drank large glasses of milk heavily laced with Courvoisier XO Cognac. I adored Peter. We were already friends from working together in London on *Salt & Pepper* and our times together with Sammy (Davis). Peter's stories were legendary. We would sit side by side laughing as one tale merged into another.

Me, Hefner, and Robert Culp at the mansion, 1977

There was also the revolving door of guys and gals that changed with the seasons; I could never keep up. And not everything was roses for me, of course, as idyllic as the mansion might have been. One thing in particular that struck me as odd was Bill Cosby's demeanor. Mr. Cosby, as he liked to be called, would always sit at the head of the table like the god of show business that he was. There would often be a good-natured banter going on back and forth between everyone at the table, and Mr. Cosby managed to pointedly ignore me all the while, no matter who was there and on every single occasion. We could be sitting side by side or facing each other two feet across the table, and his behavior was always the same. If I said something to him, he would turn his head away and talk to someone else. It was embarrassing and uncomfortable. One day, I had said something to Mr. Cosby, and he stood up and walked out of the room. I asked Peter, "Why does Mr. Cosby ignore me all the time? I mean, *walk out of the room and ignore me?*"

Peter just smiled, took a big slurp of well-laced milk, and patted my arm. "Oh, darling. He just doesn't like you, that's all."

I was devastated. America's dad, the funniest man on television . . . didn't like me?

I didn't know how lucky I was.

As the weeks and months went by, the mansion became a second home. I often wondered why it was never referred to as just that, a home, or

"Hef's place," but it was always "the mansion." Sondra, Dick and Annie Stewart, Mel Tormé, Richard Brooks, and Robert Culp became my go-to pals, along with Shel Silverstein, whom I truly treasured. Shel was one of the leading cartoonists for Playboy magazine as well as a musician, having written music and lyrics for Johnny Cash's hit song "A Boy Named Sue." Shel was a true renaissance man—a musician, author, and poet. He gave me two of his books, *The Giving Tree* and *The Missing Piece*. I was so taken with the innocence and simple philosophy of both stories and have never looked at a tree or a circle in the same way since. He had a brilliant mind and a unique view of life. Shel and I stayed good friends for years, even after I'd moved to New York.

When Bob Culp asked me out, I was flattered and surprised. I was the odd girl in the mélange of this unique family, not part of Hef's gorgeous bevy of blondes and not on the hunt for a famous arm with which to attach myself. I suppose I was "safe." And I blended in. I thought of myself as "Sondra's roomie," so being asked out by a famous actor was not what I expected, and I was shocked and excited all at the same time.

Along with being a lovely, kind man and very funny, Bob Culp was a well-known actor whose time had pretty much passed by—which was extremely hard for him. For three years, he'd starred with Bill Cosby in the successful series *I Spy*, of which he wrote a bunch of episodes. Bob treated me as if I were the most exceptional person in the world; he welcomed me into his home like family, any day, any time. I also adored his two teenage boys, Jason and Joseph, with whom I've stayed friends to this day. Whenever we didn't go out or up to the mansion, Bob used to plonk me on his couch and run episodes of *I Spy*, one after the other, after the other. There are eighty-two episodes, which I think he had every intention to show me. I believe, over the time we were together, I did make it through about thirty. Usually he only sat with me when the episodes he wrote came on, otherwise he would stand silently behind the couch at the bar counter. When the show was done, he'd come and sit down beside me.

"What do you think?" he always asked.

"It's a good show. Lots of fun." Pause.

"Why do you think that?" I really didn't have an answer, so I fluttered around how it was funny and he and Cosby had such good chemistry and . . . I didn't have much else. It was somewhat embarrassing, I didn't have any deep thoughts about this particular TV show, and more than anything, I didn't understand the point of watching this thing hour after hour—by myself.

Recently, I asked his son Jason about it.

"What *was* that? Why did he have me watching *I Spy* every day and asking what I thought?"

"He was showing you himself," Jason said.

"And he didn't think I got it after thirty episodes?"

"He was enamored with you and wanted you to see who he was and what was very dear to his heart. *I Spy* was his greatest moment, a moment he knew he could never recapture, even though he spent most of his life trying."

Enamored? I had no idea. He'd kept that a big secret. Or . . . well . . . I probably was totally unaware, being buried in my own insecure world—no one could possibly be "enamored" by me.

Now it all makes sense. Now I understand. LA/Hollywood was, and still is, a merciless and frequently cruel town where you needed the spine of a rhino to cope with the inevitable trickle-down of your show business career. You swam in a sea of piranhas, who allowed you to shine for a while—*their while*—until the light started dimming over your head. Then perhaps they deemed to allow another light to flicker for a brief moment, and then they were done with you and it was on to the next Don Johnson, Tom Selleck, Farrah Fawcett, or whoever was "the face" of the moment. It was frustrating; I couldn't seem to lift the burden of sadness from Bob. I simply didn't know how—how could I? My years had not yet taught me how to recognize the curtain that people pull close around themselves to hide their pain—pain that must *never* be seen, especially in this town.

Bob was very close to Hef, as well as Cosby, and I used to say silent prayers that *Mr.* Cosby wouldn't pop by Bob's house for a visit while I was there, even though I knew Bob knew we had somewhat of a frosty relationship. Well, we never talked about him, and he never showed up. Another shout out to baby Jesus. I still can't figure it out: during the following years, over *sixty women* were violated by this man and . . . nothing? My best guess is that there was a strict code of loyal silence among the men—*his* men, loyal friends who shadowed and threatened the women, thereby protecting him. Jim Brown was one of Cosby's closest, and I can just imagine this six-foot-two, 231-pound bear filling some poor girl's front doorway to "chat" about what a "good" idea it would be to stay silent and say *nothing*.

At the time, I just chalked Cosby up to being a rude and somewhat unpleasant guy. Many years later, my dear friend Patty Joe Mastern—the Bunny Mother, first at the LA club, then Chicago—told me her terrible story and how she had been threatened to never speak of it or her life would be ruined. Phone calls would be made to her with warnings to say *nothing*, and one day, out of the blue, Cosby sent her a potted plant for her office. Too creepy. Today, justice did briefly prevail—albeit a lot late, but as of this writing, Cosby (yeah, no more *Mr.*) has served three years for drugging and sexually assaulting Andrea Constand at her home in 2004. It is a small vindication for the other sixty women whom he'd violated since 1965, as unfortunately, on June 30, 2021, the Philadelphia Supreme Court overturned the conviction and freed Cosby. But, I look back on those infrequent occasions when he and I actually made eye contact. He saw me and I saw him. I really do believe there's something to be said for the reptilian brain.

Chapter 38

Meet the White Wizard

One day, Sondra had to speak to Mary, Hef's secretary. She needed some money, and if you were "the girlfriend," Mary O'Connor was your go-to person. She was a kind but tough woman who spent more time with Hef than anyone else. She was his trusted secretary, fierce protector, and confidant for more than four decades. Hef adored her, and she died at age eighty-four still working at the mansion.

Sondra had grabbed my arm, giggling. "I have to go and see Mary," she said. "Wanna see Hef's bedroom—upstairs? It's a trip."

"Okay." I know I should have sounded more thrilled, but I think I was more nervous than anything. I knew Hef as this kind man with a brilliant mind, and I suppose I didn't want to see this potentially scary side . . . or did I?

Let's not bullshit—of course I did, nervous or not.

We climbed the staircase, had a quick visit with Mary, and then Sondra guided me down the corridor into what I had come to think of as "the room of infamy." It was dark, with shades closed tight against the bright sunshine of the day. The room was draped in deep blue, satin and silk, with a huge silk-shrouded round bed in the middle of the room. There was an elaborate stereo system with a large viewing screen above. Suddenly, my eye caught something in the corner, and this "something" was what I can only describe as a large "apparatus." I turned my head sideways a couple of times, trying to figure out what it was, and Sondra laughed.

Then I got it.

The "apparatus" bore a vague and distant resemblance to a gynecological chair, with elevated side footrests to qualify, but much larger and with more "things" attached. I think it was also dark blue. It looked like something that solely belonged in a hardcore porn movie. I took a step back, fearing it might grind into life with the roar of a 1968 Mustang and start rolling toward me (your fault, Stephen King!).

Sondra sensed my alarm and guided me away.

"Wanna see his closet?" she asked.

"Sure." Oh God, what was in *there*?

She led me through the bathroom, which was a typical bathroom with no extra contraptions, and into the adjoining closet, which opened up to an expansive dressing room with floor-to-ceiling mirrors. She opened one of the doors to reveal a twelve-foot rack of Hef's silk pajamas—an ocean of purple, blue, black, ivory, magenta, and aquamarine that went on and on. I shivered again, but this time with huge relief that Hef had no interest in me other than as a friend of Sondra's. He still rarely spoke to me, except perhaps during a movie, and that was good—great actually. I would never have to be engulfed in those pajamas. I think and still do believe that I was so much not his type, that he simply didn't "see" me. In short, the upstairs and late nights in the grotto were for the inner circle. Whatever went on behind closed doors was a total and complete mystery to me, and that was fine. It was absolutely none of my business, and that was fine too.

On Fridays and Sundays, dancing and socializing usually finished up around midnight, and then Hef would head down to the game room outside the house at the end of the gardens. One night, around one a.m., everyone was either with Hef or they'd gone home. I was on my way to say good night and give Hef my usual thanks for his hospitality, when walking past the dining room, my eye caught the saddest sight: John Belushi sitting at the head of the dining table, alone in the dark, in front of a dinner plate piled high with cocaine. His head hung over the plate as he rubbed his finger slowly across his nose and mouth. On impulse, I walked in and sat beside him, but he didn't even see me—just kept dipping his finger into the plate and rubbing it across his nose.

"Mr. Belushi?" I said, gently touching his arm. He lifted it to get rid of my hand. I tried again—he looked terrible. "Maybe it's time to go home?"

He turned his head, staring at me with bloodshot eyes, then dropped his chin back to his precious plate. It was the curse of the times—cocaine was everywhere and on everyone's person. I tried it once, and it didn't take but a few seconds to skyrocket to the planet of euphoria. I loved everyone! Everyone was my best friend! My life was amazing! I was going to be a superstar! I had the energy of a marathon runner, and who needed sleep anyway? I had to make plans to . . . do more stuff!

That feeling lasted about forty-five minutes.

The slide down to normality . . . to the beginning of depression . . . was effortless. It wasn't hard to understand the obsession. The "high" was the crazy, happy place we all craved, the top of the roller coaster, but the comedown was brutal—hence, the single-minded need for more to get you back to that crazy happy place. Now you were past a couple of lines to grams, then more grams, then entire evenings of "partying." You didn't care about the hundreds of wasted dollars; you didn't care about the nosebleeds and the endless banter of meaningless chatter that poured out of your mouth, the ridiculous promises and plans you made, never to be achieved. It didn't matter you were swallowing dozens of Quaaludes to accompany the "high" and level it out so you could have ceaseless sex with . . . whomever. And . . . you didn't know you were slowly killing yourself because the devil had invaded your sanity. After a few days of "partying," thankfully, my logical and calculating brain took precedence over my temptation. It was a false and extremely dangerous road to a very dangerous place. I quit forever.

I looked at the plate piled high—I tried one more time.

"Mr. Belushi . . . ?"

"John," was all he said.

Three years later, John Belushi was found dead in Bungalow Three at the Chateau Marmont Hotel on Sunset Boulevard. He'd died from a combined overdose of cocaine and heroin. I never said anything to anyone about that night in the dining room. It really wasn't my business, although the loneliness surrounding this extraordinarily talented man, sitting head down, hovering over a plate of death, struck me as incredibly tragic. But, again, not being part of Hef's intimate circle, I realized there was really no one to tell—and if I had, would it have saved him? Probably not. What could I have done? That night, realizing there was nothing I could do, I left and went down to the game room, where Hef was at the Pinball Wizard.

"Hef?"

He turned and smiled. "Yes, dear?"

"I know I do this every week..."

"That's all right." His voice was always soft and kind.

"I just want to thank you for a wonderful evening and how much this means to me." His arm wrapped around my shoulder, giving me a squeeze.

"You're always welcome, anytime." And then it was back to the Pinball Wizard.

Did I know Hugh Hefner was both Dr. Jekyll *and* Mr. Hyde?

Did I know he'd turned his devoted girlfriend, Sondra—my best friend—into a drug mule, forced to retrieve his cocaine on a regular basis?

Did I know he filmed all of the young, innocent women he'd had awful sex with in his bedroom, more than often without consent—*and* kept the tapes?

Did I know he'd sexually assaulted my best friend's dog?

Did I know Hugh Hefner was a monster?

No. I didn't.

Taking an aside here for a moment, this has been my real dilemma of late: how to respect and acknowledge the horror recently revealed about the most famous man in America. But I feel I should; I feel I must—to honor the countless young women violated by this deeply perverted and, yes, evil man.

In January 2022, the documentary event entitled *Secrets of Playboy* was aired on A&E, where the vivid and shocking truth was exposed of the dark, underworld life within Hefner's enclave at the Playboy Mansion. I watched as the show revealed the countless young women and my darling friend Sondra telling their horrific stories about what he had done to them. Sondra had suffered the most. He'd broken her and, watching the television, my heart broke with her. I had known none of it. Yes, I'd seen her come home crying, but being buried in my own struggle for survival—it's not that I didn't care; I was just too overcome with my own problems to think it was much beyond a young girl in love, crying—like we all did.

And . . . again . . . I never felt uncomfortable, nor did I see anything sinister in Hugh Hefner. For all the years I knew him, he was a man who barely knew me, who had been nothing but polite and welcoming. Did he know what Cosby was doing? Probably. How could he not? Cosby was one of his best friends. Did I know that Thursday nights the mansion turned into a house of sexual horrors?

Nope.

All I knew was Sondra's friendship and the freedom to come and go from this beautiful home where I had made friends, where I felt I had somewhere to belong in this relentless show biz city. I'd had so many wonderful evenings in that house and made some very good friends with people you only saw on screen or stage. Some of them were just lovely, and most of them memorable, like the one evening I was standing at the patio bar waiting for the currently absent, pretty bartender, when I became aware of a very tall man standing next to me. I didn't really pay attention until I felt a hand touch my shoulder and the voice of Atticus Finch glided into my ear.

"Do you think we're going to wait long?"

I looked up . . . and up, into the eyes of Gregory Peck. It took me a minute to recognize who it was, then I straightened up and, with my best British composure, said, "I think he went to get more ice." At that moment, the bartender arrived, and we got our drinks.

"You're British." Oh, that voice.

"Yes, I am."

Gregory Peck and I (insane, right?) went on to spend a wonderful hour talking about everything but movies. Finally, he looked at his watch and told me it had been a pleasure, but he had another engagement. He went over to Hef, shook his hand, and left before dinner, and I never saw Gregory Peck at the mansion again. I think scantily clad blonde ladies with breasts almost popping into the fresh air was just too much for him—but that one hour of heaven is indelibly seared into my memory.

I had also met and become great friends with Leslie Bricusse (it was like two Brits finding each other in the LA Badlands), the talented and wonderful man who, along with Anthony Newley, had written some of our most iconic stage and screen productions. Leslie called me "Beloved Bora," and we spent many wonderful times going to dinner, giggling at the craziness of this city, and visiting friends. One of our friends was Sammy Davis, now happily married to the beautiful Altovise, who, to mark his twenty-fifth year in show business, had just bought him the ultimate status symbol, a brand-new Cadillac Seville, which retailed at $12,400. The car's interior was covered with the famous Gucci symbols—Gucci-decorated seats, armrests, and dashboard—bumping the car's price to $22,900. And, just in case you were not one of the fortunate to examine the interior on a spin around the block with Sammy, Altovise had made sure the car had the famous red-and-green Gucci stripes painted all around. It kind of looked like a Gucci suitcase on wheels. Just nutty.

"Darling, Sammy wants us to see the car—he is tremendously excited!"

Leslie and I pulled into his driveway, and there it sat in all its ghastly glory. Sammy was beyond thrilled and proudly showed us the full set of Gucci luggage that was included with the car. Oh my God—more "G's"! It actually made me dizzy—but it was a priceless moment that definitely warranted a great deal of humorous conversation. That Caddy was the talking piece for weeks.

Chapter 39

Feeling the Burn

A few weeks later, I left the Melting Pot and went to work at the Moustache Café on Melrose. It was a hip, busy restaurant where I definitely made more money. They made these chocolate soufflés that were a nightmare to serve—the chef would bellow when they were ready, his voice rocking the restaurant, and we had to *run* into the kitchen to pick them up before they collapsed. The maître d', Monsieur Alain (from Reno, Nevada, *not* the South of France as claimed), would hear the chef booming and clap his hands at any one of us passing by.

"*Le soufflé! C'est pré! Maintenant! Marche, vite!*"

And we would run.

Michael the bartender was a Brit, cockney and very funny. He proudly confided he was here "incognito," hiding from a well-known British gangster whom he'd testified against in court. I later found out that *he* was the gangster on the run from his own gang! But Michael was a Londoner who made me laugh, had horses and a dog, and . . . well . . . horse, dog, and funny forgives everything. During the dreaded Sunday brunches, all the Beverly Hills fab and famous would swarm in with their Beverly Hills children, dressed appropriately in the customary Oshkosh designer of the day. These precious darlings would snap their sticky fingers at us, calling for service. Finally Michael and I cooked up a plan—just before the French omelets and eggs Benedict, he would drop a generous shot of vodka into the kids' orange juice. I have to admit, it was beyond hilarious to see all the parents wondering why their precious angels were sound asleep. Yes, we were dreadful, and yes, I am not a mother (at least not of humans), but the finger snapping had gotten to be too much.

In my continuing effort to become part of the LA lifestyle, I had joined Jane Fonda's Workout studio in West Hollywood. Recently opened, it had become "the place to be seen." I signed up and became a regular. Mostly, I took this amazing and delightfully painful stretch class from Doreen Rivera, a woman talented beyond boundaries, who was to become my best friend for the next forty years. An accomplished dancer, she'd recently recovered from a terrible car accident where they told her she would never walk again, and with true Puerto Rican sassiness, she had told them, "You're right. I won't walk—I'll dance!"

Still in the recovery process, Doreen taught class, sitting legs stretched out on the floor, barking at us to pull our limbs to places they'd never been. It was great. I was there every day, taking Doreen's class, and I even *once* took Jane's aerobics class, a terrifying experience. The woman was a nonstop powerhouse of unrelenting movement; from the minute you walked into the room, there was not a second of wasted time.

"Push it! Work it! Feel the burn!" was Jane's mantra, which she roared with deep conviction above the loud, pulsating disco music. One day, I was pumping my arms up and down, stepping on and off a bench at an insane pace, thinking this actually might be the day I died, when I noticed a man standing beside me, also attempting to do this impossible task, managing only a slow shuffle with the occasional foot making the step-up. He was barely moving, breathing rapidly, and loudly exhaling short whistles of air. I glanced over at him again and realized it was her seventy-five-year-old father, Henry Fonda, looking as if he'd just opened the doors to hell. He was very pale, and I was worried he was going to drop—maybe this was his day too. I could see the headlines:

Doreen Rivera, 1979

"Henry Fonda and British Girl Drop Dead During Jane Fonda Workout."

He stopped shuffling and headed slowly to the door, weaving in and out of the sweating workout disciples. I was relieved to see Jane's gaze follow him—surely she would go over to see if he was okay? I slowed down and stopped pumping, waiting for her to approach him and check in; she didn't. I stopped moving, thinking, *Should I make sure he is . . . ?*

"Push it! Work it! BURN!" blasted into my ear as Donna Summer "Worked Hard for the Money," and I kept pumping. After class, I went outside to the tiny patio, collapsed onto a wrought iron chair, and lit up what I believed was a well-earned cigarette. Through the smoky haze of that glorious first puff, Jane came out on her way home. She walked past me, then suddenly stopped, turned around, and stared at me with what was either anger or contempt—I wasn't sure. She stood tall and kept staring—it was a moment. I was slightly afraid.

"Err, thank you, Ms. Fonda, for a great class. I hope your dad . . . Mr. Fonda is okay."

She said nothing, and finally the silence and the stare broke.

"Those things will kill you," she snarled, then turned and walked down the path. I never took her class again—it was way too scary—but occasionally I'd look in through the window (you could hear Jane's voice through the double-paned glass) and watch the devoted disciples pushing their poor bodies to the brink of collapse. I stayed safe with darling Doreen, stretching my unused limbs to pain and more pain—good pain, as it was minus an impending heart attack.

I was very content in my daily routine of the Moustache Café, taking Doreen's class, and going up to the mansion with the occasional turn at the Improv. Bob Culp and I had decided to just be friends—much better idea. We would have been miserable; the affair would have worn down, and I was too young to be with a man who needed a woman and not a girl. I was comfortable, aside from the daily agony of unused muscles being brutally attacked, and we all know what happens when you get comfortable. You become complacent, losing any drive to push forward and take risks; you actually become emotionally lazy. I didn't care. I loved it—bring on emotional laziness! Compared to what I'd been through for the past sixteen years, this was heaven. No Mother, no late-night evictions, no living in a war zone, no being poor, no panicking every time the phone rang or there was a knock at the door . . . this was peace with the world.

The biweekly phone calls to Mother continued, and darling Michael let me use the phone at Bonwit. I didn't have the freedom of a long conversation in the mahogany-paneled phone booth at Hef's, but actually, it was better because it kept my calls, and therefore Mother's tirades, short. Nevertheless, Mother still kept threatening to come and visit, exaggerating her loneliness and misery and how I'd deserted her. But I had become the master of the excuse.

"Mummy, darling. It's five thousand miles! What about your bad leg? Sitting for fourteen hours?" I don't think I'd ever called her "darling," but it worked. Any impending visits had just been thwarted. At least for the time being.

One lovely sunny day, I was reveling in my groovy life, sitting by the pool at Hef's, when Dorothy Stratten came out of the house and sat beside me in one of the lounge chairs. I can honestly say, I have never seen anyone so beautiful. Very much like Sharon Tate, her face was luminescent with a pure goodness that came from within—she was the kind of woman that could cause car accidents. I could tell she was shy and a little bit anxious, but hey, this place was fiercely intimidating.

"Hello, my name is Dorothy," she said, introducing herself.

I was about to reply when Mel Tormé pulled up a chair beside me. His voice resonated with great intention.

"What do you want to do, Juliette?"

"Do?" I was taken aback. "Do with . . . ?"

"Your life. What do you want to do with your life?" He was serious. I knew Mel had a sense of humor, so I quipped back.

"I'm doing it."

He shook his head in frustration. "You are a young, beautiful woman. You're very smart, with your whole life ahead of you. What are you going to do with it?"

I didn't think for a minute I was beautiful. Beautiful was sitting beside me, and this was not the town where being smart mattered, and . . . I didn't want to be a movie star or a rock-and-roll sensation. I was lost for words.

"I don't know. I haven't thought about it. LA seems only to be about show business . . . I mean . . . I do sing a bit."

"Do you love it?"

"I love being on stage."

"Are you good? Do *you* believe you're good?"

"I don't know. I get horrible stage fright. Don't you?"

He brushed it off. "No, never. Are you prepared to work harder than *anyone* else?"

I thought about all the comedians at the Improv, at The Comedy Store, working harder and harder for however long it took—if it ever "took."

"I don't know," I told him.

He smiled and stood up.

"Don't become one of *them*," he said, indicating all the girls lounging by the pool. "They're going to grow old one day, and this will be their big memories; this will be their *big* story they'll tell again and again." He paused. I had nothing to say. He pressed my hand. "Get up and get going. Think about it."

He gave me a peck on the cheek and went back into the house. I can't imagine what had prompted his marching out to the pool to straighten me out, but . . . I knew he was right. Mel Tormé had come out to find me specifically to say what he said. Trouble was—I felt blank. Did I really have to *do* something *more* with my life? Hadn't I done enough? This was nice, this was fun, this was easy.

But another voice piped up from somewhere deep in my core. *This isn't reality!* that voice said. *It's an escape! How long can you sit by swimming pools with insecure movie stars and half-naked gorgeous women . . . albeit extremely sweet, half-naked gorgeous women?*

I turned back to continue my chat with Dorothy just as Hef came up, took her hand, and led her away. She looked back and waved.

"See you soon!"

The happiness in her voice was infectious. I waved back.

Dorothy had been "discovered" as a teenager in 1977 by Paul Snider, a small-time promoter and pimp who wanted glitz, glamour, fame, and fortune—and he would do anything to get it. He'd had a legitimate business as a promoter for auto shows at the Pacific National Exhibition in Vancouver, but he'd wanted more, so he joined a drug gang in the city. But this creep with the black Corvette could never quite pull off the big score when it came to drugs—ironically, he actually hated drugs. Nobody trusted him, and because of his fear of drugs, he finally lost a lot of money to loan sharks, and the gang fellas hung him by his ankles from the thirtieth floor of a hotel. He fled town, ending up in Los Angeles where he tried pimping on the fringe of Beverly Hills society. After a few near-misses with the law and women who stole from him, he ran back home.

Paul met Dorothy while she was working at a Dairy Queen in Vancouver. He immediately became her boyfriend. She was an innocent eighteen-year-old girl, and he was a twenty-seven-year-old con man. He saw everything he needed in her beauty and genuine innocence, so after ingratiating himself into her life, he persuaded Dorothy to pose naked for him and then sent those naked pictures to Playboy. Hef, blown away by this beautiful young girl, immediately brought her to live at the mansion, choosing her to be the 1979 August Playmate of the Month. Paul, seeing big bucks, announced he was her manager, moved to LA, and quickly married her. He was relentlessly possessive and slunk around inserting himself into everyone's conversations. Poor Dorothy felt so obligated, she ignored everyone's advice to dump him.

I was there one beautiful summer evening when Hef was throwing one of his famous "Midsummer Night's Dream" parties, always a lavish affair put together for all his closest friends and, of course, a bevy of gorgeous girls. The party was set in the garden of the mansion, and Dorothy waved to me as Hef escorted her into the house to dance. Suddenly, two of the security guards came rushing into the garden looking for Hef. We all pointed them to the house, and they barreled in. Of course, we all followed. I knew Joe, the head of security, very well. He was a jovial ex-cop from New York City who also carried two .45s and a set of custom-made spiked brass knuckles. The guards whispered into Hef's ear, and he promptly sent Dorothy upstairs to Mary. Joe and his guys then ran out and down the driveway.

Paul Snider was climbing the wall. He was coming to get Dorothy and take her away from Hef and everything Playboy. He was over and on the ground when, by Joe's recount the next day, he came face-to-face with those lovely brass knuckles and a .45 two inches away from his head. The guys dragged him by his neck out onto the street, warning Paul if he *ever* tried this again, he'd be hurt so bad his mother wouldn't even recognize him.

And the rest is a short, heartbreaking story.

On August 14, 1980, I was living in New York when, armed with a 12-gauge, pump-action shotgun, Paul raped and murdered Dorothy at their home in LA. He shot her through the eye, making sure he destroyed everything exquisite, then turned the gun on himself.

She was only twenty years old.

It gave me a jolt of an all too familiar feeling—that of being helpless in the face of a madman. No matter how smart and savvy I thought I was, escaping Palestinian terrorists with big guns, smacking men over the head with a coffeepot—if I had been desperate for a break in this super brutal city, I could have easily wound up with the wrong guy and been found lying dead, with my head blown in on some stranger's bed.

After the murder, Hef was quoted as saying, "There is still a great tendency . . . for this thing to fall into the classic cliché of 'smalltown girl comes to Playboy, comes to Hollywood, life in the fast lane.' That is not what really happened. A very sick guy saw his meal ticket and his connection to power, whatever, slipping away. And it was that that made him kill her."

Did Hef care? Some say not.

Chapter 40

The Audition

One day, out of the blue, Oliver called me. He'd left London, moved to Marina Del Rey, and married his cousin Sylvia. All I could think of was the song "Sylvia's Mother," which Shel had written for Dr. Hook. I stumbled for words.

"You married your *cousin?*" Creepy.

"Darling, she's my *second* cousin, all above board and perfectly normal!" He was chipper and calm at the same time.

"Did you get a green card?" I asked, pretty much knowing the answer—he knew I didn't have mine.

"Of course, darling. First order of business!"

"Did you steal the band's money?" I had to ask.

He was swift and smooth in his reply.

"Such a huge misunderstanding! All's well. I left on totally amicable terms and now I'm here! Let's get to work! Have you been singing?"

I didn't believe a word he said, but he *was* here, and I *wasn't* singing, and now perhaps that could all change. My life *certainly* had to change.

"Yes. A bit." I knew I sounded despondent. "I occasionally sing at the Improv."

"What about Playboy? Don't they have a supper club with a band and singer in every Playboy Club around the US? And London? Even Jamaica?"

Light bulb!

"Yes, they do! And those clubs are called 'Lainie's Room.'" It took a minute. "Ollie! What a brilliant idea!"

"I think so too," he said, somewhat smug in his brilliance. "Do you know Lainie?"

"Yes, but not very well." I went on to explain how I lived with Sondra and spent most of my spare time at the mansion, and that I had met Lainie Kazan on numerous occasions, and we got along terrifically. Lainie was a fabulous, larger than life powerhouse who consumed you with her infectious energy. She'd been introduced to Playboy by posing in the October 1970 issue of the magazine and was now good friends with Hef, who'd named all the club's entertainment rooms in her name. The honor was well deserved, as she was a truly extraordinary singer.

"Well then, it shouldn't be too difficult to ask her."

I nodded. It would just be a matter of getting around to the asking, which of course was petrifying.

Around the time of Oliver's arrival, I'd been dating a fun guy, Peter, who was the roadie for Barry Manilow. Manilow was going to be a part of a simulcast, live-televised extravaganza show, *The Stars Salute Israel at 60*, with Israel's Prime Minister, Golda Meir, and Peter had casually asked, "Hey, you wanna come watch the show from backstage?"

Seriously? Was he kidding?

He was decidedly not. On the day of the show, he picked me up and, when we arrived, put me in the Green Room where everyone waited before they went on. He left me standing among Mikhail Baryshnikov, Carol Burnett, Kirk Douglas, Tom Cruise, Paul Newman, Barbra Streisand, and Henry Fonda—all casually chatting to each other. I was awestruck. I saw there was a large table set up with tea and coffee and an impressive spread of food, and, at the same time, I noticed Tom Cruise talking to Mikhail Baryshnikov. Suddenly I wanted to ask him, could he really *jeté* six feet in the air? Did I feel brave? No. But, nevertheless, I took a step forward and ran smack into Gene Kelly, smiling the smile of the unforgettable. My knees went weak.

"Sorry! We seemed to have had the same thought," he said with those dazzling white teeth. I saw him swinging from the lamppost with the umbrella.

"We did! Yes, we did!" I said in a very high-pitched voice.

Oh my God. It was Gene Kelly.

He smiled again, walked me over to the table, and poured a cup of tea.

"My guess is you're British?" He chuckled. My knees weakened a little more as he looked over to the monitor where Sammy Davis was taking his bows. "Whoops, I'm on next! Great to meet you! Here." He handed me the teacup and, with the grace of those dancing feet, he was out the door. I stood for a second holding the cup. I had just met Gene Kelly. He'd poured tea for me!

"Something, isn't he?" came from a voice beside me, and I turned, coming face-to-face with Carol Burnett. This was almost too much.

"Yes. He is. Very . . . something." My sense of reality had gone out the window. These were not just famous people—these were the elite. No one was trying to cozy up to a big-time director, writers weren't carrying their rolled-up scripts trying to catch an eye—these were the privileged, the royalty of Hollywood, forever safe and secure in their high-chair kingdoms. The cup was starting to rattle on the saucer, and quickly, Carol took my arm.

"Come, sit. I was on earlier, so I'm done. You're British, right?"

Sammy Davis, holding a cocktail and lighting a cigarette, waved to me as he walked into the room.

"Yes, I'm British. Did you know Sammy Davis's car is entirely upholstered by Gucci?" Why did I just say that? She roared with laughter—ice broken, and for over an hour, Carol Burnett and I drank tea and talked about everything. I told her I'd moved here from London and was sort of singing. I told her *Gone with the Wind* was my mother's favorite movie. She asked all kinds of questions about me and my life, and was just the kind and wonderful woman (genius) that she is.

"Do you want to be in show business?" she asked.

"I think so."

"Good idea to make a decision, and if you do, remember . . . this town eats people."

I laughed; this town could never even come close to Mother when it came to chomping on my soul.

"Thank you, Carol. Good advice." She put her cup down and stood up.

"Would you like to watch Barbra from the wings?"

"Oh, yes, absolutely. Of course! Thank you!"

We walked to the wings as Ms. Streisand glided by. She said "hi" to Carol, glanced at me, and swept onto the stage. Carol whispered in my ear, "She's painfully shy and gets horrible stage fright." Barbra started singing and . . . well, we all know, it was mesmerizing. I was inspired. I could hear Mel's voice in my head—and now Carol's as well.

Make a decision.

Oliver's suggestion to talk to Lainie about singing for Playboy was a call to action. We met a couple of days later to make a plan. At home, I asked Sondra how I could talk to Lainie professionally about singing for Playboy.

"Lainie's performing here at the LA club for the next few weeks," she said. "I'll take care of it." Sondra loved a mission, and to cut a very winding story short, Sondra talked to Hef who talked to Lainie, and a night out to the Playboy Club with all the girls was organized. She was amazing. I owe her so much.

The evening arrived. We all met at the mansion and stepped into the longest limo I'd ever seen, arriving at the Playboy Club with a fanfare of heads swiveling as Hef, dressed in a slick Yves Saint Laurent suit, led the way behind the manager, who seated us at a huge round table laden with bottles of champagne nestled in various silver ice buckets. It was a phantasm of gorgeousness. "Look!" went the mouths in the crowd. "It's Hugh Hefner!" Most of the girls with us were dressed in their absolute best scanty outfits, giggling as every male head turned in drooling awe, totally ignoring their dining companions. Wives and girlfriends were not impressed with our entourage and silently cursed as their dates stared mesmerized at the almost exposed breasts and mini-mini dresses. Lainie performed and I was blown away—she did a version of Earth, Wind & Fire's "Fantasy," where you might as well have been at their concert. She was that good. After her set, she came and sat with us.

Sondra broke the ice.

"Juliette wants to sing for Playboy. How can we make that happen?"

"Would you like to sing now?" Lainie asked.

Gripped with a mild terror, my mouth moved. "Actually, I'm really not prepared." Could I have sounded more British?

"She's British," Sondra said to Lainie, who stood up and took my hand. "You're cute, but you'll have to talk to Sam Distefano."

I gulped. Wasn't that Mad Sam, the notorious Chicago gangster? All right, I was cool. I knew folk in Vegas. I had "friends." I'd be fine. As my mind rambled, I realized Lainie was still talking to me. "He's the vice president and musical director of Playboy. He books all the acts, so he has to come and see you perform first."

"Okay. No problem. I can do that. Perform. Absolutely." Relief. Gangsters don't make good musical directors.

Lainie smiled. "He also books acts for the Riviera Hotel in Las Vegas."

"Oh, cool. Great." My confidence belied my voice of certainty. I had nothing, no songs prepared, no show, no outfits—nothing—and here was maybe a chance for Playboy *and* Vegas? Oh crap! Be careful what you wish for, right?

All was not lost—I did have Oliver. The next day I called him.

"We're on! We're auditioning for Playboy and maybe Vegas. We have to put on a show—somewhere—soon."

And with that we went to work. He had a piano in his apartment, or rather *Sylvia* had the piano in *Sylvia's* apartment (she'd made that crystal clear), where we would sit for hours, putting together a show. Sylvia wasn't thrilled with this invasion of her home, husband, and the disruption of mealtimes. She didn't care for me, making it quite apparent with her silence and acerbic door slamming. I didn't like her either. She had beady, suspicious eyes that followed my every movement, which was unnerving. Plus, she reminded me of my mother, but we had work to do, and work we did. Oliver wrote a touching song, "Play the Song You Used to Play." I loved it, but Oliver wasn't sure. He didn't think it was good enough and thought it was way too long at six minutes.

"Let's ask the master!"

Oliver looked puzzled as I picked up the phone. "Who's the master?"

"Leslie, darling!" I cooed into the phone. "I'm preparing a show to audition for Playboy, and we have a song my friend and piano player, Oliver, has written. He thinks it's too long. Could you have a listen?"

"Of course. Come over for tea tomorrow. Is four p.m. all right?"

"Lovely! Thank you, darling—we'll be there." I hung up.

"Leslie who?" Oliver was confused.

"Bricusse, Leslie Bricusse."

Oliver's mouth dropped open. "Leslie Bricusse?" he stammered.

"Yup. We're pals."

And Oliver, in his best Noel Coward, replied, "Of course you are."

The next afternoon, over a much-appreciated cup of British tea (P.G Tips), Oliver sat down at Leslie's piano and played his song. I was a bit concerned. He was right—six minutes is long, but when he'd finished, Leslie just shook his head.

"Oliver. You have *immense* talent; that song is a small film." He laughed. "I wish I'd written it!"

We too laughed, but it was the laugh of immense relief. Here was the master of some of the most memorable songs and shows of our time saying the words "immense talent! I wish I'd written it."

Oliver was almost tearing up. "Really?" he asked.

"Yes, darling, *really*. More tea?" he said, holding up a blue and gold patterned teapot. I told Leslie there was also an Anthony Newley song I wanted to do, "The Man Who Makes You Laugh," but I'd only ever seen him do it on Michael Parkinson's TV Show in London. I asked if he knew where I could find the music, and Leslie took a piece of paper and scribbled a phone number.

"Call him. He's home in London—he'll send it to you," Leslie said casually.

"Just . . . call him?"

"Yes."

"Don't you need to call first? An introduction?"

"Not at all. He'll be tickled."

And here we go again. The next morning, heart pumping with the terror of calling a stranger—*an incredibly famous stranger*—I picked up the phone, prepared to go through a barrage of secretaries and assistants and . . . Mr. Newley himself answered.

"Hello." That soft-spoken voice was unmistakable, and my voice went at top speed.

"Oh, hello, Mr. Newley. Leslie Bricusse gave me your number—we're good friends—and he said I should call and ask you . . . well . . . if I could maybe get the sheet music for 'The Man Who Makes You Laugh'? I love it and it feels special and I'm doing a show for Playboy—actually it's an audition—and maybe Vegas, and I would be so honored . . . to be able to sing it and . . ." My babbling was ridiculous. Isn't fear just awful?

"Do you know what the song is about?" he asked.

"No, gosh, I'm sorry. No, I don't. A clown?"

"Comedians. It's actually a whole story I squeezed together to make a song, I'm so glad you like it."

"Oh, I do. I have known and worked with many struggling comedians, and . . . well, it's very moving. I love comedians."

"It's a tough life, being funny," he said.

"Yes . . . it is. Funny is hard. Especially when you don't feel funny."

There was a pause before he asked, "Are you a comedian as well?"

"Oh, no, but I know so many and they're the hardest-working people and the least appreciated in all of show business." I could feel him smiling as my babbling continued. "I've been singing at Budd Friedman's Improv, and I have infinite respect for all the struggling comedians out there trying to get a break and what a tragedy it could be—last year one jumped off the roof of The Comedy Store."

He listened and didn't say anything for a minute. When he finally spoke, he said, "What's your address? I'll send you the sheet music tomorrow. Just piano?"

"Yes, please, and thank you . . . so . . . very much. It's a privilege." I gave him my address.

"Thank you for calling. Good luck." And that lovely, soft voice was gone.

Three days later, the music arrived. I carefully took it out of the envelope and almost cried—it was handwritten. A brief phone call begot a heap of kindness. Thank you, Anthony Newley—you were a special man.

Oliver and I finished putting the show together and started rehearsing, and we also started looking for a venue. In those days, there were lots of small nightclubs all over LA where you could book the room for a single night. You didn't have to audition, and usually within a few weeks you could get a Saturday night. Then it was your job to fill the room with an audience, a horribly stressful task. The club would charge a cover charge with a two-drink minimum, and at the end of the night, the act would get the cover charge. I wanted somewhere small that seated a respectable, intimate audience so I didn't have to get a ton of people to fill the room. Nothing is quite so sad as someone doing their show to the few friends they'd begged come see them. I was confident I had a good Playboy crowd, so somewhere around fifty seats would work well—better a bit crowded than bare chairs.

We found the perfect place: a small club with a great bar called F. Scott's located down a side street off Pacific Avenue in Venice. It seated seventy-five comfortably at round wooden tables, and the small stage had an upright piano—all we needed. Oliver jumped up and tinkled the keys for a few minutes, nodding in approval, as a well-tuned piano with all the keys working was critical. We booked the room for a Saturday, four weeks in advance.

Now we had a deadline.

Now I was moving.

Between working at the Moustache, rehearsing with Oliver, working at the Moustache, stretching my butt off at Fonda's with Doreen, working at the Moustache, and waitressing at movie premiere parties—which was monstrously awful—I spent as much time as I could at the mansion gathering an audience. Sondra was a godsend, instructing *everyone* they were coming.

I was exhausted. I'd had a hundred invite cards printed and handed them out, hoping that maybe half would show up. Leslie took a bunch, letting me know the British TV star Bruce Forsyth was here visiting and they would come together, along with whomever else he could rustle up.

"Darling, Liza's in town. I'm sure she'd love to come. Would that be fun?"

My heart dropped into my feet.

"Oh, no!" I said, consumed with panic. Leslie's eyes widened. "Darling, that's such a lovely thought and how kind of you, but"—my brain grappled for anything—"perhaps not this time? I haven't sung for a while and—well—I *am* doing her songs and . . ." I ran out of words. For a second, I flashed back to my mother not wanting to go to tea. But this was different—to have Liza Minnelli sitting in front of me, listening to *her* songs sung by a kind of okay singer was an awful, awful thought. Leslie got it.

"I understand, she's a force. Best keep it simple with just friends."

The weeks flew by and Saturday arrived; Oliver and I had rehearsed in the room the day before. We arrived early and saw thirty tables had been arranged around the stage and more, all the way to the back wall. Ms. Streisand and I had something in common. Stage fright is a special kind of pain; when it's over you can't remember what it felt like, but in the moment . . . the goblins had arrived, swirling around the bottom of my stomach and making me feel sick. Real people were coming, and the swirl was building momentum, perched to paralyze me to total, dry-mouthed dread, when Oliver gave me a big hug.

"It's going to be brilliant."

How the hell did he know? It might be, or it might be the most disastrous thing I'd ever done. Half an hour before the show, I was sitting in the tiny room off stage right, listening to the hum and buzz of people arriving, my brain ticking in an effort to distract me from my own terror.

Okay. That's good. Maybe I'll get twenty. That's fine, we'll seat them close to the stage. That'll work . . .

"Darling!" Oliver swooped in, beaming with excitement, the words falling out of his mouth at lightning speed. "It's full! To the max! Standing room at the bar! *Everyone's* here! I had no idea Leslie was bringing Bruce Forsyth, my idol! Kate Jackson from *Charlie's Angels* is here! Did you know Shel Silverstein was coming?"

"Yes."

"Another friend?"

"Yes."

"Darling! I also saw Mel Tormé!"

"Did you see Sam Distefano?" I asked as calmly as my heart-stopping panic would allow. He was the one I really needed to be here.

"Yes, he's sitting at the bar—there were no free tables!"

The manager put his head around the door. "Ready?" he asked.

I nodded. Maybe I could make a run for it out the back door, or just drop dead. That would be good . . . who could blame me if I up and died?

And then I was onstage.

The roar of applause was deafening, everyone was smiling, and my terror evaporated. A beaming Oliver sat down at the piano and started vamping the first few bars of the opening song.

The rest of that night is history. I can only describe it as magical. The songs went well, Oliver and I had such great rapport, jibing back and forth . . . everyone loved it. I stood onstage, looking out at more than seventy-five people clapping, cheering, and laughing. The show ended up being two hours long, as I filled the space in between songs with banter back and forth with the audience, which was easy, as I knew so many faces. I sang "The Man Who Makes You Laugh" well enough that Mr. Newley himself would have been proud. At the end of the show, Sam Distefano beelined straight across the room.

"Would you like to do a tour for Playboy?"

"Oh. Yes, please! Thank you!" I tried not to gush, but how could I not?

The Audition

Singing at F. Scott's

"You would start here in LA and then a month in Chicago and New York. Afterward we can talk about the Playboy Resorts, Lake Geneva, Great Gorge. Those could be regular gigs. Do you have a green card or a work permit?"

Crap. I shook my head, seeing my career toppling down the drain. "No, I don't," I told him, the woe in my voice apparent.

Sam waved it away. Inconsequential.

"No problem. We'll get you an H-1 visa. It's a temporary work permit, valid for as long as you work for Playboy."

That night I got home about two a.m. I sat in the driveway, staring out the window into the pitch-dark street. Amazing things rarely happened to me. I had never considered myself talented at anything, really. I knew I could entertain people and I knew I could make them laugh at life's absurdities and I absolutely knew I could keep us all alive in a crisis—yup, *there* was my real expertise.

Sondra came bouncing down the steps and opened the door, the words jumbling out of her mouth.

"Why are you sitting here? I'm so happy for you! We'll fill the club on your opening night!" I knew she would—Sondra was a relentlessly good friend.

The next day, I had to go to Playboy's office to fill out papers for my visa and sign the contract. Sam said it would take about two weeks for everything to go through, including my work permit, which worked out well, as Lainie was closing soon. I would open in LA, then on to four-week stints in Chicago and New York, running concurrently. I quit the Moustache and told Doreen my good news. Jane Fonda's Workout would have to live without me, which I was sure wouldn't give Jane any sleepless nights. (We'd regularly interacted on the porch over the cigarette situation.)

While at the Playboy office, I called my mother with the good news.

I should have known better.

"Oh, that's nice. Will you be coming home to sing at Playboy here?" she asked.

"I don't know. They haven't said. I think this is just for the US clubs," I said, knowing this would be a "thing."

"Well, that doesn't make sense. There's a Playboy here. In London." She sounded indignant.

"I know, but I don't know. As I said—"

"I know what you said. Are they paying you?" she demanded.

"Of course." How long was this going to last?

"I suppose you don't really want to come home anyway. What are we going to do about Christmas?" It was never going to end.

"I don't know," I replied. I was weakening.

"Fine. I hope you at least let me know. I could always come there if my leg . . . well, you don't want to hear about me . . ." She was moving into whining. I had to end it.

"Sorry, mum, they're waving at me. I have to go."

And that was that. No congrats, no "well done," just . . . when was I coming home to her.

Chapter 41

Leaving Is the Hardest Word

Opening night in LA was a memorable experience. Once again, everyone showed up, including Hef with Sondra and *all* the Playmates, Harry Reems, Shel Silverstein, Mel Tormé, and Bob Culp as well as my ever-faithful Dick and Annie Stewart, and Joe, our ever-loyal security guard. Leslie had left back to England but sent me flowers and a lovely card. Michael and Ashley were there, and I made sure they were seated next to Hef's table. By the end of the night, we'd had another wonderful show. Hef came over, shook Oliver's hand, and hugged and kissed me for the first and only time in the three years I had known him! I almost felt famous!

One of the highlights of the night had been singing with my good friend Carol Connors, who'd generously written a duet for us. Carol truly was one of a kind, a twice Oscar-nominated singer-songwriter who, at sixteen, wrote the hit song "To Know Him Is to Love Him" with the group The Teddy Bears. Fame had rushed in fast, and she was now more notably known for her collaboration with Bill Conti on the Oscar-nominated song "Gonna Fly Now," theme to the movie *Rocky*. We had been friends pretty much since I'd moved in with Sondra, and I just loved her single-minded purpose; no party stone was left unturned and no one was safe in their secrecy. Carol had an unrelenting social antenna, eternally crackling on high beam.

My opening night at the Playboy Club LA, 1979

My four weeks were over all too soon. After the last show, as the lights went down, I had a pang of sadness—I was going away for two months but I felt it would be longer, if not permanent. I have no idea where that thought came from, but it resonated loud and clear. It wasn't a happy thought—I didn't want to leave. I'd miss this odd and wacky crowd I'd genuinely grown to love, who'd taken me in as family and now given me this wonderful opportunity. I'd miss my dearest Doreen who'd become my sister, and I thought I'd even miss Ms. Fonda's glaring eyes, but I knew I couldn't make LA my home anymore.

When I was at the office signing contracts, Sam had told me Oliver could not be included as a member of the tour. Every club had a regular paid house band—including a pianist—and Sam said he wasn't needed. They'd allow it as a courtesy here in LA but if I wanted him to play the rest of the tour, I'd have to pay him out of my own salary. Playboy was paying me $1,500 a week, which in those days was a lot of money for an unknown club singer, plus they were paying travel and housing. But I would also have to pay Oliver's housing and travel expenses.

I couldn't.

And I wouldn't.

Oliver had been with me for a loyal five years. I was a coward and I'd put this conversation off for way too long. While we were packing up at the end of the last night in LA, Oliver was busy folding charts on the top of the piano.

"Ollie?" I felt like shit.

"Yes, love?" He was positively beaming as he walked over flipping the latch closed on his briefcase.

"I can't take you on tour with me."

"What?" he said, dropping his briefcase. "What do you mean?" His shock was palpable.

"They won't include you in the contract. Every club already has a house band—this was a courtesy—here in LA." I suddenly felt terrible that I'd waited until now to tell him.

"I can't believe . . . after all our hard work, you're just leaving me behind?" Tears welled up in his eyes.

"I'm sorry. That's what they said."

Understanding the predicament with Playboy's house bands, he offered, "I'll pay for my own housing and travel—give me five hundred a week and I'll be happy. Could you do that?"

"No, I can't. I have to send money home. I can't give you anything and . . . oh . . . I'll need the charts." The twenty-odd songs he'd spent long hours writing for me—charts that would normally cost about $150 a piece—for which I'd paid nothing.

"Can you think about it? Will you? It's always been us together." His voice was shaky, but I remained stone cold.

"No, I can't. I have to send the money to Mum." I said this part with all truth—I was very much still "indebted" and under Mother's spell.

He nodded. There was nothing to say. He bent down, picked up his briefcase, and walked out.

I'd just broken the heart of someone I loved very much, and I'd done it—without a thought. Yes, my mother still ruled my life. I was still afraid of her and still felt this indissoluble burden to be her caretaker, a duty I'd assumed since I was ten years old, staring at an oxygen tank at the end of my father's empty bed. She didn't need caregiving—she had a nice apartment in the West End of London and with three pensions from the ever generous British government, and money to spare—she certainly didn't need my hard-fought earnings. Nevertheless, she cried impending poverty on pretty much our every phone call. It was weird, speaking to her was like speaking to a jilted boyfriend—someone I'd walked out on. She would frequently say things like, "When you left me . . ." or "A house divided falls." And her favorite one of all: "The umbilical cord stretches to infinitum."

It was a creepy, ugly mess. Lying had become a natural progression of our every conversation. My deceit was efficient and successful and my dismissal of Oliver . . . shameful. Our friendship was over. I'd shown that I was devoid of any compassion for another person. and the love and collaboration we'd had . . . well, I'd managed to destroy with one quickly made decision. Looking back, I still can't believe that was me. I think about that day all the time. I can still see Oliver packing that briefcase and I continually wish I'd had then one ounce of the compassion I've learned to own.

I do have a long list of questions I will be submitting upon arrival at the Pearly Gates—if I get there, that is.

Hey, God. Why did you waste youth on the young and give us wisdom when we're old and wrinkly and all the shit damage has been done and therapists are getting rich, huh? That was some pretty bad planning.

I couldn't see that, even from six thousand miles away, she *still* deceptively manipulated my life to appease her own mental suffering.

I couldn't see I was *becoming her.*

No one had yet said the word "bipolar." No one had begun to understand major depressive disorders, critical conditions needing carefully prescribed therapy, and in her case, probably some serious meds. In England, if you were diagnosed "not in your right mind," you'd be sent to a psychiatrist, not one in private practice but one who'd be part of a mental institution (or asylums, as they used to be called). If deemed mentally unfit (and I'm guessing my mother's go-to scary shit of banging her head on walls for no reason would have qualified her), you were committed to said mental institution. Unfortunately, it didn't matter whether you were schizophrenic, autistic, had dementia or Alzheimer's. If you were psychotically running down hallways, screaming from hallucinogenic delusions—or maybe you were just depressed—you were diagnosed within the same category of mental disease. Everyone was in the same "ward," primarily a room housing multiple patients in curtained off beds, with perhaps a common room close by where they could go and watch television or just . . . sit. Many would have preferred a private room, but without the money to "go private," you were packed in with the general population. Suicides were not uncommon, mainly in women. These asylums were dreadful, sad places, inevitably housing most mentally ill residents for the rest of their lives.

Consequently, left to her own devices and with no help or treatment and no understanding of her condition, my mother remained trapped in her own frightening nightmare—never telling anyone (one *never* discussed private matters, even with friends you'd known for twenty to thirty years) and living in a world of paranoia and torment, clinging to me for survival. The few friends she'd make would eventually leave when *she'd* decided they were no longer worthy.

I was almost robotic when telling Oliver he couldn't come with me. I was oblivious to his feelings. All I could think of was myself. What *I* had to do and what *I* needed. Oliver would be fine, I told myself. He'd met Shel Silverstein at F. Scott's and at my Playboy show, and Shel immediately recognized his *immense* talent and hired him to work on his music, writing charts for his songs. Consequently, Oliver soon became a daily fixture at the Playboy Mansion's piano so, in my dishonorable mind, he was doing just fine. I didn't think about the hurt I'd caused and the heart I'd just smashed. I had no concept of the disrespect and disloyalty he must have felt. I easily could have paid him five hundred dollars a week for a couple of months and it would have been the right thing to do—he was my partner. I got Playboy because of *our* hard work, not to mention the twenty charts he'd written. He was the reason I had any show to do at all. But I'd done the unforgivable and shut him out. My other folly was to ask my mother.

"What should I do?"

"You don't need him—he's too expensive." Her answer was short—a proclamation I blindly obeyed.

Two weeks later, I was on a plane to Chicago. Flying out, I watched Venice Beach retreating below; I saw myself and my beloved Doreen having lunch at the Fig Tree before linking arms for our customary stroll down the boardwalk, hoping the Moroccan guy with the best Pancholi oil was around. I squeezed back tears. I was going to miss Doreen and Sondra and all the friends I'd made who'd been so good to me and made my life a joy. In my purse, I carried the wonderful recommendation letters Mel and Bob had written to help secure my work visa. I was going to miss my beloved, smoke-belching Cadillac I'd spontaneously sold for five hundred dollars to a very happy, slightly overweight, bespectacled accountant at the Moustache Café, who couldn't quite believe he now owned an authentic, drug-busted golden Caddy!

I didn't want to leave.

As the city disappeared below and the blue sky enveloped us, I thought about what a strange town LA was. It wasn't really a City of Angels—it was more an enveloping cloud of illusory hope, constantly fueling the dreams of the innocent to be *someone*, to be famous, to be *seen*, to be adored and admired and to willingly pay the price of that almost impossible climb. Some made it but most didn't, and some died trying.

I didn't want to leave.

I'd been fortunate. This town had been exceptionally good to me, and I was deeply grateful to Sondra and Playboy. I had nothing but memories of wonderful people, kindness, glorious weather, and fun. For three years, I hadn't been scared or cold or living in a constant state of anxiety and exhaustion. I had started to feel how easy it was to be comfortable and complacent, falsely secure in a youth we all believed would never end. At that moment, the plane hit some turbulence and bumped hard, pushing me back in my seat and back into reality. Hollywood doesn't accept "old." It was simply not cool. It didn't matter how many famous people were your "dear friends." Eventually they would fade away. Those groovy party invites would also slowly disappear, then were gone forever as the attention systematically reverted forward toward the new, bold, and beautiful rolling in daily from every small town in America. Unless you were in the business as a performer, or agent, or an executive prepared to climb that other impossible ladder to the corner office, there wasn't much else to strive for.

I didn't want to leave.

I was on my way to Chicago and a new adventure. I had a purpose, a job, and oh joy, I was momentarily legal, though this extraordinary opportunity was no accident. Everything that had happened wasn't luck. Tired of watching me luxuriate in easy and fun, I think the universe was shoving me out before I got trapped behind the rose-colored glass walls of this very addictive town and Hugh Hefner's mansion. I looked out the aircraft's window and noticed we were in the clouds—it almost felt like I was escaping, running far, far away from compromising my spirit. *And for what?* I thought. To be part of the "group"? To "belong" to something that was . . . what? Nothing—just a temporary and fleeting fantasy that I had honestly never thought about leaving. I remembered sitting on the plane out of Geneva, my life barely still in my hands, then leaving Beirut, Hakim's face behind the glass with his hand on his heart. I seemed to have escaped a lot.

I didn't want to leave.

I realized Mel and Carol were right, and I think they would approve; I'd made the move to *doing* something! I believed it was going to lead to something else and something else and something else . . . somewhere. I had no idea what all those "somethings" were, and they didn't seem to include any "someones."

Oliver was but a memory I'd pushed away.

I didn't want to leave but . . . my gut and the committee in my head were telling me a Very Important Part Two of my life was about to begin.

And it was.

And it did.

THE END (for Now)

Acknowledgments

To say "thank you" sometimes feels somewhat inadequate. My first thanks and gratitude is to Greenleaf Book Group for having the faith to take me on and give me this brilliant opportunity. There are so many others, that without their undying support and encouragement, this book would never have been written. My dear friend, coach, and mentor James Cunnings—thank you for pushing me to write this mad story of my life. Your continuing positive encouragement was a lifeline, especially when I was ready to throw the thing out the window. Thank you to dearest Harry Groener and his beautiful wife, Dawn Didawick. Your friendship and constant enthusiasm for my work were infectious and gave me great confidence. Thank you also to the lovely Juliet Landau for your wonderful support. You went out of your way to help me and I will never forget it. Thank you to Sondra Theodore—for your kindness back when I so needed a friend. My heart is always with you. A massive thanks and as many hugs as she'll take to my dearest, talented friend and chief mentor, Debra Englander. You have been my teacher, advisor, and number one cheerleader for the past two years. I wouldn't be here writing this without you, and there would be no book. My eternal gratitude to you comes from deep within my heart. Huge thanks to Patti Jo Masten, a great friend and one kick-ass Bunny Mother. Thank you to my dearest friend and writer extraordinaire Cathy Scott, for your constant help and support. Thank you also to Geoffrey Berwind, who turned my life around. And of course, my deepest heartfelt thanks to Yusuf Islam/Cat Stevens. You taught me to feel and cherish what we all have when we are fortunate enough to find it.

None of us can do this alone. Yes, of course we write alone, always, but when you have someone who loves you from their soul and that love is pure and unconditional—someone who gives you the encouragement just when you need it, someone who patiently suffers through every season of *The Bachelor*—that's when you know you can keep going. That's when you know you are blessed. For all that I want to thank my beloved husband Jason Watt, who has been my rock and champion supporter the whole way. I love you, honey. I thank you and I am honored to have you stand beside me as I travel along this literary adventure.

About the Author

JULIETTE WATT is a produced playwright and an award-winning soap opera writer for ABC Television's *One Life to Live* and *Loving*, garnering two Writers Guild Awards and a nomination for a Daytime Emmy. As a playwright, her acclaimed play *Night of the Bear* was produced by Tony Award–winning actress Carole Shelley at The Studio Theater, New York City. Juliette's second play, *The Invitation*, was produced by The Barrow Group at the American Place Theater, New York City.

Juliette's accomplishments include: serving as a stunt horse rider for MGM studios; a fifteen-year career as a cabaret singer, touring the world with a successful one-woman show; working as a Playboy Bunny in London, then later appearing as the headliner in their cabaret lounges in Los Angeles, Chicago, New York City, and London, England. For the last twenty-three years, she has been an ATP pilot and master flight instructor, teaching all levels in nineteen different aircrafts. In 2003, she worked for Best Friends Animal Society as the face/spokesperson of the organization during national events. In 2005, in the aftermath of Hurricane Katrina, Juliette was dispatched by Best Friends Animal Society to New Orleans, where she spent a year flying her own airplane on animal rescue and transport missions—reuniting pets all over the country with their people, and taking homeless pets to new homes, rescue centers, or shelters. She was also the spokesperson for all media coverage. From August of 2005 to March of 2006, seven thousand animals were rescued and cared for by the Best Friends team.

Juliette is also an active member of the Denver Speakers Bureau, performing workshops and speaking engagements around the country, as well as coaching clients on compassion fatigue. Juliette currently lives in Pagosa Springs, Colorado, with her husband, three rescue dogs, three rescue horses, and two goats.

www.ingramcontent.com/pod-product-compliance
Lightning Source LLC
Chambersburg PA
CBHW060407080526
44583CB00012B/501